INSIDE THE CANADIAN JUDICIAL SYSTEM

JUDGES
AND
JUDGING

PETER MCCORMICK AND IAN GREENE

JAMES LORIMER & COMPANY, PUBLISHERS
TORONTO, 1990

Cover photo: Arthur Tilley, Masterfile

Canadian Cataloguing in Publication Data

McCormick, Peter
Judges and Judging
Includes bibliographical references.
ISBN 1–55028–334–0 (bound) ISBN 1–55028–332–4 (pbk.)
1. Judges—Canada. 2. Judicial process—Canada.
I. Greene, Ian. II. Title.
KE8290.M33 1990 347.71'014 C90–095147–8
KF8775.M33 1990

James Lorimer and Company, Publishers
Egerton Ryerson Memorial Building
35 Britain Street
Toronto, Ontario M5A 1R7

Printed and bound in Canada

5 4 3 2 1 91 92 93 94 95

Preface

The advent of the Canadian Charter of Rights and Freedoms in 1982 has made Canadians aware, some perhaps for the first time, of the quiet but extensive policy–making power that exists behind the judicial robe. Like all constitutional documents, the Charter is written in vague language, with indeterminate phrases and ambiguous expressions. Over time, though, judges make decisions about the meaning of that language, piling one precedent after another to provide more precise definitions. Because of this process, it has become evident that the personalities and backgrounds of the judges are as important in explaining the impact of the Charter on Canadian society as the wording of the document itself. As a result, Canadians have become increasingly curious about what kinds of people judges are and how they make their decisions.

Take, for example, the phrase "freedom of religion." A broad definition of this principle would have the effect of expanding individual freedom, while a narrow definition would provide the state with more scope to limit individual liberty. If judges give "freedom of religion" an expansive definition, the state will not be able to prohibit the smoking of marijuana for religious purposes. If they narrow the concept, the state could possibly order a blood transfusion for the child of a Jehovah's Witness when that child's life was in danger.

In its decisions since 1982 the Supreme Court has sharpened up the legal definition of "freedom of religion" in four major ways. First, the Court has declared that freedom of religion prohibits legislatures from enacting laws (such as the old Lord's Day Act) that are designed to promote particular religious practices.[19] Second, the Court decided that laws that have the *effect* of promoting particular religious practices violate freedom of religion even if they were not intended to do so.[21] Third, it ruled that laws creating "common pause days" indirectly violate freedom of religion, because those whose weekly holy day is not the common pause day suffer a disadvantage. Even so, a common pause day may be acceptable if reasonable attempts are made to accommodate those whose holy day falls at a different time of the week.[21] Fourth, the Supreme Court decided that provincial laws requiring a permit for religious schools and specifying a minimum curriculum in such schools do not violate freedom of religion.[22]

By the end of the twenty–first century, the Supreme Court decisions will most likely have created ten or fifteen pages of these kinds of sub–definitions of freedom of religion. The same will hold true for all the other phrases in the Charter because they are all somewhat unclear — a necessary condition for a general constitutional document which has practical limits to its length.

The process of clarifying ambiguous language in laws is known as judicial policy–making. Its most dramatic manifestation comes in the interpretation of constitutional documents like the Charter and in the country's top court, but judicial policy–making also occurs less visibly in the realm of ordinary law, at all levels of court. For example, in 1988 a University of Saskatchewan mathematics professor was charged for allowing his dog "to run at large" after he was found walking the animal in a park without a leash. In Provincial Court the professor argued that the city by–law only required him to have control of his dog, and that he had control without a leash because the dog was trained to obey him. The judge agreed with this interpretation and because the decision was not appealed the city suddenly had a new policy for control of dogs in parks.

One critical aspect of judicial policy–making is that different judges can come to very different conclusions about how the same law should be interpreted. During the summer of 1989 the Quebec Court of Appeal declared that the Quebec Human Rights Code should be construed so as to guarantee a fetus the right to life. The Supreme Court of Canada came to exactly the opposite conclusion.[30] Conflicting judicial decisions about the Charter's application to abortion laws, Sunday closing legislation, unions, drunk drivers, and compulsory retirement have drawn attention to the fact that the Charter could be interpreted in a variety of different ways — many of them equally plausible.

The purpose of this book is to fill in some of the gaps in our understanding of how these decisions and interpretations get made — of judges and judging in Canada. Building on interviews with judges and collected data about judges' backgrounds and decisions, we intend to describe and demythologize the decision–making process at all levels, from the Provincial Court at the bottom of the judicial totem pole to the Supreme Court at the top.

We are taking on this task because outside of the legal profession, the judicial process is shrouded in mythology. Personally, we have had this mythology starkly illustrated by the reports of our students who attend court sittings as part of class research projects. Most have never been in a courtroom before, and they admit that their expectations are based primarily on U.S. television series like *L.A. Law* or *Perry Mason*. They expect lawyers to make brilliant and dramatic presentations that last a minute or two at most. They expect judges to exude wisdom with every gesture and to demonstrate superhuman insight into the absolute truth. They expect the issues and processes to be so complex that they'll feel lost.

Reality, they discover, is startlingly different. Some crown attorneys and defence counsel appear not to be very familiar with the cases they are handling, and they seem to stumble around looking for an argument. Many cases seem so straightforward that the judges' faces take on a noticeably bored expression. Only occasionally will a student report a dazzling, well–prepared presentation by a lawyer, or a complex and interesting case, or a judge who stunned the courtroom with a profound oral decision.

In spite of the routine nature of the majority of cases, most judges have developed a decision–making strategy that they can apply to both the routine cases and the complex ones. Our position is that although judges generally try to be as impartial as possible, they cannot help but be influenced by factors such as their social backgrounds and the particular styles of decision–making they have unconsciously adopted. To analyse these influences is not to criticize judges (unless being human is a fault), but, ideally, to provide information that judges and litigants can use to promote higher standards of impartiality in the adjudicative process.

Our study has a national perspective, although most of our information comes from Alberta and, to a lesser extent, Ontario. Between us, we interviewed 91 judges at all levels of court in Alberta and Ontario. The Alberta interviews focused especially on the decision–making process. We have also collected basic biographical data for a sample of 277 judges across Canada. We asked Alberta judges to fill out questionnaires on their backgrounds, and 116 (or 67 per cent) of them kindly responded. (This total includes 63 per cent of the Provincial Court judges, and 74 per cent of the superior court judges.) Finally, several retired Supreme Court of Canada judges have been gracious enough to grant interviews.

One of us (Ian Greene) conducted the Ontario interviews in 1979 and 1980 as part of his Ph.D. research, and with financial assistance from the Centre for Criminology at the University of Toronto. He selected a representative sample of 40 judges, 10 from each of the Supreme Court of Ontario, the District Court, the Provincial Court (Criminal Division) and the Provincial Court (Family Division). A third of these judges were selected at random from the Judicial District of York (the Toronto area), a third from a group of ten counties centring around Hamilton, and a third from a group of eight counties clustering around Sudbury. These three regions were thought to represent Ontario's diversity. In addition to the judges, representative samples of 32 trial lawyers, 30 crown attorneys, and 32 court administrators were interviewed; they were selected at random from the centres in which the judges in the sample resided. (Trial lawyers were defined as lawyers who made, on average, at least one court appearance per week, which included only 40 per cent of all lawyers. Court administrators were defined as the chief administrative officials in each court location.)

In 1982 and 1983 we received grants from the Alberta Law Foundation and the Canadian Institute for the Administration of Justice to conduct a similar study of Alberta judges, court officials, and trial lawyers, but with more emphasis on the social backgrounds of the judges and the judicial decision–making process. We selected a random sample of 41 judges across the province, 20 from the Court of Queen's Bench and 21 from the

Provincial Court. We also interviewed 10 of the 11 judges sitting on the Alberta Court of Appeal at that time. We interviewed all of the judges separately and in person, with one of us (Peter McCormick) conducting all but two of the interviews in 1984 and 1985. The other groups — a random sample of 44 trial lawyers, 15 court administrators, and 9 crown prosecutors — were interviewed by student research assistants in 1982.

We succeeded in interviewing all but two judges in Ontario and two in Alberta from the group originally selected. Of those four only two judges flatly refused an interview, and we were not able to schedule interviews during our research phase with the other two. All of the lawyers agreed to be interviewed, as well as all the court administrators and all but one of the crown attorneys in Ontario. In Alberta we were unable to achieve our target of 30 crown prosecutors and 30 court administrators because permission to conduct the interviews was not received from the Attorney General's department until two weeks before the research assistants had to return to university. However, because of time made available by this circumstance, the research assistants were able to interview a random sample of 29 civil and criminal litigants whose trials had just been completed, as well as 11 witnesses involved in these trials.

It seems only fair to provide some information about our own backgrounds, since the judges we study were kind enough to provide us with so much information about theirs. Both of us have a doctoral degree in political science, and neither is a lawyer. (It may be of interest to readers that political science and sociology were the first academic disciplines to study law and legal systems in a systematic way using social science theory. The political science study of law is our field of specialization.) One of us is the son of an Alberta Provincial Court judge, and the other is the grandson of a British Columbia magistrate; these family connections help to explain our interest in the study of judges.

In the following text, cases are referred to by numbers in square brackets; the numbers correspond to a list of cases that appears at the end of the book. Bibliographic references are contained in a separate list. Numbers in round brackets refer to specific articles or books if an author has more than one entry in the list of references.

The Plan of the Book

The book has descriptive, analytical, and critical tasks to perform. Part I, encompassing chapters 1 to 3, is primarily descriptive. It covers the adjudicative process in Canada, the system of judicial appointments, and the social backgrounds of judges.

A study of judges that avoided their political and physical setting would not be terribly informative. It would be like a history of the great Canadian hockey players that proliferated in anecdotes and scoring stats but ignored the role of the fans, the owners, and the media. The first chapter analyses the role of courts in our political system and the adjudicative process. It describes how cases such as those involving the Charter wend their way from the lower courts to the Supreme Court over a period of years, and how the complex system is sometimes used by lawyers for strategic advantage.

Chapter 2 investigates how lawyers become judges. It describes the various methods of appointing judges in Canada and traces how we have moved from a system based almost entirely on patronage considerations to one in which patronage plays a somewhat lesser role. We also address the question of whether the new appointment procedures result in the selection of the best qualified judges. The critical element in this chapter concerns the appointment process, which we feel is still too wedded to the political patronage system in some parts of the country.

In Chapter 3 we describe the social backgrounds of Canadian judges — their social class, ethnicity, education, careers, and achievements before becoming judges. We draw heavily on the data we have collected ourselves and suggest that the backgrounds of judges might be the cause of some unconscious bias in decision–making. The solutions are for judges to become more aware of how they are different from ordinary Canadians, and for the system to make more judicial appointments from among women and members of visible minorities.

Part II, comprising chapters 4 through 7, constitutes the analytical section of the book and is based on our interviews with judges in Alberta and Ontario. Chapter 4 explores how judges adapt to their role. We compare the reasons given by judges for wanting to become judges with their actual experiences on the bench.

Chapters 5 to 7 dissect the judicial decision–making process. Approaches to decision–making vary with the kind of court, and chapter 5 centres on the trial courts. It deals with decision–making both with regard to the substantive issue before the court and to the sentencing decision. Decision–making in the appeal courts is the subject of Chapter 6, while Chapter 7 highlights the Supreme Court of Canada. Readers should keep in mind that our description of decision–making is based primarily on the judges' own accounts, so that we have at best represented only a part of the reality of the process. But it is a part that certainly cannot be discounted in its importance.

Part III, comprising chapters 8 to 10, examines the role of judges in the law–making process and suggests ways in which the adjudicative process might be reformed.

In common law jurisdictions, which means all Canadian provinces except for private law matters in Quebec, judges are expected to base their decisions, as much as possible, on precedent cases. But there are ways and means by which judges can depart from precedent, and sometimes when this happens judges can be said to be entering into the policy–making process just as surely as when they establish new precedents. In chapter 8 we try to penetrate the idea of 'precedent' to see how it really works for a judge making a decision.

One of the most controversial current issues in the law and politics field in Canada is whether judges serve society best by applying a broad interpretation to the law to take into account changing conditions (an "activist" approach), or whether they should leave that task to the legislative and executive branches of government (a "restrained" approach). We take up this issue in chapter 9 by considering what judges think about it. We also address the question of how the judges' backgrounds influence their decisions in Charter of Rights cases.

In our concluding chapter we apply our findings to the issue of court reform in Canada. We suggest that as Canadians become more aware of how judges decide cases — especially high–profile cases like those involving the Charter of Rights — they will demand some changes both in the way judicial appointments are made, and in the adjudicative process itself.

Peter McCormick
Ian Greene

Acknowledgements

We are grateful to many people for their assistance and support. Without the encouragement and advice of Professor Peter Russell, this book would never have been written. Professor Russell kindled Ian Greene's interest in studying courts and judges, and supervised his thesis research, some of which is reported in this book. Professor Russell also encouraged both of us to undertake our study of the Alberta judiciary, and provided a great deal of invaluable advice along the way.

Research involving interviews is costly, and we are grateful to the Centre for Criminology at the University of Toronto for assisting with the Ontario research in 1979 and 1980, and to the Alberta Law Foundation and the Canadian Institute for the Administration of Justice for their generous support of the research in Alberta. We are especially indebted to Marc Gold, Research Director of the Canadian Institute for the Administration of Justice, who was always ready to take timeto deal with the administrative issues related to publication. We should note, however, that the views expressed in this book are our own, and do not necessarily reflect the positions of these organizations.

Carl Baar, Timothy Endicott, Jane Haynes, Jim MacPherson, Peter Russell and Judge Pamela Thompson read the manuscript and provided us with some cogent insights. Virginia Smith, our editor at Lorimer, and Robert Clarke, our copy editor, gave us numerous pertinent suggestions; it is impossible to thank them enough for their recommendations, good humour, and encouragement. Professors Ted Morton and Mike Withey at the University of Calgary unselfishly provided us with their research data on the Charter of Rights decisions of Alberta judges. The following people read parts of the manuscript, and we are indebted to them for their comments: Karl Friedmann, Marc Gold, Peter Hogg, former Chief Justice William Howland, former Chief Judge C.A. Kosowan, Chief Justice J.H. Laycraft, Lorraine McCormick, Chief Justice Kenneth Moore, Margaret Moore, Eilonwy Morgan, George Szablowski, Martin Thomas, Chief Judge E.K. Wachowich, Blenus Wright, and Allan Young. All of these people contributed toward improving the manuscript, but we take full responsibility for its shortcomings.

We also received assistance and helpful comments from undergraduate and graduate students too numerous to mention, but we are especially thankful to Shannon Bell, Heather Black, Jim Cassimatis, Tom Cerrone, Orest Chabursky, Betty Charalambopoulos, Anne DeMelo, Pam Denecky, Josh Hawkes, Judi Hoffman, Laura Horton, Yoav Kaplun, Andy Knight, Alex Kotkas, Lisa Lambert, Michelle Lewicki, Wayne Mah, Suzanne Maisey, Gus Marcelino, Diane McCallum, Charles Moore, Richard Quon, Jack Santos, Perry Silver, Inga Smulders, Pat Vadacchino, Joseph Vecchiolla, and Nina Yaramelli. We are also thankful for the patience and assistance of our office staff, including Jean Bowers, Lana Cooke, Betty Knapp, Angie Ritter, and Anne Stretch. Staff at the computing centres at the University of Lethbridge and York universities were called on frequently to resolve the difficulties we ran into when transferring manuscript and data files by electronic mail across the country; they include Daniel Bloom, Marshal Linfoot, Peter Madany, Ali Makooie, Jamie Savage, and Russ Wilton. There were others who provided support in a variety of important ways, including Irving Abella, Peter Gabor, Lorene Harrison, and Joanna Morgan.

We are grateful to Gerald Gall, Mde. Justice Ellen Picard, and Mr. Justice William Stevenson for their support during critical phases of the project. We wish to express a special thanks to all of the judges, lawyers, crown attorneys, and court staff whom we interviewed.

Most importantly, we are indebted to our wives, Lorraine McCormick and Eilonwy Morgan, without whose constant encouragement and tolerance for our long working hours the project would never have been completed.

P.M. & I.G.

Contents

To
Donald V. Smiley
one of the most understanding and insightful
persons we have known
who encouraged us with advice and humour

Part I

Adjudication, Appointment, and Backgrounds

1

The Courts

The judicial process has always had a certain mystique surrounding it. The ambience created by robes, a specialized jargon — often an anglicized latin — and a formal and complex court structure tends to discourage lay persons from learning about legal issues.

But the legal world is not as difficult to penetrate as one might imagine. Legal professionals are simply another group of specialists who have adopted a set of standard work procedures and who use code words to converse in a kind of shorthand. To begin with, the judicial system in Canada operates under a number of basic concepts, and if we understand those concepts we can also more easily understand the judicial decision–making process.

The Purpose of Courts

Throughout history most governments have established institutions for resolving disputes. These institutions are almost always called courts because in earlier days disputes were settled by the monarch from his throne in his courtroom.

There are three practical reasons why governments would want to establish courts. First, the orderly resolution of disputes between citizens, besides being a desirable alternative to combat, is a prerequisite for all other state activities in complex societies. Second, the more that citizens can rely on the even–handed enforcement of the contracts they make with each other, the more they can specialize in commercial activities and trust the trade relationships they enter into. Third, the fair resolution of disputes between the government and the citizen enhances the government's authority and legitimacy.

Courts, then, are government–sponsored dispute–resolution centres in which officials called judges have been given the power to decide controversies. The process by which disputes are settled in courts is known as "adjudication." Courts are successful to the extent that (most) citizens consider the judges to be fair whether they win or lose, and therefore voluntarily comply with judicial decisions. Fairness implies that judges be impartial, meaning that they are not biased in advance for or against any of the parties in a dispute. One way of promoting impartiality is by providing judges with "independence," which means that they are not be- holden to any of the parties in the disputes that come before them, including (and especially) the government.

Judicial independence is an essential feature of adjudication. But how can judges be independent from the government when the courts are considered to be one of the three branches of government, alongside the legislature and the executive? Moreover, judges are appointed and paid by the executive branch of government and have their offices and support staff provided by the executive branch. The Supreme Court of Canada wrestled with these issues in the *Valente* decision of 1985.

The Valente Case [31]
and Judicial Independence

While driving his car at high speed along a street in Burlington, Ontario, in 1981, Walter Valente struck and killed three girls on their bicycles, as Paul T. Heron recounts in his commentary on the case. Valente was charged with dangerous driving, a Canadian Criminal Code offence that carries a potential jail sentence.

Shortly after the Charter of Rights came into effect in 1982 the case came to the Provincial Court in Ontario, the lowest court in the judicial hierarchy. If we think of Canadian courts as a four– tiered hierarchy, the "capital 'P'" Provincial Courts are on the bottom, and above them are the "small 'p'" provincial superior trial courts, the provincial superior appeal courts, and finally the Supreme Court of Canada.

Valente instructed his lawyer, Noel Bates, to keep him out of jail, and Bates turned to the Charter of Rights, which declares that any person charged with an offence has the right to a hearing before an "independent and impartial tribunal." Bates was aware that Provincial Court judges do not have the same constitutional guarantees of independence as judges who are higher on the judicial ladder.

Our constitution declares that provincial superior court judges — judges on the second and third tier — can be removed from office only if the Senate and House of Commons jointly pass a resolution to this effect; the public nature of this procedure makes it difficult to remove judges and thereby protects them from retaliation for making decisions that displease individual cabinet ministers. The constitution also requires that the salaries of the provincial superior court judges be established publicly through a law of Parliament, thus preventing the Minister of Justice from arbitrarily reducing the salaries of judges who decide contrary to the government's wishes.

There are no such written constitutional guarantees of the independence of Provincial Court judges, so Bates argued that Provincial Court judges are not independent. He held that because the Provincial Court judge charged with hearing Valente's case was not independent, the judge had no authority to decide the case.

The Provincial Court judge considered the argument to have merit (some Provincial Court judges have for years been irritated that the superior courts have a higher constitutional status, and have unsuccessfully pressed the provincial government to take appropriate action), so he disqualified himself and referred the independence question to the Ontario Court of Appeal. Valente lost in the Court of Appeal; he appealed to the Supreme Court of Canada and lost again.

The Supreme Court held that judges are independent if three conditions are met. First, judges must have "security of tenure," meaning that they cannot be fired because the government disagrees with their decisions. Because Provincial Court judges in Ontario (and most other provinces) can be removed only after a judicial inquiry has determined that the judge should be dismissed, this condition was satisfied. Second, judges must have "financial security," a legislated right to a salary, so that the cabinet cannot secretly manipulate judges by raising or lowering their salaries or by threatening to do so. Third, judges must have "institutional independence," or the ability to control administrative actions in the courts that could affect judicial decision–making. The Supreme Court felt that the Ontario law that outlines the terms and conditions of the employment of Provincial Court judges met these three conditions, and that constitutional safeguards, while advantageous, were not strictly necessary.

The "security of tenure" condition means that judges in Canada are given permanent appointments that continue until the mandatory retirement age, which is 75 for superior court judges and 65 or 70 for most Provincial Court judges. (In New Brunswick, there is no compulsory retirement age for Provincial Court judges.) Under extraordinary circumstances a judge can be dismissed, but not by a cabinet minister or legislature acting alone. A judicial inquiry must take place to investigate the allegations of wrongdoing, and the inquiry must recommend dismissal. A judge cannot be removed for making an error in law, but only for behaviour inappropriate for a judge, such as taking a bribe or not fulfilling court–related duties. The reason why a judge cannot be removed for an error in law is that vengeful litigants with plenty of money to litigate, disappointed with a judicial decision, might harass a judge by pressing for his or her removal. If such situations could occur, a judge might be inclined to decide in favour of well–known "trouble–makers."

We asked the judges we interviewed in Ontario and Alberta to tell us what judicial independence implied to them. Although all the judges told us that it meant that no one — especially cabinet ministers — could interfere in the decision–making process, some judges thought that the principle had additional overtones. A third of the judges thought that judicial independence meant that the judiciary should control the flow of cases through the courts, and a few (13 per cent) thought that judges should have *complete* control over all aspects of court administration. Half the judges thought that judicial independence implied that even the chief judge could not give orders to the junior judges regarding case–flow management decisions. This lack of consensus about some of the implications of judicial independence has ramifications for the judges' perceptions of their role (see chapter 4).

Adjudication

Adjudication is a process by which the two parties in a dispute (the litigants) put their case before a neutral third party (the judge) for resolution. The judge makes a decision based on an objective set of standards (the law), and this decision can be enforced by the coercive powers of the state. Usually, one party to the dispute wins and the other loses; decisions that result in compromises or simply "split the difference" are rare. The judge must reach his decision by first determining the facts of the case and then applying the law to those facts.

(To be sure, these are the types of case that form the core of the court's adjudicative function; not all actual cases look like this. For example, some court cases are *ex parte* — they go uncontested or by default — meaning that the second disputant is invisible. As well, the court is often called upon simply to ratify a decision reached elsewhere, as in many modern divorce cases, and the "dispute" is largely a fiction. The core of the court's role, however, is a dispute involving the legal rights or obligations of two or more parties.)

Disputes that go to court are either *public* or *private*. Public law disputes are those in which the government is a party. These include criminal law, administrative law, and constitutional law cases. Private law disputes are conflicts between two private (or corporate) persons. These include real estate transactions, contracts, family law, and suits for negligence.

Adjudication is, of course, just one of many methods of dispute resolution. In *negotiation* the two disputing parties attempt to resolve their dispute without the aid of a neutral third party; they do not necessarily look to external objective standards and there is usually no enforcement mechanism obliging the parties to reach an agreement or to abide by it. In *mediation* the parties turn for help to a neutral mediator, who simply assists the two parties to negotiate but cannot impose a settlement. In *arbitration*, the neutral third party — an arbitrator — may impose a binding settlement but is not usually bound by the same strict set of objective standards — the whole body of law — as a judge.

Courts use the adjudicative method because of the need for predictability. Mediation and arbitration produce more varied outcomes, which certain parties can perceive, rightly or wrongly, as an indication of favouritism. At the same time, adjudication is not ideally suited to all disputes. Disputes involving parties who want a quicker and less formal procedure, and disputes in which the state has no compelling interest, probably do not belong in court.

In private law cases, adjudication is ideally the dispute resolution method of last resort, to be used only when negotiation, mediation, or arbitration are impossible or fail. The adjudicative service is provided by the state so that a method of last resort will be available — so that private disputes can be settled without the disruption of public order.

In public law cases involving disputes between the state and private citizens, countries adhering to the principle of the rule of law submit such disputes to adjudication to promote the perception that the government is fair. The rule of law means that government officials may act only as authorized by legitimate laws — which usually means laws enacted by elected legislatures — and that the law must be applied equally to everyone. When the state uses adjudication to resolve disputes between, for example, the law enforcement authorities and the persons they accuse of crimes, it intends to ensure adherence to the rule of law.

Two great legal systems have developed in the world: the common law system and the civil law system.

The Common Law System

The common law system is based on the judicial system of England and Wales, and its origins can be traced to the time of King Henry II in the twelfth century. Henry II inherited a justice system based primarily on local, traditional courts, so that the rules of commerce and the criminal law varied from one locality to another. Such a system not only discouraged inter–regional trade in England but also promoted disunity. The king and his advisory council created legislation to standardize some of the criminal and commercial laws across England, and the council itself heard disputes arising out of these laws.

Before long, the council experienced a "caseload crisis" not unlike backlog problems in many of today's courts. Travelling justices were appointed to relieve the pressure on the council and to provide a more convenient dispute–resolution service for the king's subjects. As caseload pressures continued, central courts separate from the king's council were created. The travelling judges together with the judges of the central courts had jurisdiction to settle certain disputes even in the absence of decrees from the king's council. Records were kept of their decisions, and judges began to refer to these records of old cases when deciding new cases. As much as possible, the precedents set by the old cases were followed in the new cases according to the principle of *stare decisis* ("let decided matters stand"). This judge–made law became known as the "common law," because it was judge–made law that the judges applied to all social classes across England and Wales.

According to the rules of *stare decisis* as they have developed over the centuries, every court must follow the precedents established by a higher court in the same court system, and the precedents of the highest court "trump" those of any lower courts. In the absence of conflicting precedents established by a higher court, a court usually follows its own precedents. The precedents of higher or equal status courts in another common law jurisdiction are influential, but not binding. For example, U.S. Bill of Rights precedents are often cited in Canadian Charter of Rights cases, but they are only sometimes followed. Precedents must be followed only when the facts in the current case and the precedent case are substantially the same. If a judge considers the facts in a current case to be significantly different, the judge may "distinguish" the precedent, and thus depart from it.

All courts in Canada must follow precedents established by the Supreme Court. The Supreme Court itself almost always follows its own precedents. In the mid–1970s the Court announced that it might occasionally overrule its own precedents (or those established by the Judicial Committee of the Privy Council in London, England, which was Canada's highest court of appeal until 1949) if it considered those precedents to be clearly wrong or inappropriate. Since that time, according to Peter Hogg (1), the Supreme Court has overruled fewer than ten precedents. Such overruling will not occur frequently because it would destroy the predictability of the adjudicative system. However, because judges can "distinguish" appropriate precedents, *stare decisis* is not quite as rigid as it might first appear.

One of the most difficult issues for judges is to decide when to follow *stare decisis* and when to "distinguish" a precedent case (that is, leave it aside as not relevant). Our survey of Alberta judges' views on this difficult question indicates that the majority of judges at all levels think that *stare decisis* should be followed in an almost mechanical fashion, although some judges strongly believe that rigid adherence to tradition falsely assumes that all wisdom is in the past. (See chapter 8.)

In addition to *stare decisis*, a second essential characteristic of the common law world is the adversary system. According to the adversarial approach, it is the responsibility of the litigants to present the judge or judges with all the facts and theory needed to make a decision. Judges have neither the responsibility nor the opportunity to carry out an independent investigation of the facts. Although they do sometimes research legal theory and precedents on their own, they are not usually provided with all the resources necessary for this work because they are expected to rely primarily on the information presented by counsel for the litigants.

Only in recent years have Supreme Court of Canada judges and provincial appeal court judges been assigned law clerks to assist them with their legal research. Trial court judges rarely have such assistance. Thus, if judicial decisions seem to take into account only a narrow range of possible fact situations or legal interpretations, this is often because the lawyers presenting the case have narrowed the considerations in advance.

In the U.S. Supreme Court, law clerks sometimes play a major role in writing judicial decisions. As Bob Woodward and Scott Armstrong have shown, some Supreme Court justices do little more than proofread the decisions written by their fresh–out–of–college clerks. In our own research, we found that law clerks in Canada do not play nearly as influential a role in appeal court decision–making.

A third characteristic of the common law system is that judges do not receive specialized training in judging, but are appointed from among the ranks of lawyers. This tradition dates from thirteenth–century England. In the preceding century the quality of the king's judges had begun to deteriorate, perhaps because the kings were too busy with crusades and disputes with nobles to give the courts the attention they needed. The judges and court officials were poorly paid, and even though all the judges were clergymen, many resorted to accepting bribes. As a result, the end of the twelfth century saw a public outcry about corruption in the judicial system. In response, Edward I appointed a royal commission to investigate in 1289, thus setting a precedent to be followed by governments for centuries thereafter when confronted with public dissatisfaction with the administration of justice.

The commission found that about half of the judges in the common law courts were corrupt, and the king fired them. He was forced by circumstances to look outside the clergy for replacement judges. For about a century some businessmen had specialized in advising litigants about how to proceed in the increasingly complex judicial system. Edward appointed some of these "lawyers" to fill the vacancies in the judiciary. His solution to the crisis soon became a tradition. By early in the fourteenth century, lawyers had completely displaced clerics as judges in all but one of the royal courts. These lawyer–judges have ever since continued to wear robes in the clerical tradition.

The Civil Law System

The common law world includes most Commonwealth countries and the United States; the rest of the world has adopted the civil law system, which developed in continental Europe beginning at the end of the eighteenth century. University scholars had become fascinated with Roman law, and they urged governments to adopt uniform codes of law based on the old Roman codes. For example, Napoleon I supervised the codification of French private and criminal law into a set of unified codes. The codes are organized in a logical sequence, from general principles to specific rules of law.

Judges in civil law countries usually receive specialized training as judges; it is not assumed that the training and experience of a lawyer by themselves are appropriate for judicial duties. In France, for example, those who want to become judges attend basic law school for a year; they can then attend the National School for Jurists if they score high enough on an admissions exam. After a year at the School and a year and a half as an apprentice, they are appointed as a judge in one of the lower courts. They can be promoted up the judicial hierarchy by more senior judges, who assess their ability.

Another important difference between the common and civil law systems is that civilian judges place less emphasis on precedent than common law judges. According to the civil law approach, whenever the code is unclear judges look for guidance to the general principles in the code, the reports of the "codificateurs" (the framers of the code), and finally scholarly writings — all before researching precedent judicial decisions. A third difference between the two systems is that civilian judges may often conduct their own investigations of the facts of a case; this is known as the "inquisitorial" approach. They need not rely entirely on evidence presented by counsel for the opposing sides.

Canada's legal system incorporates elements of both the common law and civil law approaches, although common definitely overshadows civil law. After conquering Quebec in 1759, the British authorities attempted to obtain the support of Quebeckers by allowing the colony to maintain its civil legal system in the private law field. Today, Quebec's legal system adheres to the civil law approach for private law matters, although the inquisitorial style of adjudication is not nearly as evident as in most other civil law countries; precedent plays a larger role because of the influence of common law. In public law matters, Quebec is a common law jurisdiction, like all the other provinces and the federal government. The Supreme Court of Canada, which is required by law to have three judges from Quebec, acts as a civil law court when it hears private law appeals from Quebec and as a common law court the rest of the time; understandably, Quebec scholars and judges have some reservations about the viability of this dual role.

Impartiality

In common or civil law countries that adhere to the liberal political ideology — liberalism stresses the maximization of individual freedom, the limitation of governmental powers through laws enacted by representative legislatures, and equality in the application of the law — judges are expected to be as impartial as possible. Impartiality implies that judges must hear a case with an open mind, without being biased in advance toward any of the litigants. Absolute impartiality is a human impossibility, but the more that judges can demonstrate impartiality, the more respected and credible will be the adjudicative process.

A number of practices and principles have developed to promote judicial impartiality. The most important is the principle of judicial independence, as elaborated by the Supreme Court in the *Valente* case. Other methods of promoting impartiality are the presumption that judges will disqualify themselves if a litigant is a family member or associate, the prohibition against judges holding a second job, and the expectation that judges will, upon appointment, sever their association with groups that are likely to litigate or that advocate particular courses in public policy (such as political parties or anti–abortion groups).

The Canadian Court Structure

As the caseloads of courts grow in response to new laws, changing values, and population increases, governments tend to create new and more specialized courts, the result being a complex hodge–podge. Canada is no exception to this trend, but in addition Canada's court system has had to respond to another factor: federalism.

Some federal countries have established two separate hierarchies of courts — one to hear cases arising out of federal laws and the other primarily to hear cases arising out of state or provincial laws. The United States provides an example of this "dual" court system. In 1867 the Fathers of Confederation rejected the dual court model in favour of what Peter Russell (6) calls an "integrated" court structure. The goal of the integrated approach is to allow for most cases arising out of both federal and provincial laws to be heard in the same court system, a system in which both the federal and provincial governments have some responsibilities.

At the very top of the system, however, the provinces currently have no responsibility, reflecting the desire of some of the Fathers of Confederation for federal dominance of the Canadian political system. The 1867 constitution granted the federal Parliament the power to establish a Supreme Court of Canada — which it did in

1875 — to appoint all its judges and to determine its jurisdiction. The Supreme Court has the constitutional and statutory authority to hear appeals involving cases arising out of both federal and provincial laws.

A significant number of Supreme Court cases involve constitutional interpretation: they settle disputes about the extent of federal and provincial powers and disputes about the extent to which the powers of both Parliament and the provincial legislatures are limited by the Charter of Rights. It seems curious that this important court, which acts as a referee between the two orders of government, is staffed by appointees selected only by the federal order. The Meech Lake Accord set out to reduce this anomaly by giving the provincial premiers the right to nominate candidates for the Supreme Court, with the final selection to be made by the prime minister. Even with the failure of the Accord, it is possible that the provincial governments may gain the ability to be consulted over Supreme Court appointments through more informal channels.

As of April 1, 1990, the eight ordinary judges on the Supreme Court of Canada, who are known as "puisne" (pronounced pyoo'–ney, meaning "junior") judges, earned $166,800 per year. The chief justice earned $13,400 over and above the base salary.

The architects of the Canadian constitution decided to adopt a more fully integrated approach, based on courts for which both federal and provincial governments have responsibilities, immediately below the level of the Supreme Court. They did this for several reasons, although the possible inconvenience of a dual court system to the public was only a minor consideration — if it was considered at all. More importantly, the commitment of most of the anglophone Fathers of Confederation to a strong central government resulted in the idea that the federal government should have the power to appoint provincial superior court judges; this federal power made the idea of separate federal courts seem less attractive. As well, the provincial superior court judges of the time opposed the establishment of a rival system of courts. Perhaps the most important consideration was the fact that if the federal government was empowered to make appointments to the prestigious provincial superior courts, the new government would have at its disposal wonderful patronage opportunities that would encourage ambitious lawyers to work for the federal political parties. The result was section 96 of the British North America Act (renamed in 1982 to become the Constitution Act 1867), which gave the federal cabinet the power to appoint provincial superior court judges, as well as provincial county and district court judges. Consequently, these federally appointed provincial judges became known as "section 96 judges."

The superior courts have trial and appeal divisions. The trial divisions are known by such names as Queen's Bench, Supreme Court, or High Court. The appeal divisions are usually known as The Court of Appeal of the province. The trial divisions have jurisdiction over serious and moderately serious Canadian Criminal Code cases and over private law cases involving sums of money exceeding the monetary limits of the small claims courts, and these courts preside over jury trials.

Canada's system of courts is modelled on the court system of England and Wales. Many superior court judges in England and Wales were travelling justices who held "assizes," or hearings, in the major county centres at least twice a year. If litigants did not want to wait for an assize, they could travel to London where the superior courts sat more frequently. Before Confederation the colonial governments had established superior courts on the English model, with travelling justices holding assizes in county towns twice a year. In the early years, because of the difficulties of travel to provincial capitals, local merchants demanded that judges be appointed permanently to sit in major centres outside the capitals. In response, in Upper Canada in 1794 Lieutenant-Governor Simcoe established a number of "district" courts in the major centres. The judges in these courts had an "inferior" status, but were empowered to hear many of the kinds of cases that superior court judges would otherwise hear. Litigants could often choose between having a case settled before a district court judge, or waiting for a superior court judge's assize. The other common law colonies followed suit, with the result that eventually all the provinces except Quebec had district courts (sometimes known as county courts).

There may have been a marked difference between the abilities of district court judges and superior court judges in the past, so that it was worth maintaining the separate existence of the two courts to give litigants in outlying areas the chance to choose between a quick hearing before the district court judge, or waiting for the superior court assize where the services of a "better" judge would be available. With the development of higher standards in legal education, however, the pool of available talent for the county and district courts increased, so that the rationale for maintaining the county or district courts and the superior courts as separate entities diminished.

For example, our Ontario interviews indicated that three–fifths of the trial lawyers, crown attorneys, and court administrators did not consider the superior court trial judges to be superior in ability; outside of Toronto, this proportion jumped to three–quarters. Spurred on by this change in perception as well as by the desire for greater efficiency in the court system, since 1975 all provinces with county or district courts except for Nova Scotia, Ontario, and British Columbia have merged their county and district courts with their superior courts — and Ontario and British Columbia have started the merger process.

There are about 800 provincial superior, county, and district court judges in Canada. The puisne superior court judges earn $140,400 per year, while puisne county and district court judges earn $135,400. The chief and associate chief judges earn $13,400 more than the puisne judges.

Section 101 of the Constitution Act 1867 gave Parliament the right to establish not only a "general court of appeal" (Supreme Court) but also other federal courts "for the better Administration of the Laws of Canada." (Such federal courts, however, cannot hear federal Criminal Code cases; these cases must be heard in courts established by the provinces.) Pursuant to section 101, Parliament established the Exchequer Court in 1875 to hear cases involving federal taxes, patents and copyrights; until 1887, the six judges of the Supreme Court of Canada also served as Exchequer Court judges. In 1971 Parliament abolished the Exchequer Court and replaced it with the Federal Court. The jurisdiction was expanded to include federal administrative law cases. The Federal

Court has two divisions, one for trials and one for appeals. In 1983 Parliament created a third section 101 court — the Tax Court of Canada — to hear certain cases arising under federal taxation laws. The Federal Court now has 27 judges, and the Tax Court has 15.

Ottawa is responsible for providing the administrative support services for the Supreme Court of Canada, the Federal Court, and the Tax Court, as well as for appointing and paying all the judges of these courts. Federal Court and Tax Court judges earn $140,400 per year. The chief justices and associate chief justices of these courts earn $13,300 more than the puisne judges.

All of the other courts in Canada, including the provincial superior, county, and district courts, are established by provincial legislatures, and their administrative support is provided by the provincial governments. These provincial courts, which among them employ nearly 1,800 judges, conduct all trials for cases arising out of either federal or provincial laws (except for the relatively few trials conducted by the Federal Court or the Tax Court).

The provincial legislatures have created two basic types of courts: "superior" courts and "inferior" courts. The superior courts have jurisdiction over the most serious criminal cases, including jury trials, civil or private law cases except for small claims cases (which are cases involving a set maximum that varies from $500 to $15,000, depending on the province or territory), and appeals from the inferior courts.

All the provinces have at one time had an inferior court known as the "Provincial Court." Unlike the provincial county, district, and superior courts, the provincial governments have the constitutional power to appoint all the judges to these "capital-P" provincial courts; therefore, following the lead of Peter Russell (6) we will refer to them as "pure provincial" courts. (It should be kept in mind that there are four kinds of courts established by the provinces. From "lowest" to "highest," these are the "Provincial," "county and district," "superior trial," and "superior appeal" courts. The fact that most provincial legislatures have chosen to name the lowest of these courts "*the* Provincial Court" often creates confusion.) The Ontario and Quebec legislatures have recently renamed their pure provincial courts the "Ontario Court of Justice Provincial Division" and "Court of Quebec" respectively. Before the late 1960s, Provincial Court judges were known as "magistrates" or "police magistrates."

The pure provincial Courts are by far the busiest courts in the country, with over 90 per cent of all the cases heard in Canadian courts. Even though these courts have provincially appointed judges, our constitution gives the federal Parliament the right to assign them the responsibility for conducting trials under the federal Criminal Code. Therefore, a large portion of the caseload of the pure provincial courts is composed of minor to moderately serious violations of the federal Criminal Code. As well, the pure provincial courts hear cases under the Young Offenders Act, provincial offences such as highway traffic violations, and some family law cases such as adoption, child neglect, child and spousal abuse, and enforcement of maintenance orders. The pure provincial courts also hear small claims cases involving civil suits up to a maximum of between $500 and $15,000, depending on the province. (In New Brunswick, Prince Edward Island, and parts of Ontario, the provincial government has chosen to appoint persons already sitting as federally appointed judges to hear small claims cases. These judges, therefore, have both federal and provincial appointments.) There are nearly a thousand pure Provincial Court judges in Canada, and they earn between $70,000 and $105,000 per year, depending on the province they preside in.

In addition to the Provincial Court judges, most provinces have created positions for lower–status adjudicators who are usually called "justices of the peace," or JPs. These officials often double as court clerks, and few of them have legal education. (Moreover, according to one of our studies, less than 30 per cent of the head court administrators in local courts, most of whom were also JPs, had any university or college training.)

The JPs hear cases involving minor provincial or municipal offences, such as parking offences, but are occasionally given jurisdiction over some relatively serious cases. For example, in 1984 an Ontario resident, Charles Currie, was liable to a fine of $10,000 in a case before a JP. Like Valente, Currie claimed that the adjudicator was not independent as required by the Charter, but unlike Valente he won his case before a superior court judge. At the time, JPs did not have security of tenure, their salaries could arbitrarily be varied by the deputy attorney general, and many of them received a fee for service so that some of them favoured by the police had higher incomes. As a result of the Currie case, Peter Russell (6) has noted that the Ontario legislature approved amendments to the Justices of the Peace Act which provided JPs with more security of tenure, put the rosters of fee–for–service JPs under the supervision of Provincial Court judges, and removed the deputy attorney general's ability to vary salaries. When the case reached the Ontario Court of Appeal, the judges took into account these changes and found that JPs met the Charter's test for independence. However, this ruling came before the Supreme Court's decision in *Valente*, and the Supreme Court has yet to rule on the standards of independence for JPs.

Although JPs do perform adjudicative functions, we have not included them in our count of Canadian judges. This is partly because their status will remain unclear until the Supreme Court of Canada makes an authoritative decision on the matter, and partly because JPs do not have the educational background or experience associated with being a "judge" in the common law world. (In Quebec, there are more than 150 "municipal court judges" who hear cases arising under municipal by–laws and minor traffic offences, but in Montreal, Laval, and Quebec City, they have a more extensive jurisdiction, according to Russell (6). We have also excluded these officials from our count of judges.)

According to law, federally appointed judges must be selected from among lawyers who have been qualified to practise law by a provincial or territorial law society for at least ten years. Before the 1960s, the provincial legislatures did not require their magistrates to be lawyers. Since the transformation of magistrates' courts into the Provincial Courts, legislation in all the provinces except Alberta and Newfoundland has required that Provincial Court judges be selected from the bar. Even in Alberta and Newfoundland, however, as Russell (6) has observed, very few non–lawyers are appointed.

Reform–minded political scientists such as Peter Russell (6) and Carl Baar and judges such as Thomas G. Zuber have criticized

the provincial court systems for being too hierarchical, too difficult for the average citizen to understand, and too fragmented to
allow efficient operation. The Ontario Liberal Party's attorney
general Ian Scott was the only provincial attorney general in this
century who attempted a major restructuring of the provincial
court system. In 1989, following the recommendations of the 1987
Zuber Commission Report, Scott announced some significant reforms. The first phase of the reform, now under way, creates an
Ontario Court of Justice including all judges other than those in
the Court of Appeal. This court has two divisions: General and
Provincial. The General Division includes all superior court
judges (except those on the Court of Appeal), all District Court
judges, and the small claims court judges. The Provincial Division
is formed from the criminal and family divisions of the old
Provincial Court.

Besides the change in name, this reform has two major aspects
to it which may influence court reform in the other provinces.

Figure 1.1 Canadian Court Structure

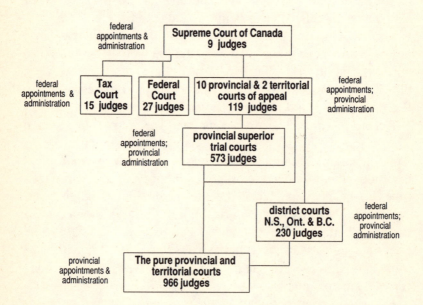

Table 1.1 Number of Judges in Canada, 1990

Judges of Canadian Provincial Courts, 1990

| | Federal Appointments | | | Provincial Appointments | | |
| | Appeal | Superior Trial Cts | County/District | Provincial* | | |
Regular** or Supernumerary	R S	R S	R S	R S	Total	Judges per 100,000 pop.
B.C.	13 8	36 3	46 4	123	233	7.8
Alberta	11 3	57 6		110 1	188	7.8
Saskatchewan	7 1	29 6		46	89	8.8
Manitoba	7	33 2		37 2	81	7.5
Ontario	16 4	48 9	145 25	252	499	5.3
Quebec	18 6	139 14		289	466	7.0
New Brunswick	6	23 5		24 4	62	8.7
Nova Scotia	7 1	12 1	10	39	70	7.9
P.E.I.	3	4 2		3	12	9.3
Newfoundland	6 2	19 2		28 1	58	10.2
N.W.T.	***	3		5	8	15.4
Yukon	***	1		2	3	11.8
Sub–totals	94 25	404 50	201 29	958 8		6.8
	119	454	230			

573=superior courts
803 = all federal appointments in prov's.   966   1,769

* Provincial Court totals include the Court of Quebec and the Territorial Courts.
** Supernumerary judges have reached retirement age, but have been reappointed for a specified period on the recommendation of the chief judge or judicial council or have opted for semi-retirement prior to retirement age.
*** The appeal court panels in the territories are made up of some combination of the territorial superior court trial judges and court of appeal judges from British Columbia (for the Yukon) or Alberta (for the N.W.T.).

Pure Federal Courts

Regular** or Supernumerary	R	S
Supreme Court of Canada	9	
Federal Court Appeal Div.	10	1
Trial Div.	14	2
Tax Court	13	2
Sub-totals	46	5
Total	51	

Total federal and provincial judges: 1,820
Judges per 100,000 population in Canada: 7.0
Sources: Number of judges: *Canada Legal Directory*, 1989.
Populations used to calculate number of judges per 100,000: *Canada Year Book*, 1990 (1988 estimate).

First, to promote greater efficiency the administrative services for all the courts have been merged and reorganized on a regional basis rather than a "level of court" basis. Second, Scott hoped eventually to merge the General and Provincial Divisions into one trial court. The federal government will have to cooperate to bring about this unified court, because the Provincial Division judges will need federal appointments to attain the same status and jurisdiction as the superior court judges in the General Division. If federal cooperation is attained, Ontario will be left with just two courts: a unified Ontario Court of Justice which will handle all civil and criminal trials, and a Court of Appeal.

Since Confederation Ontario has tended to lead the other provinces in reform of the legal–judicial system. For example, in 1968 the province established the Provincial Court out of the former local magistrate's courts. Within 15 years all the other provinces had followed suit in what Peter Russell referred to as "a remarkable demonstration of Ontario's influence on provincial public administration." (Russell [6], 126) If the reforms of the Ontario court system that Scott initiated are successful, this example may lead to similar changes in the other provinces.

Chief Judges and Justices

Each level of court has a judicial head known as a "Chief Judge" (the title used in the Provincial and district courts) or "Chief Justice" (the title used in the superior courts). Many of the courts have associate chief justices or judges to assist their respective chiefs with their administrative duties. The chiefs are selected by the prime minister (in consultation with the minister of justice) for federal appointments, and by the appropriate provincial attorney general for provincial appointments. The chief is either selected from among sitting judges (which is the usual practice) or appointed from outside the court.

The duties of the chiefs and associate chiefs vary with the nature of the court. In all the Provincial Courts, the chief judges assign judges to particular judicial districts and devise plans for assigning judges temporarily from less busy courthouses to more busy courthouses to assist with case processing. As well, the chief judge may want to influence how specific judges are assigned to cases when a court centre has more than one judge.

For example, in some multi–judge courthouses, cases are grouped together in certain courtrooms according to type (such as highway traffic offences, minor criminal offences, major criminal offences, offences involving women), and judges rotate monthly among the various courtrooms. This system can promote the practice of "judge–shopping" or "judge–avoidance," whereby lawyers invent excuses to delay until the judge they want turns up in the courtroom, or until the judge they want to avoid is absent. A third of the Ontario judges we questioned thought that this practice of judge–shopping or judge–avoidance contributed to unnecessary delays in the system. Another system of managing case–flow is to assign a case to a particular judge who will eventually hear the case regardless of delays.

In the district and superior trial courts, the chief judges and justices design the system for assigning cases to judges. The chief justices of the superior courts set the travel schedules for the judges' circuits. In the courts of appeal (including the Federal Court of Appeal and the Supreme Court of Canada), the chief justices decide on the make–up of the appeal panels, and they preside over the "conferences" — discussions after hearings — of the panels which they have assigned themselves to.

In the provincial court system, there is a mixture of circuit points (courts presided over by a single non–resident judge for a set number of days per month), and local court centres in the larger towns and cities with a number of resident judges. Each multi–judge court at the Provincial or district level in each local court centre has a "senior judge." The senior judge is appointed by the Chief Judge, and is often the longest–serving judge in the local centre. The senior judge handles the administrative duties at the local centre on behalf of the chief judge.

Most jurisdictions in Canada have created positions for judges who have either reached the mandatory retirement age or chosen early retirement but wish to continue judging on a part–time basis. These semi–retired judges are known as "supernumerary" judges, and account for about 6 per cent of Canada's judges.

Dignity and Decorum

Courts are potentially violent places. A 10:00 a.m. visitor to almost any of the Provincial Courts in Canada's larger cities will see the courtrooms for ordinary criminal cases filled with dozens of people waiting for trial. The "docket," or list of cases scheduled for that day, is posted beside the courtroom door, and it may list 50 to 100 cases, including some dealing with breaking–and–entering, assault, and perhaps robbery. The people in the courtroom include accused persons, victims of crime, witnesses, and friends and family of these people. Accused persons and victims eye each other in close proximity. Witnesses are angry because their cases may already have been adjourned several times and each adjournment has made the witness miss a day of work. Security is often provided by an aging official whose primary job is to give directions to people entering the courthouse.

We questioned the judges about how they could keep order in an atmosphere like this. This response from an Ontario Provincial Court judge was typical:

> When I first became a judge, I thought that the whole idea of wearing robes was ridiculous. During the summer, the chief judge isn't so particular about having the judges wear robes because the courtrooms are so hot. So I decided to go to court one day without my robes. It was the worst day I've ever had. First of all, no one knew who the judge was. People were arguing and bickering in the courtroom, and I thought some fights would break out. The next day I came in my robe, and I had no problem keeping order.

Robes, then — worn by judges in the common law world since the early times when judges were clerics — are not worn just for tradition's sake, but because of the strong sense of authority vested in them, an authority that has a pacifying effect. They also serve another function, as illustrated by an Ontario Supreme Court judge's comment:

> When my orderly comes to help me put on my robe in the morning, it changes me. It makes me realize that I am about

to enter the courtroom and perform a very important function. I must listen to all the evidence impartially, and then make some decisions that may have a tremendous impact on people's lives. I have to leave my own prejudices and preferences behind for awhile and I have to take that role seriously. I don't think I could concentrate as well on that role without my robe. I think that the robe also reminds the people in the courtroom — lawyers, witnesses, and litigants — that they also have an important and serious job in the courtroom.

Several judges also told us that in addition to the way they dressed, the way they were *addressed* helped them to concentrate on the judicial role. Provincial and district court judges are addressed as "Your Honour," and superior court judges are addressed as "My Lord" or "My Lady." (This is because in the English system, superior court judges usually *were* lords.) The judges often made a point of telling us that they did not take these forms of address seriously outside the courtroom, but that nevertheless they thought they served a function.

When all else fails to keep order in the courtroom, judges can cite a disorderly person for "contempt of court," which was originally a common law offence with a maximum sentence of life imprisonment. In some Canadian jurisdictions, statutes regulate the judges' ability to cite for contempt, but the maximum penalties are still severe. Before the Charter, even those criticizing judges outside the courtroom could be charged with contempt. The idea behind this power was that if citizens lose respect for judges, the consequences in terms of potential social disorder are serious; therefore the criticism of judges — even if accurate — cannot be tolerated.

In 1986, Harry Kopyto, a radical Toronto lawyer who was later disbarred, was convicted of "scandalizing the court" (a form of contempt where charges are laid by the Crown) for complaining that the courts and the police stick together like "Krazy Glue." A reporter picked up his remarks. Kopyto was eventually acquitted of the charge when the Ontario Court of Appeal panel found that freedom of expression in the Charter of Rights takes precedence over the law of contempt, at least in this case.

It is perhaps a tribute to the atmosphere in courts created by the formal trappings and the judicial robe that judges rarely need to resort to citing for contempt to keep order. On the other hand, the concern — some might even say preoccupation — of some judges with their own dignity and decorous proceedings can, of course, have a down–side as well: many citizens (and not only those burdened with guilty consciences) can be totally intimidated and demoralized by the ordeal of appearing in court, even as a witness.

Half of the court personnel whom we interviewed in Ontario (judges, trial lawyers, crown attorneys and court administrators) said that judges tended to develop a "swelled ego" because of their role in the courtroom. They often referred to this tendency as "judgeitis." Like any persons in positions of authority, including the police, medical doctors, and professors like ourselves, it is sometimes difficult *not* to develop an unrealistically inflated self–view. In chapter 4, we analyse in more detail how judges adapt to their roles.

Judicial Discipline

Persons who feel that a judge has engaged in behaviour inappropriate for a judge may complain to one of the judicial councils: to a provincial judicial council for Provincial Court judges, or to the Canadian Judicial Council for federally appointed judges. Provincial judicial councils vary from province to province but usually consist of senior judges, or a combination of judges, lawyers, and lay persons.

The Canadian Judicial Council is composed of all federally appointed chief justices and judges, and associate chief justices and judges of the provincial superior, district, and county courts, and of the Supreme Court of Canada, the Federal Court, and the Tax Court, a group consisting of 39 judges in 1990. In the 1987–88 fiscal year, the Canadian Judicial Council received 47 complaints, according to its Annual Report. In 1989–90 the number of complaints jumped to 83, almost double. None of the complaints from the public produced enough evidence to warrant a judicial inquiry. Judicial councils represent an uneasy balance between "keeping the judges in line" and "protecting the judges" from groundless complaints; the fact that other judges play so large a role in the process may beg the question of which of these two functions is more important.

Procedures have developed in all liberal countries to promote fairness in the adjudicative process. In the common law jurisdictions these procedures are known as the "rules of natural justice." They include many of the legal rights now enshrined in sections 7 to 14 of the Charter of Rights, such as the presumption of innocence, the right to an impartial and independent judge, and the right to counsel. Another of these principles is that litigants have the right to appeal a trial judge's decision at least once.

Appeal Courts

Courts that are specifically established as appeal courts hear cases in panels of three judges or more. This is because appeal courts frequently have to decide difficult questions about the meaning of the law, about which reasonable judges could differ. It is considered that several heads are more likely to make better decisions than one.

Provincial appeal courts usually sit in panels of three judges, although the court itself is usually composed of many more judges than this — for example, six in New Brunswick, and twenty–four in Quebec (including supernumerary judges). For more complex cases, a panel of five or even more can be struck, although by the late 1980s this was becoming increasingly unusual. In 1987, there was only a single reported decision of a provincial court of appeal using a seven–judge panel, and in 1989 the three prairie provinces handled their entire caseload without a single panel larger that three judges. Although the chief justice determines membership in the panels and assignment of cases to panels, he or she usually takes into consideration the preferences of the regular appeal court judges, and spontaneous last–minute substitutions or rotations are not uncommon.

The Supreme Court of Canada

In a complex court structure like Canada's, there are usually several levels of court above the court in which a case was originally heard, so that more than one appeal is possible. For a second or third attempt, the opportunity to appeal is sometimes limited to cases in which judges grant permission to appeal. This permission is called "leave to appeal."

Very few litigants have a right to appeal to the Supreme Court of Canada. Those who do are litigants whose cases involve a serious criminal offence where the provincial court of appeal rendered a non-unanimous decision about a point of law, or where the appeal court had reversed the decision of the trial court. Litigants involved in reference cases — cases based on hypothetical questions about constitutional issues which provincial cabinets submit to appeal courts — also have a right of appeal to the Supreme Court. In almost all other cases litigants must apply to the Supreme Court itself for leave to appeal.

The judges consider the applications for leave to appeal in panels of three. They rely heavily on written submissions that explain the importance of the case and on the research of their clerks, although litigants also make oral presentations. It takes the agreement of two judges out of three to grant leave to appeal. Each year, the Supreme Court receives about 400 applications for leave to appeal, and grants about 15 to 20 per cent of them. From 1981 to 1989, the Court decided from 63 to 126 appeals a year, an average of 96. According to Morton, Russell, and Withey, nearly one-fourth of the Supreme Court's caseload consisted of Charter of Rights decisions from 1987 to 1989.

Once a case is past the leave to appeal stage, a hearing is scheduled, often for almost a year after leave to appeal is granted. Sometimes, in urgent cases — such as Chantelle Daigle's abortion case — the Court may schedule a hearing within a week. The Supreme Court sits in panels of five, seven, or the full court of nine depending on how the chief justice views the importance of the case. The most common panel size, seven, accounts for about 80 per cent of the Supreme Court hearings. Nowadays the hearings typically last no longer than half a day. Lawyers for the various parties are assigned limited times to address the court — usually from 30 minutes to an hour. Small lights on the speaker's podium modelled on the traffic light system indicate to counsel when their time is up.

As soon as possible after the litigants conclude their arguments, the judges in the panel meet privately in a "conference." Beginning with the most recently appointed judge, the judges explain in turn how they think the case should be decided. After all of them have spoken, it is usually clear whether they will be unanimous or whether they will present several different opinions. A judge in the majority group will often volunteer to write the majority opinion; otherwise, the chief justice will ask a judge in that group to write it. After writing a draft of the opinion, the judge circulates it to the other judges on the panel, and each of them may send it back with suggestions for revisions. According to an article by Madame Justice Bertha Wilson, if the writer cannot accept the revisions, the other judges may decide to write separate opinions. Opinions that agree with the outcome of the main opinion but disagree with the justification for it are known as separate "concurring" opinions. Opinions that disagree with the majority result are known as "dissenting" opinions.

In recent years the judges have been attempting to write a greater number of unanimous decisions, probably in an effort to improve the authority and credibility of the Supreme Court. Sometimes a unanimous decision is not attributed to any particular judge but is simply released as the opinion of "The Court." From 1983 to 1985, 87 per cent of the Supreme Court's decisions were unanimous, which according to Wilson (1) is 10 per cent higher than during the 1970s. (However, more recently, the proportion of unanimous judgments has been dropping, and there may be a trend for judges to write a greater number of separate concurring opinions.) The judges seem to try especially hard to render a unanimous decision for cases involving high-profile political controversies, such as the twin decisions on the constitutionality of Quebec's French–only commercial–signs provisions. [8,9] Because the process of consultation among the judges is often lengthy, particularly in cases in which the court wants a unanimous judgment, decisions may not be rendered for several months or, more rarely, more than a year after the hearing.

The decision of the Court's majority on the law can be divided into two parts: that which was required for the determination of the case before the court (the *ratio*); and "words in passing" (or *obiter dicta*), statements about the law that are not essential to the court's decision. The *ratio* for a decision is a more authoritative statement of law than *obiter dicta*, because the law is considered to be established by the decisions about concrete cases and not simply by statements of judges' opinions. A lower court will feel relatively free to disregard a statement of law by a higher court if it was made in *obiter* (although perhaps less so after a 1980 Supreme Court decision [26], as we explain in chapter 8). It is up to the judges themselves in future cases to distinguish between *ratio* and *obiter*, because the two aspects are not always clear from the text of the opinions.

The Court Maze

The adjudicative process in courts developed over the centuries as a response to the need of governments to keep order and, in rule–of–law countries, to the need of governments to be perceived as fair. Over time, court systems grew more and more complex as society expanded, more laws were established, and new courts were created to take the pressure off existing courts.

Court procedures, originally designed to promote fairness, became increasingly complex as procedural rules were modified over and over again to plug loopholes or to take new conditions into account. The law itself became increasingly dense as both statute law and common law piled up. The federal concept, which divides power over courts between central and regional authorities, has further complicated court systems in countries like Canada.

As a result the average person now tends to feel lost when confronted with the law and the legal system. Without a lawyer, an encounter with the justice system can seem like being exiled to an alien world with strange customs and an incomprehensible language. Even lawyers find it difficult to grasp the complexity of the entire system. In our interviews with lawyers, we asked for comments about the courts at all levels. Almost all the lawyers said that they specialized in practising in one or two levels of court; they simply could not comment about the rest of the system.

This tendency for court systems to become increasingly complex has created a number of problems. First, some litigants and lawyers now view the court system more as the opportunity to play a game of "beat the system" skilfully than as a dispute–resolution service of last resort. For example, half of the lawyers we interviewed were not opposed to using delay tactics for their clients' advantage in some situations, and we even spoke with a few lawyers who claimed to specialize in delay. They boasted that through various technical procedures they could keep a case out of court almost forever — if they were paid enough.

Some of the judges we spoke to complained about some large corporations that took cases they had no hope of winning to court; their strategy was to force their adversary (who could not afford to litigate a case for several years) to agree to a settlement favourable to the corporation. As well, numerous cases end up in court that could be settled more effectively and with less emotional damage by negotiation or mediation. These cases include disputes between neighbours and family disputes. Years ago, such disputes were resolved through mediating organizations such as churches or community groups, but with the increasing urbanization and secularization of society these means are no longer as readily available.

Court proceedings are sometimes used by politicians as excuses for avoiding contentious political issues. A high–profile example of this abuse of courts occurred just before the 1988 federal election. Joseph Borowski had been pursuing a ten–year court battle to obtain a declaration that the fetus is a person and is protected by law like any other person. But before Borowski's case was heard by the Supreme Court of Canada, the Court struck down the section of the Criminal Code dealing with abortion in the *Morgentaler* decision.[23] Because Borowski's case rested on challenging a section of the Criminal Code which had disappeared, the lawyer representing the federal government had only to ask the Court to quash Borowski's appeal, and the appeal would have ended. But the federal government wanted to keep the issue before the Court so as to avoid taking a stand on abortion during the election campaign: it is considered a violation of judicial independence for a politician to comment about a case before the courts. After the election, when the case was finally decided, Mr. Justice Sopinka had some harsh words about how the Supreme

Court had been used as a political weapon: "Failure [of the government to bring the motion to quash] has resulted in the needless expense to [Borowski] of preparing and arguing the appeal before this Court. In the circumstances, it is appropriate that the [government] pay to [Borowski] the costs of the appeal."

Carl Baar has shown that criminal cases can take anywhere from three months to three years *on average* to go to trial, depending on the location of the court. According to Baar, the courts in the Peel region, west of Toronto, are among the slowest in this range, while courts in New Brunswick routinely try almost all of their criminal cases within six months. In Ontario, if a criminal trial decision is appealed it takes an average of one year before it can be heard. An appeal to the Supreme Court of Canada will usually add at least another year onto the process, and often several years. Private law cases tend to take at least 50 per cent longer to get through the system than criminal cases. Thus, occasionally one comes across a Supreme Court of Canada decision concerning a factual situation that occurred ten years earlier.

The fragmentation of court services can also be a serious problem for litigants when their dispute involves an issue that the law treats as several sub–issues over which different courts have exclusive jurisdiction. This problem is especially serious in family law cases. The federal Parliament, which has exclusive jurisdiction over marriage and divorce, has conferred on the provincial superior courts the exclusive jurisdiction to hear divorce cases and associated issues such as the division of property, maintenance orders, and custody over children. Nevertheless, Parliament has given Provincial Courts jurisdiction over some related family issues, such as spousal and child abuse. Most provincial legislatures, which have jurisdiction over private law matters such as the enforcement of maintenance payments, have conferred jurisdiction for these matters on their Provincial Courts. A family with marital problems can find itself facing different trials in different courts (possibly as many as five different courts, depending on how the province has divided up its Provincial and section 96 courts), in addition to the trauma caused by the marriage break–up.

Since 1977 the federal government has cooperated with several provincial governments in establishing unified family courts as pilot projects. There are now unified family courts with federally appointed judges in Hamilton, Saskatoon, St. John's, and the eastern district of Manitoba, according to Russell (6). In New Brunswick and Prince Edward Island, all family matters were transferred to the superior trial court. In British Columbia there is a unified family court in Richmond staffed by both federal and provincial judges. In the rest of the country, however, the family court system remains seriously fragmented. The provinces seem unwilling to abandon their system of provincial family courts, and the federal government seems unwilling to give provincial family judges federal appointments. It appears that there is not enough concern with the unnecessary inconvenience and suffering that the fragmentation causes for a permanent solution to be found.

Our interviews showed that judges tend to be as frustrated as anyone by unnecessary delays, by the misuse of the court system, and by the fragmentation of the courts. Some four–fifths of the Ontario judges we interviewed think there is a problem of unreasonable delay in the court system. As well, two–thirds of these judges had thought out strategies for reducing delays. Three–quarters of them were frustrated by what they considered to be unnecessary delays caused by trial lawyers, and two–thirds of them wanted greater unity in the court system. But given the judge's role as an impartial third party and the principle of judicial independence — which erects a very high fence between judges and the governmental authorities responsible for court administration — judges are not in a good position to take action to reduce abuses and delays and to promote court unification.

Trial lawyers constitute another group that could potentially advocate for reforms that would help to make the court system the public service it was intended to be. However, the Ontario interviews showed that on the whole, trial lawyers are not terribly interested in reform. Only half of the Ontario trial lawyers felt that there was a problem of unreasonable delay in any court, and fewer than half favoured greater unity in the court system. Three–quarters said they had rarely or never made suggestions to improve the efficiency of the courts. Only two–fifths said that they had ever belonged to an organization that they thought was trying to improve court administration — a revelation that says a great deal, given that all lawyers belong to at least one provincial law society, and most belong to the bar association. If the court system is to be reformed, the pressure for reform will most likely have to come from outside the legal profession.

2

Judicial Appointment in Canada

When one thinks of judicial appointments in Canada, political patronage comes to mind just as surely as sand is associated with deserts. Patronage (the use of appointed positions to pay off party loyalists or political debts) in federal judicial appointments became a key factor in deciding the outcome of the 1984 federal election. During the televised debate between John Turner and Brian Mulroney, Mulroney criticized Turner for appointing five Liberal MPs to the bench not long after Turner became prime minister.

Turner said he had no choice in the matter. Former prime minister Trudeau was planning to make the appointments before leaving office, but because the Liberals had only a slim majority in the House of Commons, these appointments would have left Turner, the new prime minister, with a minority government. To save the Liberal majority Trudeau agreed not to make the appointments as long as Turner agreed to appoint the judges after the election was called. Mulroney accused Turner of failing to do "the right thing." This critical moment left Mulroney the victor in the debate and was a key factor in his subsequent electoral victory. It is open to question, though, whether Mulroney himself has since done "the right thing" about reducing patronage in his federal judicial appointments.

Like the United Kingdom, Canada fills judicial vacancies through executive appointment, formally by the representative of the Crown but in practice by the federal minister of justice or provincial attorney general (with the prime minister or premier having the right to make the most prestigious appointments), depending on which court the appointment is to be made to. The appointee is selected from the ranks of experienced practising lawyers.

This description of the appointment process, however, is deceptively straightforward. It does accurately differentiate Canadian practices from those of many U.S. state courts, where the judges are elected by the general public for specific terms. In most cases, however, these judicial elections are merely confirmation elections. When judicial vacancies occur, non–partisan nominating commissions interview candidates and provide a short list to the state governor. The candidate selected by the governor serves a probationary year and then faces the confirmation election. No other candidates are on the ballot for that particular position, and voters can either confirm or reject the judge. Re–confirmation elections are usually held at intervals of six or twelve years. In the federal courts in the United States, elections do not occur; judges are appointed by the president.

The Canadian practice is also distinguished from the bureaucratic career pattern of continental Europe, where people choose a career in the judiciary straight out of university, starting at the bottom and working upward through a combination of merit and seniority, as described by Henry J. Abraham. Beyond that, however, the declaration that Canadian judgeships are appointive positions implies a uniformity that does not by any means exist.

In fact, there are three different appointing procedures which correspond to three categories of courts: the pure provincial courts sometimes referred to as "capital–P" Provincial Courts, the section 96 courts (federally appointed judges in provincial superior, county, and district courts), and section 101 courts (the Supreme Court of Canada, the Federal Court, and the Tax Court). Each category of court is subject to a different appointing power and procedure, and each is currently undergoing dramatic evolution. One thing that all three procedures have in common is a history of political patronage, although today patronage is becoming a less important factor in appointments to some Canadian courts.

Provincially Appointed Judges

The responsibility for appointing judges to the pure provincial courts lies exclusively with the provincial governments. Appointments are usually made by the attorney general with some input from the premier and often some feedback from the provincial cabinet.

For much of the period since Confederation, the saga of these appointments is very much a story not for the squeamish. Historically these courts of inferior jurisdiction have been poorly regarded. Their pay–scales, working conditions, and status did not attract the best legally trained personnel and the double consequence of this, according to John Hogarth, was the appointment of numbers of magistrates of dubious legal competence and also of substantial numbers of lay magistrates. The unilateral power of appointment meant that patronage often loomed large, while the equally unilateral power of removal — magistrates held their positions at the pleasure of the Crown until the reforms begun in the 1960s — meant that the provincial judiciary dwelt constantly in the shadow of the provincial executive council.

The situation changed abruptly and dramatically after 1968 (but not at the same time or the same pace in all provinces), when major revisions to the provincial court structure rippled across the country. Magistrates Courts became Provincial Courts and the status and qualifications of their bench were adjusted concomitantly. For one thing, a person appointed to the provincial bench in any province almost always needs a law degree and at least five years of legal experience — although ten years is the norm in practice. (In Alberta and Newfoundland non–lawyers can receive judicial appointments, but this rarely happens.) The days of the lay magistrate are over, save for the diminishing number of such individuals appointed before the restructuring. Provincial courts have acquired a chief judge (and often associate chief judges named to preside over specific regions or special functions) with responsibilities for the recruitment and the supervision of incumbents. The number of provincial judges has also tended to increase, sometimes dramatically. Many provinces also created judicial councils (with judicial, legal, and lay representation in varying numbers and proportions) with a formal statutory role in the removal and usually the appointment of provincial judges. What has been copied across the country is the *idea* of a judicial council rather than any single model of its composition or powers, as McCormick (1) shows.

To oversimplify slightly, and to imply an inter–provincial uniformity that is still in the process of development, the process for the appointment of a provincial judge now involves a formal letter of application accompanied by a resume. Typically, the chief judge or some other individual (often another member of a judicial council) may well have had some role in prompting the application. Indeed, some chief judges have indicated that the recruitment of new judges is the most time–consuming and possibly the most important of their duties.

In Saskatchewan and Newfoundland, applications for judgeships are sent to the attorney general, who selects appointees from among the applicants when judicial vacancies arise. The attorney general's preliminary selections are screened by the province's judicial council, which may recommend that certain candidates not be appointed. In British Columbia and Alberta the application is made (or immediately forwarded) to the Judicial Council itself, which screens applicants to generate a pool of qualified individuals from which the attorney general subsequently appoints provincial judges. In still other provinces, applicants are screened by a special committee that could be either ongoing (Ontario since 1989) or ad hoc (Quebec).

In all provinces except Prince Edward Island, the judicial independence of provincially appointed judges has been enhanced by the fact that they can be removed from office only on the recommendation of the provincial judicial council after an impartial inquiry, although the precise procedures involved and the way that specific provincial councils plug into the process vary considerably from one province to another.

The result of these changes is that patronage now plays a much smaller role in the appointment of pure provincial judges than it did two decades ago. Research by the Canadian Bar Association in 1985 indicated that patronage remains an important factor in judicial appointments by provincial governments only in five provinces: Nova Scotia, New Brunswick, Prince Edward Island, Manitoba, and Saskatchewan.

Today, to an extent that was clearly not true 20 years ago, provincial judges are legally qualified and appointed only after a formal screening by a neutral professional body. They also enjoy official independence in the performance of their duties. Our survey suggests that these reforms have radically changed the traditional assumption in the legal profession that the federally appointed judges tend to be better qualified than the pure provincial judges. Nearly half of the trial lawyers and crown attorneys we questioned in Ontario and Alberta thought that these two kinds of trial judges tended to be of equal competence. Only a sixth regarded these judges in terms of the traditional hierarchy of merit; about a third thought that on the whole, the federally appointed judges were more able but that a significant number of pure provincial judges were equal to or better than their federal counterparts. Some 75 per cent of the pure provincial judges and 55 per cent of the section 96 judges thought that, on the whole, pure provincial judges tended to be equal in ability to the federally appointed trial judges.

Provincial Superior Court Judges

Given Section 96 of the Constitution Act, 1867, which provides for the appointment by the federal government of judges in the provincial superior courts and the provincial county or district courts, political connections and experience were for decades an important consideration in the appointment of provincial superior court judges.

For example, Guy Bouthillier (1) reports that 54 per cent of the Quebec Court of Appeal judges appointed between 1867 and 1972 had previously been cabinet ministers or elected legislators, and William Klein found that a third of all judges appointed by the federal government in Ontario, Quebec, and Manitoba between 1905 and 1970 had previously run for elected office — most for the party that made the judicial appointment.

Among the Section 96 appointments, patronage is now a less important factor now than it was two decades ago, but only somewhat less. In 1985 the Canadian Bar Association reported that

patronage was *not* a "significant factor" only in federal appointments in British Columbia and Quebec. Recent research done by
Peter Russell and Jacob Zeigel has shown that the patronage factor
was as strong in the first Mulroney government as it had been
during the Trudeau years. The fact that patronage has remained
the basis for judicial appointments for so many years indicates that
it did not necessarily produce bad judges. It was just that the pool
of potential judges was limited to lawyers who had paid their dues
by working for the party in power.

Interestingly, the individuals appointed for political reasons
seem to have been drawn from provincial politics as often (or
sometimes more often) than from federal politics. The list of
provincial attorneys general who later served on the provincial
court of appeal, for example, would not be a short one. This in
turn suggests the historical importance of the linkages between
the federal and provincial wings of the Liberal and Conservative
parties.

To be sure, we should not allow a distaste for the more blatant
forms of patronage to be carried too far. To serve one's country
and one's province in elected office is not a criminal offense but
an honourable calling and cannot realistically or fairly be treated
as a total disqualification for subsequent judicial appointment.
Indeed, there is a case to be made for preferring that the higher
provincial courts contain some proportion of judges whose service
in public life has alerted them to the complexities of the legislative
process and the nuances of political reality as well as the techni-
calities of "black letter" law, given the degree of discretion with
which judges are often faced.

Our point about patronage, then, is meant to indicate the prev-
alent career patterns for judicial appointment rather than to con-
demn out of hand the individuals involved, but with a double
caveat. First, where political connections and professional competence both carry obvious weight in deciding who should serve
on the bench, it follows that an unusual degree of political clout
may sometimes be enough to offset a much more modest level of
legal ability. Second, the all–important appearance of judicial
neutrality may be undermined by an all–too–evident connection
between judges and partisan political leaders. The connection

often appears all the more sordid where the relevant political experience had more to do with party fundraising than with public service in cabinet. It is also fair to add that the calibre of judicial appointments has often been open to criticism.

Real change did not come until the 1970s, with what we might call the "Ratushny Revolution," so named for Ed Ratushny, assistant and later advisor to a series of Liberal justice ministers (including John Turner, Pierre Trudeau, and Otto Lang). Responding to the ongoing criticisms and determined to raise the quality of judicial appointments, the Department of Justice established a network of contacts in every province, including senior judges, deans of law schools, and prominent lawyers, to put forward the names of outstanding candidates. Informal enquiries would follow to create a pool of competent and outstanding lawyers for consideration for judicial appointment, and the minister of justice could draw on this pool when vacancies occurred.

As a final step, the names of potential appointees were sent to the National Committee on the Judiciary of the Canadian Bar Association to perform a last screening function by ranking them as "well qualified," "qualified," or "not qualified" for the proposed appointment. The new procedure resulted in a series of excellent appointments, and in his retrospective account of the process Ratushny points with pride to many of the judges appointed. It is reasonable to suggest that the broad net used for the initial name hunt was probably more significant in its effects than the final screening process.

One problem with the "Ratushny Revolution" was that its head–hunting and screening process was only as strong as the resolve of the minister of justice, and political considerations could short–circuit its operation. Precisely because it had no formal (let alone constitutional) sanction, the procedure could be bypassed, and political connections could shoot some candidates past others whose claims rested purely on professional achievements and disinterested recommendations. Even the final approval by the Canadian Bar Association committee could be evaded if the pressure of time and circumstances made it desirable to do so, as occurred in at least two cases during the rash of patronage appointments when John Turner replaced Pierre Trudeau as prime minister.

The Ratushny system proved itself capable of generating excellent judges, but the off–switch remained under partisan political fingers, and when the switch was turned off, it was business as usual for patronage. A second problem was that the Canadian Bar Association committee was not asked to comment on the "elevation" of judges from a lower court to a higher one, and a significant proportion of section 96 appointments are elevations.

The patronage factor in federal judicial appointments often meant that when the same party was in power in a province as federally, consultation would occur between the federal justice minister and the provincial attorney general regarding prospective section 96 appointments; when the same party was not in power, no consultation occurred. This pattern led to an ugly dispute between the federal and provincial authorities in Saskatchewan in the early 1980s. The Liberals had been in power in Ottawa since 1963 and had used their authority to ensure that few lawyers who were not good Liberals received appointments to the section 96 courts in Saskatchewan. When a Conservative government came to power in the province in 1982, it was determined to force the federal Liberal government to consult with regard to judicial appointments.

Saskatchewan's strategy was to reduce the size of its section 96 courts each time a judge retired so that the federal cabinet would have no judicial vacancies to fill. This standoff continued, according to Peter Russell (6), until the Conservatives came to power federally in 1984. John Crosbie, the new justice minister in Ottawa, committed himself to consulting both with the relevant provincial attorneys general and with the relevant chief justices before recommending new section 96 appointments to the cabinet.

In the 1984 election campaign, Mulroney's TV–debate promise to end patronage appointments resulted in the Conservative government establishing consultative committees on federal judicial appointments in each of the provinces — a policy that did not come into effect until just before the 1988 election. Essentially, the recruitment stage was transferred from the Department of Justice to the Commissioner of Federal Judicial Affairs, who receives applications and decides whether the applicants meet statutory requirements. As well, the screening function of the Canadian Bar Association committee was decentralized to five–person assessment committees (the membership of which is not made public) set up for each province and territory.

These assessment committees consist of a nominee of the provincial or territorial law society, a nominee of the local branch of the Canadian Bar Association, a federally appointed judge nominated by the chief justice of the province or territory, and one nominee of the federal minister of justice and one of the provincial or territorial attorney general. The committee is limited to reporting that a candidate is or is not qualified, and cannot, for example, rank applicants or highlight their fitness for specific courts or positions.

During the first year of operation of the new system, the government did not publicly advertise the new appointment procedure. Consequently, most of the applicants considered by the new consultative committees were names already on file with the minister of justice under the old system. The result, according to Peter Russell and Jacob Zeigel, is that patronage probably remains a major ingredient in federal judicial appointments — a situation not likely to change unless the consultative committees are given the power not only to screen candidates presented by the federal executive, but also to actively recruit good candidates to apply for judicial positions.

In addition, if the secrecy surrounding the committees was reduced so that the names of the committee members were made public and if each committee would produce an annual report (listing such facts as the number of applications considered, but not the "rating" given to each applicant), the process could be made both more accountable and credible.

Like the pre–1988 appointment system, the elevation of a sitting judge to a chief justice's position or to a higher court is not referred to these committees but is dealt with instead by the federal justice minister in consultation with the chief justice and the provincial attorney general. The Russell–Zeigel study and Peter McCormick's investigations show that such promotions make up a large part of the federal judicial appointment process.

For some three–quarters of all such elevations, the same political party made both the initial appointment and the elevation. This suggests (but does not prove) that patronage continues to be a factor in such decisions.

According to the research by McCormick, five of every nine appeal judges are promoted from the Section 96 trial bench, and they average nine years of trial bench experience prior to elevation. In only two decades in this century, the 1930s and 1950s, have judges with trial bench experience made up a minority of appellate appointments. Of the 239 provincial court of appeal judges for whom reliable information is available, 64 had been candidates for elected office, or provincial or federal representatives, or members of provincial or federal cabinets (including seven who had served as attorney general). Three others had been involved exclusively in municipal politics. Eight had served as crown attorneys or assistant crown attorneys, and ten had been members of the public service. Sixteen were drawn from academic ranks, with several years of full–time university appointment. Among 171 provincial court of appeal judges in this century about whom information could be obtained, the most common reasons for leaving the appellate bench were, not surprisingly, retirement (71 cases) or death (60 cases).

Even among the court of appeal judges there was an important number of elevations. Sixteen appeal judges were appointed to the Supreme Court of Canada (more than half of them since 1970), and 18 left the appeal bench to become chief justice of the provincial superior trial court. As Russell (6) points out, summaries of this sort may well understate the degree of political affiliation because they catch only the most publicly visible connections.

Federal Judges: The Supreme Court

At Confederation the basic structure of provincial courts already existed and was simply formally acknowledged and continued. There were no federal courts, nor were any federal courts directly established by the British North America Act. However, Section 101 of the BNA Act (now the Constitution Act, 1867) authorized the Parliament of Canada to create courts, and Parliament duly established the Supreme Court of Canada, the Federal Court (formerly the Exchequer Court), and the Tax Court. For all three courts, the same appointment procedure was used: the unfettered discretion of the Governor–General in Council, which under responsible government means the cabinet, which in actual practice means the minister of justice and the prime minister.

Judges of the most longstanding of these courts, the Supreme Court of Canada, are appointed and paid by the government of Canada, serving on good behaviour until age 75. As for all judicial appointments by the federal government, the minister of justice plays a major role, but the prime minister also tends to be personally involved in appointments to the highest court in the land. There is no formal requirement for any consultation before the appointment is made, nor is there any necessity of a formal ratification by any other body before the appointment becomes effective. The modest approval procedures adopted for Section 96 judges — such as circulating the names of possible appointees to the Judiciary Committee of the Canadian Bar Association or the new consultative committees for comment — seem not to apply to Supreme Court appointments.

One limit on federal discretion has been built into the Supreme Court Act since the beginning. That is the requirement that one–third of the justices be selected from the bar of the province of Quebec — a stipulation that *may* now be constitutionally entrenched by virtue of s.41(d) of the Constitution Act, 1982, although as Peter Hogg (1) notes, the experts disagree on this matter. In origins and logic, this requirement is not an example of regional representation, but rather a recognition of Quebec's unique civil law system and of the consequent concern that it not be undermined unwittingly at the hands of common law judges. However, the practice in appointments has been to treat the other six positions as belonging to specific regions as well: Ontario normally has three justices, the four Western provinces two, and the Atlantic provinces one, although brief departures from this convention are not unknown.

For the Supreme Court's first 75 years, as James Snell and Frederick Vaughan document so graphically, the major problem was simply getting good lawyers to serve. Trapped between the established prestige of the longstanding appeal courts of the central provinces and the final appellate authority of a Judicial Committee prepared to overrule it rather casually, the Supreme Court was not seen as the crowning achievement of an outstanding legal career, and many nominees refused appointment. The result was something of a vicious circle: many of the best lawyers would not serve because the Supreme Court was not seen as deserving of prestige and high reputation, and the Court could not earn such a reputation because the best lawyers often declined to serve on it.

The circle was only broken by the amendment to the Supreme Court Act in 1949 that patriated final appellate authority by abolishing appeals to the Judicial Committee. (The abolition of the right to appeal was not retroactive, so cases initiated before 1949 continued to wend their way to London through the 1950s; the last major JCPC decision in Canadian law was decided in 1954.) The truly supreme Supreme Court is a development of only the last 40 years, and the high–profile Supreme Court of only the last 20.

Patriation, and the status of a final appellate body, only highlighted the logical flaw of the Supreme Court's origins. Although it has since 1949 served as the final arbiter of intergovernmental disputes over jurisdiction, it is created and staffed unilaterally by the federal government. In the hockey game of Canadian jurisprudence on federalism issues, Team National gets to bring its own referees. As Peter Hogg (2) points out, the question "Is the Supreme Court of Canada biased in constitutional cases?" is one that recurs by the very nature of things every time the federal government "wins" a major argument in the courts. It's a question that reflects a logical and defensible fear on the part of provincial officials.

One trend that is clear in Supreme Court appointments is the salience of previous judicial experience. Of the 16 judges appointed to the Supreme Court of Canada since 1970, 13 have been elevated from a provincial superior court, and one was elevated from the Federal Court. There are, clearly, logically sound reasons for this trend: a smoother transition to new judicial responsibilities, and a proven track record of competence and judgment that reduces the risk of disappointing performance.

However, the trend can also be seen in another light. Judges are trained professionals who value rigorous logic and thoughtful consistency, and they give not only decisions but also written reasons for those decisions. From this, it follows that judges generate a written record of the predilections and value preferences that constrain and colour their judgment, in the form of reasoned convictions about issues like those arising from the Charter and federalism. The professional qualities for which judges are deservedly respected make this record a reliable predictor of future performance. This record is part of the background against which a prime minister makes appointments and can be a major component of the choice. So far, it does not appear that prime ministers have used their unilateral power to stack the court with judges favouring a particular line or style of decision-making, although there are a handful of spectacular counter–examples.

It is therefore only to be expected that the debate on constitutional reform of the last quarter–century would time and again have raised the question of a provincial role in Supreme Court appointments, to create a truly neutral Supreme Court able to adjudicate impartially (and to be seen to have done so) in constitutional cases. The Victoria Charter — approved briefly by all 11 governments in 1970 before Quebec's premier Robert Bourassa withdrew support at the last moment — would have required consultation and agreement between the federal minister of justice and the attorney general of the province from which the appointee came, with elaborate arrangements if the two could not reach agreement. More recently, the Meech Lake Accord would have given provincial premiers the right to propose nominations for Supreme Court vacancies, leaving nothing but a choice and a veto to the national government.

It is, of course, an open question as to whether the effect of a provincial role in judicial appointments would have a real impact, or whether it would simply contribute to the status and effective power of the Supreme Court itself. However appointed, the judges of the Supreme Court of Canada stand at the apex of the Canadian court system. Whether they uphold or reverse the lower court decisions that come to them, and whatever the reasoned arguments they present, their decisions of necessity become a statement of the single unified conception of law that binds all lower courts. Arguably, the prime minister might "lose" some influence and discretion by a less unilateral appointment process, but the Supreme Court itself would gain in the sense that it could no longer be attacked as the creature of the national government.

Breach of "Good Behaviour"

To help guarantee their "independence," judges can be removed from office only for a breach of "good behaviour." In the common law, Peter Russell (6) notes, "breach of good behaviour" includes only "improper exercise of the office, neglect or refusal to perform the duties of the office, or conviction for a serious criminal offence involving moral turpitude." (p. 176)

Since the *Valente* decision in 1985, which established that judges may be removed only for breach of good behaviour after an impartial inquiry, it has been unclear whether the political authorities that have the ultimate responsibility for removing judges — Parliament or the provincial cabinet or legislature, depending on the court involved — have the constitutional authority to broaden this definition. Given this decision, it is possible that such inquiries will confine themselves to the common law approach to good behaviour. Since *Valente*, the only recommendations for the removal of judges have come from inquiries into the behaviour of Provincial Court judges, and all of the recommendations have adhered to the common law concept of "good behaviour."

In Ontario inquiries were recommended by the Ontario Judicial Council with regard to two judges, but the inquiries never took place. In 1987 it was alleged that a Windsor judge threatened to hold in contempt of court anyone who tried to enforce the City of Windsor's parking bylaw. (*The Globe and Mail*, March 1, 1989, A2) A judicial inquiry was established, but before it convened the judge reached retirement age, which ended the matter.

In 1989 a Toronto judge presided over the trial of a man charged with assaulting his wife. According to *The Globe and Mail* (February 14 and March 1, 1989, A1), the judge blamed the wife for the assault and ordered her to be handcuffed and removed from the court. The attorney general asked the Ontario Judicial Council for a report on the conduct of the judge. The Council ordered an inquiry, but before it could take place the judge resigned.

An inquiry in Nova Scotia, also in 1989, recommended that a Provincial Court judge be removed for committing a crime that violated the "moral standards of the community." The judge had been convicted of assaulting his wife, and resigned to avoid being fired. (*Toronto Star*, April 17, 1990, A3.)

In 1988 two Manitoba judges were accused of involvement in a parking ticket scandal. It was alleged that some Provincial Court judges and magistrates (nowadays, magistrates are court officials who hear minor traffic cases under the supervision of a judge) had a practice of accepting gifts in exchange for cancelling parking tickets. One Provincial Court judge and one magistrate pleaded guilty to charges laid against them after a "plea bargain." (A plea bargain is an agreement by an accused person with a crown attorney to plead guilty in return for a reduced charge or a more lenient sentencing recommendation. The guilty plea avoids the necessity of a trial and so is beneficial to the crown attorney, and of course the sentencing recommendation and reduced charges are beneficial to the accused if he or she is guilty. A large proportion of guilty pleas in Canadian courts are a result of a plea bargain.) The judge retired shortly before his conviction. The chief judge of the Provincial Court was also charged in relation to the ticket–fixing scandal, but was acquitted. The provincial Judicial Council nevertheless investigated and criticized him, but concluded that his behaviour did not warrant his removal as a judge. However, he was demoted to the position of an ordinary judge. (*The Globe and Mail*, December 2, 1988, A10; and Nora Underwood et al. in *Maclean's*, April 24, 1989.)

Throughout Canada's history there has never been an example of a federally appointed superior court judge who has been removed through joint address of the Senate and House of Commons. (In England, where a similar procedure applies, only one judge has ever been removed.) During the twentieth century, the only example of proceedings being initiated for the removal of a superior court judge involved Mr. Justice Leo Landreville in 1966. It was alleged that ten years earlier, before Landreville was a judge, he had used his influence as mayor of Sudbury to help the

Northern Ontario Natural Gas Company obtain the franchise for the distribution of natural gas in Sudbury. He was acquitted of criminal charges against him, but a royal commission inquiry found that his behaviour had not been to the standard required of a judge. The fact that justice minister Pierre Trudeau initiated proceedings to remove the judge precipitated his resignation, as Russell (6) recounts.

In several cases, superior court judges have resigned after embarrassing publicity about their behaviour has appeared and before an inquiry into their behaviour could be set up. Perhaps the best–known recent example of this concerns Davie Fulton, a former federal justice minister and Progressive Conservative leadership candidate, who was appointed to the trial division of the British Columbia Supreme Court in 1973 by the Trudeau government.

As Jack Batten relates, Fulton's reputation was tarnished by a series of unfortunate events beginning in 1979, when he was charged and then convicted of impaired driving. Soon afterwards, a Vancouver prostitute published her memoirs and claimed that Fulton had been one of her clients, along with B.C. chief justice John Farris. Farris resigned from the bench, but Fulton claimed not to know the prostitute and brought a libel suit against her. Before the case got to court, the prostitute admitted that Fulton had not been her client — the client had been another lawyer named David.

The stress caused by this incident led Fulton to resume drinking, and in 1981 he was again convicted of impaired driving. Because this was a second offence, he had to spend two weeks (on weekends) in jail, and so he resigned from the bench rather than face an inquiry by the Canadian Judicial Council. It is heartening to learn from Batten that Fulton, who had an excellent reputation both as justice minister and as a superior court judge, stopped drinking and went on to a successful career in private practice with elements of public service, such as heading a government inquiry into the land claims of the Lubicon Lake Indians in Alberta in 1985.

There are two recent examples of formal inquiries into the conduct of superior court judges. The first occurred in 1981 when Mr. Justice Thomas Berger of the British Columbia Supreme

Court spoke at a university convocation in November and criticized the November 5 constitutional accord for ignoring the rights of Native Canadians and Quebeckers. His remarks had also appeared in *The Globe and Mail*.

Mr. Justice G.A. Addy of the Federal Court objected to Berger's intervention in politics and wrote to the Canadian Judicial Council to complain that Berger had violated judicial independence. The Council initiated an inquiry by a committee of investigation composed of three judges. The committee reported that Berger's foray into politics was a violation of judicial independence so serious that in the future, judges guilty of similar actions should be removed. The reasoning was that Berger's statements would cause him to appear biased when hearing future constitutional cases or cases involving Native rights. As well, when a judge makes a political statement, this is a tacit invitation for politicians to reply, thus dragging judges further into the political arena. (In fact, Prime Minister Trudeau did comment publicly on Berger's pronouncements. According to Russell (6), Trudeau said, "I just regard that [Berger's statements] as the judiciary getting mixed into politics.... I hope the judges will do something about it.")

The full Canadian Judicial Council agreed that Berger had acted improperly, but did not regard his offence as serious enough for removal from the bench. The Council reprimanded Berger and left it at that. Berger eventually resigned from the bench in any case, possibly in response to the distress caused by the Council's formal inquiry.

The second inquiry concerns the conduct of the five judges of the Nova Scotia Court of Appeal who in 1983 had finally acquitted Donald Marshall, Jr. of murder after he spent 11 years in jail for being wrongfully convicted. Although the Court of Appeal acquitted Marshall, the judges wrote that Marshall was in large measure to blame for his plight by attempting to rob the murder victim and lying about this in court. In 1987 and 1988, a royal commission investigation into the miscarriage of justice around the Marshall affair concluded that the Court of Appeal was wrong to have blamed Marshall. The Commissioners wrote that

The Court [of Appeal] used the evidence before it — as well as information that was never admitted into evidence — to "convict" Marshall of a robbery with which he was never charged, and concluded, in our view erroneously, that Marshall had "admittedly" committed perjury. The Court's further suggestion that Marshall's "untruthfulness ... contributed in large measure to his conviction" was not sustained by the evidence before the Court.... We have concluded that the Court's decision amounted to a defence of the criminal justice system at the expense of Donald Marshall, Jr. in spite of overwhelming evidence that the system itself had failed.

In 1990 the attorney general of Nova Scotia requested the Canadian Judicial Council to investigate the propriety of the behaviour of the five Court of Appeal judges, especially with regard to whether they had misused their office or exceeded their authority.

Only four federally appointed judges at the county and district court level have been removed. Unlike superior court judges, county and district judges can be removed by the cabinet, but only after an impartial inquiry. The most interesting example of the removal of a district court judge occurred in Manitoba in 1933. Judge Lewis St. George Stubbs had become converted to socialism. In his role as a surrogate court judge, Stubbs discovered in 1929 that a recently deceased Winnipeg merchant had signed three wills, two leaving large sums to charity, and one leaving his assets to his family. It turned out that none of the wills was valid, but Stubbs felt that the wills stipulating the charitable donation represented the true desire of the deceased merchant, and he suggested that the Manitoba legislature should intervene to bring this about.

In the meantime the family succeeded in obtaining an order from the Court of Appeal to gain access to the estate. Thereupon, as Dale Gibson and Lee Gibson recount, Stubbs held a public meeting in a theatre to denounce the Court of Appeal and press for legislative intervention. Stubbs also published pamphlets criticizing the appeal court. Complaints were made to the federal minister of justice, but the Liberal government which had appointed Stubbs refused to act. Meanwhile, the Manitoba legislature reduced Stubbs' stipend as a provincial surrogate court judge; as a result, Stubbs chastised the attorney general in comments he made in his court, going to far as to call the attorney general a liar.

After the Conservatives came to power in Ottawa in 1930, a judicial inquiry was appointed to investigate complaints that Stubbs had misbehaved. The inquiry determined that Stubbs' attacks on the Court of Appeal at the public meeting and in his pamphlets "did great harm to judicial institutions" and therefore constituted judicial misconduct. As well, it stated that calling the attorney general a liar in court and in pamphlets was improper. Upon receiving the inquiry's report, the federal cabinet removed Stubbs from judicial office. He went on to become a member of the Manitoba Legislature, which was perhaps a more appropriate place to pursue his agenda for social reform.

While it is not known how many Provincial Court judges and magistrates (the term used for these judges before the 1970s) have been removed, it is safe to say that more of them have been removed than federally appointed judges. This is in part because the procedure for removal of Provincial Court judges was quite lax until the last decade or two, and in part because it has only been in the last few decades that the provincial appointing authorities have placed much emphasis on quality appointments.

In a number of cases that come before the Canadian Judicial Council and provincial judicial councils, a judge's conduct is "serious enough to be questioned and reviewed but not serious enough to justify removal." (Russell [6], 184) Such conduct might include an isolated impolite comment in court, being habitually ten minutes late for court, or a minor drinking problem. In such cases, a judicial council will often handle the issue more informally by delivering a private reprimand to the judge, for example. In many other cases, such complaints will find their way to the appropriate chief judge or chief justice rather than the judicial council, and these are dealt with informally by the chief.

In general, the few examples of judges who have been removed from office or have had their reputations seriously questioned testify to the high calibre of the Canadian judiciary. Judicial "mis-behaviour" is an exceptional circumstance, although this is not to deny that the umbrella of judicial independence is sometimes broad enough to shelter bad manners or a short temper, as documented by Nora Underwood.

Training

For most of Canada's history it has been assumed that judges need no training other than a legal education and several years of experience practising law. This approach, which is usual in common law countries, contrasts with civil law jurisdictions such as France, where would–be judges must graduate from a specialized training program for judges. After successful graduation, the newly trained judicial specialists apply for a junior judgeship, and then are promoted up the judicial hierarchy by other judges according to merit.

It is now generally accepted that while several years' experience as a lawyer is a useful background for a judge to have, it does not satisfy all of a judge's training needs. This fact becomes evident when we consider that only a minority of judicial appointees have had extensive courtroom experience and only a minority of criminal court judges have specialized in criminal law. In 1971, E.A. Tollefson proposed that new judges should receive a year of combined instruction and in–service training, and in 1973 Jean de Montigny and Pierre Robert recommended that new judges should attend a judges academy for two months.

Judicial training in Canada has far to go before it meets either of these recommendations, but some progress has been made in recent years. In 1971 Parliament established the Canadian Judicial Council in part to "improve the quality of judicial service" in courts staffed by federally appointed judges. This council, composed of all chief and associate chief judges and justices in these courts (totalling 39 judges in 1990), has both an educational and a disciplinary role. With regard to judicial education, the council conducts several week–long seminars each year, including one on judgment writing. As well, the Canadian Institute for the Administration of Justice (an organization composed of judges, lawyers, and academics, established in 1974 to promote judicial research and education) runs an annual one–week seminar for new judges with the support of the Canadian Judicial Council. The provincial judicial councils or judges associations run similar seminars for Provincial Court judges.

But although judicial education has improved during the past two decades, it remains a "patchwork quilt," to use the words of Ontario's former chief justice, William Howland, in the First Annual Report of the Canadian Judicial Council. To promote more comprehensive judicial education, the Canadian Judicial Centre was established in Ottawa in 1987. It is jointly financed by the federal and provincial governments and has a mandate "to design and coordinate educational services for both federally and provincially appointed judges." The centre has already organized frequent "early orientation" seminars for new judges to supplement the existing training sessions.

Conclusion

The selection processes for the various kinds of judges in Canada are variations on a theme, and that theme is executive appointment; the variations have to do with recent and rather marginal limits on the exercise of that executive discretion. There is a clear advantage to appointing judges rather than, for example, electing them, in that the attributes of professional competence, legal precision, and adjudicative fairness are not easily assessed in an election campaign. The disadvantage, of course, is that there is no guarantee that these qualities will be pre–emptively important in the appointive selection process either, and that they won't be overridden by other considerations such as political party patronage.

Canada inherited the tradition of appointing judges for political patronage reasons from the United Kingdom. However, early in this century this tradition changed in Britain. It became a constitutional principle that the Lord Chancellor — the cabinet minister who appoints all the superior court judges and many inferior court judges — would make the appointments based on merit.

Canada has lagged far behind this example. Some important reforms have been made in appointment procedures in recent years to reduce the patronage factor and to stress merit more while at the same time ensuring that political experience is not a factor detrimental to a judicial appointment. The reforms have been the most effective regarding the appointment of Provincial Court judges in British Columbia, Alberta, Ontario, Quebec, and Newfoundland. However, in five provinces — the three Maritime provinces, Saskatchewan, and Manitoba — patronage remains an important factor in the appointment of Provincial Court judges.

Even after the reforms introduced by the Mulroney government in 1988, party activity on behalf of the Conservatives is the single most important factor in predicting federal judicial appointments to the provincial superior courts and the Federal Court. Fortunately, for the last few decades prime ministers have resisted the temptation to make patronage appointments in the Supreme Court of Canada.

In spite of the long history of partisan political appointments to the Canadian courts, the practice of appointing judges according to their ideological orientation has not been part of our tradition — in stark contrast to the situation in the United States, where a candidate's liberal or conservative leaning is a major factor in the president's nominations for federal judicial appointments, and in the Senate's confirmation process. Because Canadian judges, thanks to the Charter of Rights, are called on to make a greater number of policy–oriented decisions than in the past, it may be difficult for the appointing authorities in Canada to continue to ignore the variable of ideology.

The governments in Canada that continue to appoint judges to reward the party faithful will most likely continue to do so unless public pressure forces them to change. Perhaps one reason why public pressure has not been much of a factor so far is that the current system has resulted in very little judicial corruption, and although judges selected according to merit might often be better judges, the judges that the patronage system has produced have in general been good judges. As well, even if partisan considerations eventually disappear, governments may nevertheless begin to select judges based on their apparent willingness to conform to the appointing authority's ideological preference.

Canadians can promote reform and prevent regress in the appointment of judges by insisting on judicial appointment procedures that are likely to result in the selection of the very best judges. In our view the most promising option available is the one adopted by British Columbia, Alberta, Ontario, and Quebec: the creation of non–partisan nominating committees that advertise for qualified judicial candidates and then present a short list of those most qualified to the cabinet minister responsible for appointments.

The membership of such nominating committees should include at least one member nominated by the provincial attorney general, one by the federal minister of justice, and one by the judiciary. As well, at least one member should be from outside the legal community. With federal and provincial representation on nominating committees for both pure provincial judges and federally appointed judges, the fragmentation of the courts might be overcome; if new judges are acceptable to both orders of government, court unification is more likely.

Judicial representation will ensure that the observations of the sitting judges about the lawyers being considered for appointment — views that could be very cogent — will be considered. And lay representation may help the nominating committees keep in mind the overarching goal of courts — to provide a dispute–resolution agency that is truly a public service.

Another issue that the public may become concerned about is judicial education — something now almost non–existent except for the legal training that lawyers receive and the recently established one–week seminars for new judges. Is the practice of law for at least ten years really the best training–ground for judges? As noted earlier, in continental Europe prospective judges must obtain specialized training in judging for a year or more as part of their post–secondary education. They must then apprentice in the court system and work their way up to the more senior judicial positions through promotions based on merit.

The weakness of the European system is that judges often lack the "real world" experience that Canadian judges all have. One wonders, however, whether the best features of both systems of judicial recruitment and training could be combined. It may also be worth considering the British practice of appointing lawyers who are prospective judges as part–time judges to begin with. If they show themselves to be competent they may well receive a full–time judicial appointment.

Another foreign innovation that could tie into judicial training is the U.S. idea of judicial performance reviews. As Dorothy Linder Maddi points out, a number of credible systems have been developed through which trial lawyers can evaluate the performance of individual judges. Judges could use the results of such reviews in their continuing education programs, much as some university professors use the results of their teaching evaluations to improve their teaching. We will return to the consideration of these innovative ideas in our concluding chapter.

3

The Background
Characteristics of Judges

What kinds of people become judges? Given that almost all judges are lawyers, and given the patronage factor, we can surmise that the majority of judges are well–educated (and therefore, by definition, in the middle or upper socio–economic class) and have participated in politics of one form or another. And given that most judges have at least ten years' experience as practising lawyers before becoming judges, and that they retire between the ages of 65 and 75, their average age is probably in the 50s. But other than these bare–bones facts, what are the backgrounds of judges?

Moreover, what difference does it make what the backgrounds of judges are, given that judges must decide cases impartially? Isn't one well–educated and middle–aged judge going to decide cases much like any other? There is no doubt in our minds, based on our interviews with judges in Ontario and Alberta, that judges generally do their level best to be as impartial as possible. However, when they are faced with giving meaning to general phrases that could have a number of plausible meanings, such as many of those in the Charter, and there are few if any guiding precedents, the principle of impartiality may be of little assistance.

In these cases judges may apply what they perceive to be the standard of the "average reasonable person," but that perception may be influenced by the judges' personal experiences and backgrounds. It is worthwhile, then, to delve a little deeper into the backgrounds of judges and ask whether those backgrounds put them in an ideal position to assess the views of the "average reasonable person."

To consider this issue we relied on three sources of information. The first source was the biographical questionnaire filled out by Alberta judges: 116, or 67 per cent, of the judges responded, an unusually high response rate for a mailed questionnaire, which was achieved only thanks to the support of the two chief justices and the chief judge as well as follow–up contacts with the judges who did not respond immediately.

Second, we analysed the press releases of a random sample of 277 section 96 judges and provincially appointed judges from across Canada. The information from these press releases was much less rich than the data from the Alberta biographical questionnaires. However, by comparing the two sources of data we were able to establish how our conclusions about the Alberta judges could be generalized to apply to Canadian judges as a whole.

Third, we tapped other studies of judicial backgrounds in Canada, which include John Hogarth's *Sentencing as a Human Process* (1971), which described the background characteristics of 71 of the 78 Ontario magistrates (now Provincial Court judges) who dealt annually with at least 700 Criminal Code cases; Guy Bouthillier's four studies of judges in Quebec, published in the 1970s and based on information obtained from various biographical sources about judges appointed from 1867 to the early 1970s; John Porter's *The Vertical Mosaic*, which includes brief comments on the "senior" Canadian judiciary from 1940 to 1960 (he included only Supreme Court of Canada judges, plus the chief justices of the provincial superior courts and the Exchequer Court); Dennis Olsen's extension of Porter's analysis to 1973 in *The State Elite* (1980); and William Klein's study of the political backgrounds of judges in Manitoba, Ontario, and Quebec from 1905 to 1970 in his Ph.D. dissertation. In addition, there are three major sources of information on the backgrounds of Supreme Court of Canada judges. These are a biographical history of the Supreme Court by George Adams and Paul Cavalluzzo published in 1969, Peter Russell's study of the bilingual and bicultural aspects of the Supreme Court published in 1969 (9), and the history of the Supreme Court by James Snell and Frederick Vaughan published in 1985. We supplemented this information with the more recent biographies of the current Supreme Court judges which are published in *The Canadian Who's Who*.

It is obvious from the list above that not a great deal of research has been done into the backgrounds of Canadian judges. Our own study in Alberta is the only one which involves a survey of provincially appointed as well as federally appointed judges in a province.

In doing this study we compared the backgrounds of judges to those of average Canadians. The judges have no control over some of the characteristics, such as their ethnicity, sex, age, and the religion and social class they were born into. Others are a result of choice and achievement, such as marital status, prior career experience, and prior political experience.

Ethnicity

Canadian judges tend to over–represent the British and French ethnicities, and to under–represent the minority ethnicities. This is especially true in the older, more established provinces like Ontario and Quebec. John Porter and Dennis Olsen found in their separate studies that the non–British and non–French ethnicities were significantly under–represented among the senior judiciary in these provinces. On the other hand, in the newer Western provinces with their less entrenched legal–judicial establishments, the British are over–represented on the bench, but not to any great extent. For example, in Alberta 54 per cent of the Alberta judiciary is of British origin, compared with 50 per cent of the Alberta population. Peter Russell (6) notes that non–Caucasians are especially under–represented on the judiciary in all provinces. American Indians and Asians represent 6 per cent of the Alberta population, for example, but in 1985 there was only one judge of Asian origin and none of Native descent.

The over–representation of people of English and French origin among the judges is partly a result of these groups having lived in Canada longer than the other ethnic groups, with the exception of Native Canadians. Being better established in society, they have the resources to send their children to law school, and they have the political connections that in some provinces are important for obtaining judicial appointments. Thus, it is not surprising that although only 84 per cent of Albertans were born in Canada, 93 per cent of Alberta judges are Canadian–born. More important, the minority ethnic groups have been the victims of systematic discrimination for many years.

As a result it has been much more difficult for their members to pursue a legal or judicial career — a fact illustrated by the history of one of Canada's greatest judges, Bora Laskin. After graduating from law school in Toronto in 1936 and being admitted to the Law Society of Upper Canada in 1937, Laskin was unable to obtain a good position in a law firm in Toronto because he was Jewish, so he went to graduate school in the United States. He obtained a master's degree in law at Harvard University, and then was able to secure a position as a law teacher at Toronto's Osgoode Hall Law School and later at the University of Toronto Law School. Several decades later the climate had changed and Laskin was appointed to the Ontario Court of Appeal in 1965 and elevated to the Supreme Court of Canada in 1970, the first person of neither British nor French origin to attain such a position. He became chief justice in 1973.

The under–representation of the minority ethnicities, and particularly the non–Caucasians, creates problems for the justice system. Some members of the minority ethnicities are sceptical about the ability of the judiciary to fully comprehend issues in cases that involve culture–specific factual situations. It also means that the Canadian judiciary lacks the insights that could be provided in judicial decisions about equality rights if they were written by judges who had personal experiences with discrimination.

Gender

According to our survey of press releases, in 1990 only 7.5 per cent of Canadian superior court judges and 6 per cent of the provincially appointed judges were women. This gross under–representation of women is largely a product of the fact that the legal profession was dominated by men until recent years, as a result of social values and prejudice. There is now a fairly large group of women lawyers with at least ten years of experience, so it can be expected that the proportion of women in the judiciary will increase.

However, women still face barriers in pursuing judgeships that men do not. According to our interviews with women judges, some husbands strongly object to changing jobs or moving so that their wives can accept a judicial posting. And because many men still do not accept equal responsibility for child care, women lawyers with children are likely to have less career experience than male lawyers of the same age. Thus, the rate of increase in the proportion of female judges may be slower than the rate of increase in women graduates of law.

As with the under–representation of the ethnic minorities on the judiciary, the under–representation of women means, in Russell's words (6), that "insights and knowledge needed for intelligent adjudication are often lacking." Moreover, the stereotypical views that some male judges still occasionally exhibit about the "proper woman's role" may influence some judicial decisions, as Mary Eberts has demonstrated.

In an address in Toronto in 1990, Madame Justice Bertha Wilson tackled the question of whether an increased proportion of women judges will make much difference to the interpretation and application of the law. She said that women tend to have a different perspective from men on some issues. For example, in the areas of contract, real property, and corporate law Wilson said that there is probably not a separate woman's perspective. However, she said, "Some aspects of the criminal law, in particular, cry out for change since they are based on presuppositions about the nature of women and women's sexuality that in this day and age are little short of ludicrous." She cited U.S. studies that found that some male judges, in tort, criminal, and family law cases, were not impartial because their decisions were based on assumptions about the traditional role of women.

Wilson elaborated on one theory as to why men and women judges may view some legal issues differently. During their childhood, boys learn to distance themselves from their mothers to assert their masculinity, while girls learn to identify with their mothers. The result is that men tend to see the world in terms of competing rights and individual self–determination, while women stress competing obligations, relationships, and caring. According to Wilson, the male dominance over the legal–judicial system may account for the direction the adversary system has taken. It promotes battles over competing rights rather than compromise, and the rules of evidence attempt to exclude information about the general circumstances surrounding the cases — the kind of evidence that women are more likely to find relevant than men.

Wilson stressed that the goal of an impartial judicial system is not to introduce elements of female bias to counteract male bias, but rather to educate all judges — male and female — to be more sensitive to each others' differing perspectives. We might add that this sensitivity is more likely to develop with a more equal balance of men and women on the bench.

Age

Because they are usually appointed from among the ranks of lawyers with many years of experience in private practice, judges are older than the average adult Canadian.

The average age of federally appointed judges in Canadian provincial courts is about 60, and does not vary significantly from province to province. Most provincially appointed judges are several years younger, which is not surprising given the lower retirement age for most of them. Our survey of press releases indicates that the average age of section 96 judges in Canada is 59, and of provincially appointed judges, 53. In Alberta, where more complete data were available, we calculated the average age of federally appointed judges to be 58, and of Provincial Court judges, 56. The press release survey indicated that section 96 judges had served on the bench an average of 10.3 years, while the provincially appointed judges had served 10.5 years. The average age on appointment of the section 96 judges was 49, and of provincially appointed judges, 41. Supreme Court of Canada judges are slightly older, with an average age, as of February 1989, of 63. Their average age at appointment was 58.

These averages can hide the actual range of ages. Table 3.1, for example, shows the distribution of the ages of section 96 judges on appointment, according to the press release survey. Although

Table 3.1 Age of Section 96 Judges at Appointment

```
Age on
Appointment
35–39  |**********
40–44  |************************
45–49  |*****************************************************
50–54  |******************************
55–59  |****************************
60–64  |******
65–69  |**
       0          12         24         36         48         60
```

Number of s.96 Judges in Press Release Survey
(total cases for which age reported = 178)

most judges are appointed between the ages of 45 and 49, some are as young as 36 on appointment, and some as old as 66.

It appears that judges are being appointed, on average, at a somewhat younger age today than in past decades. Looking at the period 1848 to 1974, Guy Bouthillier (3) found that at the time of appointment the average age of Quebec Superior Court judges was 60, and of Court of Appeal judges (1867–1972), 55. According to John Hogarth's study, the average age of Ontario magistrates in the mid–1960s was 55.

As long as it is considered important that judges are recruited from the ranks of experienced lawyers, it is inevitable that they will be older. This may mean that judges, when making policy through interpreting the law, will find it more difficult to consider the policy implications of changing social values than the relatively younger policy–makers in the executive and legislative branches.

Religion

Judges tend to belong disproportionately to the main–line religious groups in Canada — Roman Catholic, Anglican, United Church, and Jewish — with a heavy skewing toward the more prestigious and established affiliations. In Alberta, for example, 21 per cent of the judges are Anglican, compared with 9 per cent of the Alberta population. According to our own research and that of Hogarth, those from the minor protestant religions, and non–

Christians, tend to be under–represented on the bench. (Information on religion was not included in the press release information.)

The point is not, of course, that ambitious lawyers can improve their chances to judicial appointment by joining the Anglican Church, but rather that the Anglican affiliation correlates with the higher social status that facilitates achievement and recognition. This tendency for the major religions to be over–represented on the bench is simply another indication that judges, like all elites, tend to be drawn more from the established sectors of society. This fact may make it somewhat more difficult for the judiciary as a whole to understand the differential impact that some laws (such as Sunday closing laws) may have on the approximately one–eighth of Canadians who profess to have no religion, or on those who adhere to the less prominent religions, and especially non–Christians.

Social Class

As might be expected, socially judges come disproportionately from upper–class backgrounds. In Alberta, 46 per cent of the fathers of federally appointed judges and 52 per cent of the fathers of Provincial Court judges were businessmen, lawyers, or other professionals, compared with 9 per cent of Alberta males in 1931 (which is around the time when most of these judges were born). Conversely, 37 per cent of Alberta judges had fathers who were labourers or farmers, compared with 87 per cent of the men in the province when the judges were children (see Table 3.2).

Table 3.2 Alberta Judges: Occupations of Fathers

Occupation	Fathers of Queen's Bench and Court of Appeal judges	Fathers of Provincial Court Judges	Alberta Males 1981	1931
Businessman	22%	25%	8%	7%
Labourer	24%	22%	35%	38%
Farmer	13%	15%	9%	48%
Lawyer	15%	17%	0.4%	0.2%
Other Professional	9%	10%	3%	2%
Administrative and Clerical	13%	3%	12%	3%
Teacher	4%	7%	2%	1%
Other	1%	1%	30%	1%

According to John Hogarth, 25 per cent of the Ontario magistrates in the mid–1960s had fathers who were in the labourer, farmer, or teacher categories. Bouthillier (3) notes that 32 per cent of Quebec superior court judges (1849–1974) had fathers in these categories. And George Adams and Paul J. Cavalluzzo report that only two of the first fifty Supreme Court of Canada judges were born into working–class families.

Judges also tend to be the children of lawyers to a disproportionate degree. In the Quebec and Ontario studies, 25 per cent of the judges were the children of lawyers; in the Alberta study, 16 per cent of the judges were. At the time when the fathers were practising law, lawyers constituted only about 0.2 per cent of adult males. Moreover, 60 per cent of the Quebec judges, 65 per cent of the federally appointed Alberta judges, and 38 per cent of the Alberta Provincial Court judges had relatives who were lawyers. Given the tendency of children to adopt the occupations of their parents or other relatives, this finding is hardly surprising; but it does indicate the difficulty that judges may have in identifying the standards of the "average reasonable person."

The question of whether the judiciary should be more representative of the social class backgrounds of Canadians is a difficult one. There are some critics, such as Dennis Olsen, who think that the upper–class nature of the judiciary indicates the failure of our governing system to implement the liberal–democratic value of equality. Others, for example Peter Russell (6), think that because being born in a middle–class or upper–class family (especially a family of lawyers) does provide advantages to children who aspire to a judicial career, a non–partisan appointment process structured to recruit the very best judges will always recruit judges disproportionately from the middle and upper classes.

Moreover, judges from a working–class background may not necessarily be more sympathetic to the claims of workers when those judges come to make decisions on issues that are more policy–oriented than legal. According to Russell, "Some very tough attitudes may be engendered in the person who has had to struggle and 'make it the hard way.'" There is some evidence (discussed in chapter 9) that judges from business and professional backgrounds may tend to accept more Charter claims in favour of individual litigants than judges from working and farming backgrounds.

Marital Status

The proportion of judges who are married is higher than the proportion of Canadians of the same age who are married. For example, 93 per cent of Alberta judges are married, compared with about 80 per cent of the general population in the same age bracket. (The press release data were incomplete regarding the marital status of the judges.) Only 3 per cent of Alberta judges were single or divorced — a much smaller proportion than the general population. According to Hogarth, only 4 per cent of Ontario magistrates in the mid–1960s were single or divorced. Of the twelve judges who served on the Supreme Court of Canada in 1988 and 1989 (there were three retirements), ten were married, one was single, and one was widowed.

As a result, judges may have some difficulty in understanding the problems of Canadians who are single (whether heterosexual or gay) or divorced.

Prior Career Experience

Almost all judges are recruited from the ranks of lawyers, but what kinds of lawyers? Table 3.3 shows the occupations of Alberta judges before they sat on the bench. Of these judges, 70 per cent had held more than one job, but only eighteen Provincial Court judges and three federally appointed judges had held more than three prior jobs.

Some comparisons can be made with Hogarth's data. Among legally trained Ontario magistrates, 13 per cent had worked as crown attorneys during most of their prior careers. If those Alberta

Table 3.3 Prior Work Experience of Alberta Judges						
Court	Sole Practitioner	Multi–Lwyr Firm	Crown Attorney	Gov't Counsel	Military	Police
Prov. Ct.	28%	60%	26%	26%	21%	5%*
S.96 Cts.	20%	80%	18%	20%	16%	–*
*Because most had more than one prior job, the totals exceed 100%.						

judges who worked only briefly as crown attorneys are excluded, the corresponding figure among Alberta Provincial Court judges is 16 per cent, and among Queen's Bench judges, 12 per cent. About half of Ontario magistrates had military experience. That Alberta judges had less military experience is probably because the Alberta study is 20 years more recent. (Comparisons cannot be made with the press release data because the press releases did not contain complete information about the prior careers of the judges.)

About one–fifth of the judges on each bench — on the Provincial Court, this includes only legally trained judges — considered themselves to be primarily trial lawyers before appointment; the remainder considered themselves to be both trial lawyers and solicitors, or only solicitors. (Solicitors are lawyers who handle legal work that rarely involves trials, such as real estate, wills, and contracts.) Of the federally appointed judges, 20 per cent reported that they had been only solicitors before their appointments, whereas only 7 per cent of the Provincial Court judges described themselves that way.

Of those who had been primarily trial lawyers, the Provincial Court judges had worked mostly in criminal law, whereas the federally appointed judges had worked mostly in civil (private) law. Some 17 per cent of the Provincial Court judges had spent 50 per cent or more of their time in criminal law, compared with only 7 per cent of the federally appointed judges. Similarly, Hogarth found that most legally trained Ontario magistrates who had not been crown attorneys were drawn from civil practice. Only 17 per cent of these magistrates had spent 20 per cent or more of their time in criminal law. The corresponding figures for Alberta are: legally trained Provincial Court judges — 28 per cent; federally appointed judges — 18 per cent. (No comparable figures are available for other Canadian judges.) What these figures show is that most judges who hear criminal cases have had little prior experience in criminal law. This is especially true with regard to the provincial superior court judges.

Non–lawyers may not appreciate the extent to which lawyers do their work away from the courtroom; advising clients, negotiating on behalf of clients, and drafting legal documents all make up a larger proportion of the "typical" lawyer's "average" day than court appearances. Only a small minority of lawyers appear in court as often as once a day; we found that only two–fifths of the lawyers in Ontario and Alberta made at least one court appearance per week, on average. The popular belief that lawyers spend most of their time in court in front of a judge says more about the media presentation of the law than about the real world. It also suggests a need to re–examine the complacent assumption that five or ten years of practice are necessarily sufficient preparation for presiding over a criminal courtroom.

The press release survey showed that 15 per cent of the section 96 judges had been elevated from a lower court. As well, one out of ten of these judges had belonged to the law society of more than one province before their appointment.

As Table 3.4 shows, judges are inclined to be high achievers, with superior court judges tending to out–achieve their Provincial Court brethren to some extent.

The fact that judges are high achievers is an indication that they tend to be hard–working and ambitious. It seems bizarre to criticize them for this, but it may be difficult for judges to empathize with those who are low achievers, a factor that could influence more policy–oriented decisions — such as the Charter cases affecting labour unions — as well as sentencing decisions in criminal cases.

Table 3.4 Achievements of Judges (Alberta, 1985)	superior court judges	Provincial court judges
Received a scholarship, medal, or award at university	39%	17%
Have been appointed Queen's Counsel	63%	32%
Honorary degree or title	14%	10%
Worked in a law firm with more than ten lawyers	50%	15%
Have been partner in a law firm	96%	62%
Have done some college or university teaching	30%	21%
Have published books or articles	24%	11%
Held executive position in the law society or bar association	65%	21%
Held executive position in a service club or fraternal organization	35%	43%
Have been a member of a political party	75%	60%

Political Experience

During Canada's first century, almost all the judges appointed to every level of court in Canada were supporters of the ruling party. Before World War I, many if not most of these judges had been candidates for office (successful or unsuccessful); since that time, the proportion of judges who were candidates has fallen to a level of perhaps 10 to 20 per cent of judges. This change is particularly evident with regard to the Supreme Court. According to Peter Russell (6), only two judges appointed since 1949 to Canada's highest court have been candidates for elected office.

Although progress has been made in establishing less partisan methods for making judicial appointments during the past two decades — particularly with regard to Provincial Court appointments in the more populous provinces — the current Canadian judiciary is still composed partly of judges appointed under the old partisan systems. For example, in the 1985 survey of Alberta superior court judges, three–quarters reported having belonged to a political party, and three–quarters of these belonged to the Liberal Party — the party in power in Ottawa when they were appointed. However, three out of four Provincial Court judges in Alberta had been selected according to a more non–partisan procedure. These appointments do not reflect a party bias. Although most of the judges were appointed by a Progressive Conservative provincial government, a third of the judges had belonged to the Liberal Party, and only a fifth had belonged to the Conservative Party.

As patronage begins to play a lesser role in the appointment of judges in Canada, the proportion of judges with experience in a political party will not necessarily be greatly reduced. Judges tend to be high achievers, and political activity seems to be one facet of this trait. For example, three–fifths of the judges appointed according to the non–partisan method of Provincial Court appointments in Alberta had previously been members of a political party. This prior political experience may actually help judges when they are called on to make policy–oriented decisions. As well, political experience, which brings elites into contact with people in all walks of life, may assist judges in understanding the broader

context of the cases before them, and in making sounder sentencing decisions.

The Supreme Court of Canada

Table 3.5, summarizing information from the *Canada Who's Who*
and press releases at the time of appointment, includes 14 judges
because of four retirements in 1988 and 1989. Justices Estey and
Le Dain of Ontario were replaced by Justices Sopinka and Cory.
Mr. Justice Beetz of Quebec was replaced by Mr. Justice Gonth-
ier, and Mr. Justice McIntyre of British Columbia was replaced
by Madame Justice McLachlin.

The nine judges serving on the Supreme Court in February
1989 had on average 15 years' experience in the practice of law,
and 10 years' experience as a judge before appointment to the
Supreme Court. They averaged 58 years of age on appointment,
and the average age of the judges in 1989 was 63 years. They had
served on the Supreme Court an average of 4 years. Most had two
degrees, a bachelor's degree and a law degree. Only one judge,
La Forest, had been a full–time law professor, although three had
part–time teaching experience. Thus, most of the judges had a
solid grounding in legal practice and the art of adjudication, but
none had a background in public policy analysis or in public
administration — two areas in which Supreme Court decisions
based on the Charter of Rights are having an enormous impact.

More important is the judges' training in the "school of life."
As Sidney Peck, Donald Fouts, Peter Russell (8,9), and Neil Tate
have shown, it is usually possible to identify a "liberal" and a
"conservative" wing in the Supreme Court at various points in
time. When the law is unclear, "liberals" tend to opt for an outcome that stresses equality or liberty, or that makes it possible for
governments to implement progressive social programs, or that
supports the rights of accused persons as against the great power
of the state. "Conservatives" tend to make decisions that preserve
existing inequalities or restrictions, or that restrict governments in
implementing social programs, or that uphold the powers of the
crown in criminal cases. It should be noted that the judges are not
necessarily consistently liberal or conservative on all three of
these dimensions, or over time.

Former chief justice Brian Dickson, who retired from the Court in 1990, has a reputation in legal circles as being a "judge's judge" and one of the best Supreme Court of Canada judges in the history of the Court. Although he was thought to be a "conservative" when he was appointed to the Supreme Court, through his decisions he became known as a "liberal." He was noted for his ability to empathize with ordinary Canadians, his willingness to face difficult legal and social problems, and his skill in writing persuasive judgments about them. A glimpse at his background indicates the importance of his broad range of interests and experiences in nurturing these qualities.

As Dale Gibson recounts, Dickson was born in Yorkton, Saskatchewan, in 1916, and lived during his childhood in several prairie towns and cities because his father, a bank manager, was frequently transferred. Dickson's mother was one of the first women graduates of Trinity College in Dublin, Ireland. According to Gibson, Dickson said that his interest in law was kindled by mock trials staged by his Boy Scout troop. Dickson's father was transferred to Winnipeg around the time of his son's high–school graduation; Dickson attended the University of Manitoba, finishing two years of the arts program before attending the law school. He graduated with the gold medal in law in 1938, but because there was little work for young lawyers in the depths of the depression Dickson spent two years, Blenus Wright recounts, "in the agency end of a life insurance company."

In 1938 Dickson met his future wife, Barbara Sellers. As Wright tells the story of their courtship, Dickson offered to tutor Sellers in a course on logic (since Dickson had done very well in the subject), and afterwards it seemed only "logical" that they should get married. They went on to have four children and five grandchildren.

In 1940 Dickson joined the Royal Canadian Artillery and took up a combat role in 1941 as part of the air defence of Great Britain. (It is interesting that five other recent members of the Supreme Court of Canada also served with the Royal Canadian Artillery during the Second War: Ritchie, Lamer, Le Dain, Chouinard, and McIntyre.) He returned to Canada in 1943 to attend the Canadian War Staff College, but then insisted on returning to a combat role overseas. During the battle of Falaise Gap he was wounded and lost a leg. To ensure that this physical handicap would not unduly hamper him, he has participated in numerous outdoor pursuits right through his term as chief justice, including, as Gibson notes, duck hunting, ridding horses, running a hobby cattle ranch, and swimming.

In a personal interview with Wright, Dickson described the impact of religion on his life:

> My father was a Unitarian and my mother was an Anglican, but in most of the small towns we lived in when we were young there was neither a Unitarian Church nor an Anglican. It was either Presbyterian or Methodist and later United. I went normally when we were in Winnipeg to the Presbyterian Church and I taught Sunday School in the Presbyterian Church. When I got married I was married in an Anglican Church and became interested in the Anglican faith and became Chancellor [advisor to the Bishop regarding legal, procedural and disciplinary matters] of the Diocese in Rupert's Land in the Province of Rupert's Land and in due course Chancellor for the Primate who was Archbishop Clark. During the war we had two church parades every Sunday, either Roman Catholic or Church of England, and I attended the Church of England parade. After the war we attended the Anglican Church. We still attend, but not as frequently as formerly. (p.11)

Dickson's personal values are reflected in his record of public service. According to Gibson, Dickson's history of community service work is so extensive that it is difficult to document fully.(p. 13) For example, Dickson has served as the chair of the Manitoba Civil Service Commission and as a member of the Board of Trustees of the Manitoba Law School. During the major flood of Winnipeg in 1950, Dickson was president of the Red Cross, and he took six weeks off work in his law practice to supervise four thousand volunteers. This record is consistent with the fact that a large proportion of judges have done community service, although few have done as much as Dickson. But unlike many judges, Dickson did not participate much in politics before his appointment to the bench.

After the war Dickson joined a prominent law firm in Winnipeg and specialized in business law. He became a well-known and sought-after corporate lawyer, as Gibson relates. "He did not have much courtroom experience but was a skilled advocate in many appearances before various regulatory boards and commissions. He was not very familiar with the work of trial courts, especially in criminal matters. But he had an enormous appetite for work." (Wright, p. 12)

His judicial career began in 1963 with an appointment to the Manitoba Queen's Bench. He was elevated to the Manitoba Court of Appeal in 1967 and to the Supreme Court of Canada in 1973. He became chief justice in 1984 after Bora Laskin's death. According to Dickson himself, he became interested in a judicial appointment to "follow the life of the law, rather than business." (Dickson, p. 141)

In an interview with Wright, Dickson describes a typical day as chief justice of Canada:

I get up around half past six. I get into riding clothes. I have a golf cart at the door and I go in the golf cart over to our stable which is two hundred yards away from the house and our Farm Manager has a couple of horses saddled and bridled and groomed. We ride normally through the fields and along the shore of the Ottawa River which is on our property, for about three quarters of an hour. I come back and have breakfast and then shower and change. I get picked up by my driver at about a quarter to nine or nine o'clock and get down here about nine thirty. I meet with the Executive Legal Officer for a few minutes or clear the mail and dictate replies. By that time it's ten thirty then we go to court until twelve thirty. We dispose normally of one case in the morning and one in the afternoon. I normally have lunch in the Judges' Dining Room and we're back in the court around two and go on to four and then from four to five, five thirty, clear up other questions, meet with the Registrar of the Court and whoever else wants to see me. I get home around six thirty and have dinner around seven thirty. I read whatever mail has come in and look usually at American television until nine thirty, ten o'clock and then retire. I prepare for the case mostly over the weekend or late in the afternoon or going and coming in the car because it's a thirty–five minute drive to our farm from here so I've got about an hour and a quarter to read the factum for the following day and read the Bench memo or read the Globe and Mail or Le Devoir which are the two papers I try to keep up with. (p. 25)

Some of Dickson's convictions, which are reflected in his judicial opinions, are apparent in various addresses he has given:

People like peace and security, national unity and respect for fundamental freedoms. Beyond these basics, any discussion as to what people want out of society is likely to give many answers. I would hope that in ongoing discussions hearts and minds will be directed to the quality of life rather than quantity of goods, to conservation rather than consumption and to a lowering of materialistic expectations in favour of a greater sense of sharing, nationally and internationally. (On the occasion of the installation of Mrs. Agnes Benidickson as Chancellor of Queen's University, October 24, 1980, as quoted by Wright, p. 14.)

It is my belief and contention that for the law to be just, it must reflect compassion. For a judge to reach decisions which comport with justice and fairness, he or she must be guided by an ever–present awareness and concern for the plight of others and the human condition. ("Law and Compassion," Convocation Address, University of Toronto, June 20, 1986, as quoted by Wright, p. 23.)

I dedicate myself to maintain the great tradition of this court, to search for truth and to use such judicial power as is mine to resolve fairly the basic questions about justice and liberty, the rights of the individual and the authority of the State. In the discharge of those responsibilities I will be beholden to

Table 3.5 Supreme Court of Canada Judges 1988–90

Judge	Years on Court (1988)	Place of birth	Home before appointment	Age in 1989	Marital status	No. of children	Law deg.
Dickson**	15	Sask	Man	73	Married	4	Manitoba
Beetz	14	Que	Que	62	Single	0	Montreal
Estey	11	Sask	Ont	70	Married	4	Sask.
McIntyre	9	Que	BC	71	Married	2	Sask.
Lamer***	8	Que	Que	56	Married	1	Montreal
Wilson	6	Scotland	Ont	66	Married	0	Dalhousie
Le Dain	4	Que	Ont	65	Married	6	McGill
La Forest	3	NB	NB	63	Married	5	NewBruns.
L'Heureux–Dubé	1	Que	Que	62	Widowed	2	Laval
Sopinka	0	Sask	Ont	56	Married	2	Toronto
Cory	0	Ont	Ont	64	Married	3	Osgoode
Gonthier	0	Que	Que	61	Married	5	McGill
McLachlin	0	Alta	BC	45	Widowed	1	Alberta
Stevenson	0	Alta	Alta	55	Married	4	Alberta

Judge	No. of earned degrees	Years exp. as a judge before S.C.C.	Years in full-time university teaching	Years in part-time university teaching	Years in private practice*	Year app'd to S.C.C.	Religion
Dickson**	1	10	0	6	18	1973	Anglican
Beetz	4	1	20	0	1	1974	R.C.
Estey	3	5	0	4	30	1977	R.C.
McIntyre	2	12	0	0	20	1979	Anglican
Lamer***	2	11	0	10	12	1980	R.C.
Wilson	3	7	0	0	17	1982	United
Le Dain	2	9	15	0	10	1984	Anglican
La Forest	5	4	18	9	15	1985	R.C.
L'Heureux–Dubé	2	14	0	0	21	1987	R.C.
Sopinka	2	0	0	11	28	1988	R.C.
Cory	2	15	0	0	24	1989	Anglican
Gonthier	2	15	0	0	22	1989	R.C.
McLachlin	3	8	6	2	6	1989	
Stevenson	2	15	2	9	15	1990	Anglican

*includes years working as counsel to government or a corporation
**Chief Justice, 1984 to 1990
***Chief Justice beginning July 1990.

no one save God. (On "Swearing In" as a judge of the Supreme Court of Canada, Ottawa, March 1973, as quoted by Wright, p. 23.)

It is important that judges are as aware of their own powers and responsibilities as those whose cases will be brought before them, many of whom will not own horses or have estates to ride across or chauffeurs to drive them to work. An onerous duty therefore rests with those who are charged with the tasks of recruiting and selecting judges to ensure that the candidates can handle judicial power with integrity.

In spite of the weaknesses of the recruiting procedures for federally appointed judges in place in the early 1960s, the fact that they would result in the selection of a judge like Brian Dickson indicates that while the improvements in the system since that time are welcome, the old procedures did produce some outstanding judges.

Overview

If the purpose of courts is to adjudicate disputes, the system works best when judges can apply a relatively well–developed set of rules (the law) to factual situations. The background training and experience of Canadian judges generally suits them well for adjudication, although the appointment systems that existed before the reforms of the past two decades tended to screen out many potentially good judges who lacked the right political connections, in favour of those with more modest credentials but more powerful friends.

The more that the law consists of a set of general principles rather than specific directives, the more the decision–making process in a court becomes a policy–making operation rather than adjudication. Neither courts nor judges are well suited to policy–making. Courts have little access to the research tools of social policy. The principle of *stare decisis* makes it difficult for judges to adjust to changing circumstances, or to admit policy–making errors. Judges tend to have little background experience in policy–development, except for what they may have learned from their experience working for political parties, before they were appointed to what is typically a long term.

When judges take on a policy–development role, or when they make decisions involving a great deal of discretion (such as sentencing), they often apply what they think would be the standard of the "average reasonable person." But the "average reasonable person," as seen through the eyes of a typical judge, is likely to be a high–achieving male of British or French origin adhering to one of the main–line religions, approaching 60 years of age, living in a comfortable middle–class or upper–class environment, and active in a political party. Is it possible for such judges to empathize with average Canadians, or must the judiciary change to become more representative of Canadian society? We agree with Peter Russell: neutral appointment procedures established to find the best possible judges are bound to choose older lawyers from the higher socio–economic class. Judges will most likely always have to rely on educational seminars to help them become more familiar with the views of younger and less advantaged Canadians. With regard to the other factors, especially gender and ethnicity, the judiciary should indeed be more representative of Canadian society, and this goal should be kept in mind by the appointing authorities.

The fact that most criminal trial judges have had little experience in criminal law is simply a reflection of the fact that most lawyers are primarily solicitors. Although the experience of judicial applicants should be kept in mind when decisions are made regarding which court they should be appointed to, our finding underlines the need for more comprehensive judicial training in the criminal law field. The efforts of the Canadian Institute for the Administration of Justice, the Canadian Judicial Council, the Provincial judges associations, and the Canadian Judicial Centre are to be applauded, but one wonders whether one or two weeks of training for a criminal court judge who has spent his or her entire professional career as a solicitor is adequate.

One factor that may help courts in their policy–making role is that the Supreme Court, the courts of appeal, and some lower courts may allow intervenors — parties not directly involved in a case but whose interests may be affected by it — to present arguments. For example, the federal government, a provincial government, or an interest group such as the Women's Legal Education and Action Fund (LEAF) or the Canadian Civil Liberties Association can apply for intervenor status. Such groups have the opportunity to present the judges with balanced advice from the perspective of "the public interest." Often, however, counsel for intervenors, trained in the adversary approach, miss this opportunity and simply argue for one side or the other. Moreover, in recent years the Supreme Court of Canada has begun to limit the number of intervenors it will accept in order to control its workload.

In a public address in Toronto, Madame Justice Claire L'Heureux–Dubé made an especially cogent comment: "If people were encouraged to utilize alternate dispute resolution methods and if politicians were slower to seek judicial solutions to policy problems, the public might well become less preoccupied by the heritage, background and gender of judges."

She is undoubtedly correct. However, it appears unlikely that her "best of all worlds" will come about in our lifetimes, given the propensity of Canadians to litigate, the lack of availability of alternate dispute–resolution procedures, and the great temptation for politicians to foist contentious policy problems onto the courts.

Part II

Judges' Attitudes:
The Judge's Role and
Decision-Making

4

Adapting to the Judicial Role

Some — if not most — judges undergo a personality change after they are appointed. In our interviews in Ontario and Alberta, three–fifths of the trial lawyers and crown attorneys and two–fifths of the judges themselves thought that the most common change was an inflated ego. But the changes are not necessarily for the worse; a fifth of the trial lawyers and crown attorneys we interviewed said that the good personality traits of newly appointed judges became even stronger.

What does it mean, what does it feel like, to be a judge? Clearly, a position on the bench is not a job like any other. It carries with it special obligations and special advantages, unique opportunities and unusual problems. However, simply asking the judges flat out what it is like to be a judge threatened to force them into a stilted replay of conventional clichés, or to reduce the matter to a rather flat job description. Neither approach seemed particularly promising. We chose instead a less conventional tactic. We examined how judges think about and adapt to their new role by considering their responses to three distinct and disparate sets of questions.

First, why did they accept a judicial appointment, and were they still happy with their decision to leave the practice of law? In other words, what did the position of a judge look like "from the outside" before they took it up, and how has that impression survived first–hand experience?

Second, how do they cope with the isolation (largely self–imposed) from former friends and some social situations that accepting a judgeship entails? In other words, what was the transition to the bench like, and to what extent have they made the transition successfully and left its stresses behind them?

Third, what are the qualities that judges admire in other judges and try to emulate in their own judicial performance? In other words, what does the position of a judge look like to them "from the inside" now that their first–hand experience has given them a capacity to distinguish real merit and to identify its component parts?

The first and third question could be asked of any occupational group; it is, however, significant and revealing how few employment contexts would allow the second question to have any meaning whatever.

Why Become a Judge?

In a legal system such as our own, a person does not choose to be a judge in the way people choose most occupations; rather, to become a judge a person must decide to stop the practice of law — not to start a career but rather to change career in midstream. This also implies that the decision to become a judge is made, not by young adults as an initial career decision, but by middle–aged adults well established in their profession and in their community. One feature that contributes to the status of judicial office is the fact that the careers the judges have left behind are so highly regarded. New judges accept a role, a set of obligations and expectations, with elements of both continuity and discontinuity with their previous legal careers.

The discontinuity is extreme for those new judges whose legal practice was not structured around trial court appearances, which includes — surprisingly — a majority of judges. To ask a judge, "Why did you choose your present occupation?" therefore carries different overtones from the same question addressed to any other group in our society. The declining age of initial appointment implies that this decision involves not a brief capstone of a legal career, but rather a commitment of several decades.

All the judges interviewed in Ontario and Alberta were asked why they had decided to accept appointment to the bench. All but six gave reasons for their decisions, with more than half giving more than one reason.

Of the Alberta judges, four said they had turned down a previous offer of judicial appointment, while thirty–five said that they had accepted the first such offer. The rest of the 51 judges interviewed gave no indication one way or the other. Interestingly, although several Alberta judges said they had been approached by someone (usually a sitting judge) about "letting their name be put on a list," only one indicated having "applied" for a position, although the procedure for appointment to provincial court in Alberta has for two decades involved a formal application (albeit one that is usually solicited) to the Judicial Council. This might indicate no more than a convention that appointments are offered to individuals of objective merit, and that any effort to elicit the offer devalues it.

There was a clear difference between judges who gave *practical* reasons for their decision to accept judicial appointment, and judges who gave *idealistic* reasons. There was also a distinction between judges who indicated some strong motivation of whichever type, and judges who indicated a weaker motivation. The four categories in Tables 4.1 and 4.2 indicate the four possible combinations of these factors. (For judges who gave more than one reason for accepting a judicial appointment, we include only the response that the judge emphasized the most.)

Type I responses, characterized by a desire to escape negative features of the practice of law, were fairly numerous. We describe these judges as "escaping to the bench." Type II responses identified appealing features of judicial appointment, such as security or independence. Type III responses clustered around the idea of a judicial appointment as a "new challenge" within the practice of law. Type IV responses saw the judicial appointment as the "pinnacle of a legal career" and/or the offer of appointment as a flattering honour.

Type I: "Escaping to the Bench"
["strong motivation/practical reasons"]
Without exaggeration or distortion, type I judges can be described as individuals who "escaped" to the bench, driven by something outside the position as much as they were drawn by something

Table 4.1 Reasons for Accepting Judicial Appointment: Alberta

Reasons given by judges for accepting a judgeship	Motivation for a judicial appointment		
	strong	weak	TOTAL
practical	30% (n = 15) Type I: Escaping to the bench	10% (n = 5) Type II: Practical reasons	40% (n = 20)
idealistic	24% (n = 12) Type IV: It is an honour to be a judge	36% (n = 18) Type III: Want the challenge of being a judge	60% (n = 30)
Total	54% (n = 27)	46% (n = 23)	100% (n = 50)

Table 4.2 Reasons for Accepting Judicial Appointment: Ontario

Reasons given by judges for accepting a judgeship	Motivation for a for judicial appointment		
	strong	weak	TOTAL
practical	38% (n = 14) Type I: Escaping to the bench	9% (n = 3) Type II: Practical reasons	47% (n = 17)
idealistic	11% (n = 4) Type IV: It is an honour to be a judge	42% (n = 15) Type III: Want the challenge of being a judge	53% (n = 19)
Total	49% (n = 18)	51% (n = 18)	100% (n = 36)

distinctive in it. About one–third of the judges in both provinces saw themselves as having been "pushed" into accepting appointment by undesirable or unpleasant aspects of the career they were leaving. Some accepted appointment to the bench because they had become tired or bored with the practice of law; others spoke of being overwhelmed or saturated or burnt out; still others had more specific or personal problems that directed their choice. All saw the move to the bench as an opportunity to escape, desirable not so much for itself as for the alternatives that it precluded.

Within this general type of response were three sub–groups: those who were bored with the practice of law, those who were feeling overloaded with their law practice, and those who had come to dislike the practice of law for some other reason.

Boredom

I had practised law for years, and I had had my excitement. The practice was becoming repetitious and boring, and I had already thought about leaving the profession before the question of a judgeship ever came up. There comes a time for many litigation lawyers when you have had enough, when you are ready to step back from that kind of practice. (Alberta Court of Appeal judge)

I had been in private practice for more than 25 years, and I just got tired of regular practice. I was attracted by the life style of a judge, by the fact that there was less high pressure, less overtime, and some time for self and family on evenings and weekends. (Alberta Provincial Court judge)

I was doing straight criminal law as a lawyer and found myself doing the same thing over and over. I thought I could have a greater impact on the law if I was on the bench. (Ontario Supreme Court judge)

At first, the practice of law was fun, but after 17 years I was getting stale and the work was drudgery. I told my family I wanted to become a judge, and after some discussion they agreed that I should let my name stand. (Ontario District Court judge)

Overload

Basically, I just started to feel overworked as a lawyer, I was getting tired of the job. I was a trial lawyer, doing both civil and criminal work, and it just got to be too much to be going at it night and day. It was probably what today you'd call burnout. (Alberta Court of Queen's Bench judge)

The time demands of the profession had built up to a point that I couldn't take any more, and after 29 years in practice, I thought it was time to try something different. (Alberta Court of Queen's Bench judge)

I had been 28 years in practice, and I just found myself saturated to the point of dysfunction. I was just going bonkers. (Alberta Provincial Court judge)

After 20 odd years practising law, you're ready for a change. You grow tired of having to be prepared for three or four possible trials the next day. Being a judge is appealing because there aren't so many pressures. Your work usually ends at the end of the day. (Ontario Supreme Court judge)

I was a lawyer for 23 years, and general practice was getting to be very hard work. I worked weekends, nights — there was no time to keep up with changes in the law. I wanted a change of direction. (Ontario Provincial Court judge)

Other

There had been a major upheaval in the firm in which I was a partner, and I just couldn't accept the way it had turned out. I was just about to leave the firm to set up in practice on my own when I was approached about becoming a judge. (Alberta Provincial Court judge)

There were aspects of the partnership in the law firm that I couldn't control sufficiently, and I became discontented. It was a question of outlook I guess – I found it difficult to reason with the older partners, and I thought I was being used in an unprofessional manner. (Ontario Provincial Court judge)

I just got fed up with the practice of law. I lasted six years, and I just couldn't take it any more. I was approached and asked if I would accept a judgeship. My wife and I considered it for about three weeks, especially how we would do on the lower income. In the end, I thought I would enjoy the work, my wife agreed to the lower income, so I accepted. (Ontario Provincial Court judge)

I went to Harvard Law School, and discovered that I hated law. I liked working with children, so I had in mind to become a juvenile court judge as soon as I could. (Ontario Provincial Court judge)

I just got fed up with my clients in my law practice. (Ontario Provincial Court judge)

The distribution of responses among the levels of the court is striking. Almost half of the Provincial Court judges mentioned boredom, dissatisfaction, or burnout as reasons for accepting a judicial appointment; less than one–quarter of the section 96 judges gave similar reasons. As might be expected, the higher the court in the appellate hierarchy, the lower the proportion of judges who cited negative reasons for accepting appointment. This is consistent with the idea that higher judicial appointments are intrinsically more satisfying and prestigious, so that lawyers are more likely to accept an appointment for its own sake.

Type II: "Pragmatic Calculation"
[weak motivation/practical reasons]
Five Alberta and three Ontario judges mentioned more practical and pragmatic aspects of a position on the bench as major factors in their decisions. Some said they were attracted by the security,

and others by the freedom and independence that the position offered.

> I had been an RCMP officer, and I quit to go to university with plans to become a crown prosecutor. I became a relief magistrate as a part time and summer job to make some money because I needed it for my family, and from there I was appointed straight to bench. (Alberta Provincial Court judge)

> I was a crown prosecutor at the time I was offered an appointment, and a judgeship just seemed like a better job with more independence. (Alberta Provincial Court judge)

> I have to admit that the question of security and of a pension was also part of the calculation that led to the decision to accept appointment. (Alberta Provincial Court judge)

> I had just come back from semi–retirement (I was raising my family) and the position was open. It seemed like a good way of striking back in. (Ontario Provincial Court judge)

> I was on the executive of the local Conservative Association. The attorney general was a friend of mine, and he asked me to find someone to fill the vacancy we had here for a family court magistrate. At that time, the job had such little prestige that we couldn't find an acceptable candidate. In desperation, the attorney general asked me to take it on for 90 days until someone else could be found. I accepted, and it stuck. (Ontario Provincial Court judge)

> I thought that being a judge would give me a little more non–sitting time to write articles about the law. Also, I've never been preoccupied with making money. (Ontario District Court judge)

Although the numbers are small, there is again a clear connection with the level of court involved; most in this group were Provincial Court judges. This again is consistent with the conventional wisdom that higher judicial appointments are more prestigious, while lower judicial appointment is assessed in terms more similar to career choices in other fields.

Type III: "A New Challenge"
[weak motivation/idealistic reasons]
Most judges indicated that they accepted appointment not because they were "pushed" by dissatisfaction with private practice but because they saw something intrinsically attractive about the bench. They saw sitting on the bench as an interesting, even exciting, new set of challenges within the legal profession.

> To a certain extent, I became a judge because there were things I didn't like about the way things were being handled. I thought that I could make some real improvements in that regard, and I believe that I have done so. I think I'm good at what I do. (Alberta Provincial Court judge)

> I accepted a judgeship because I was interested in people and in the prospect of helping them resolve their problems; I have always felt that a trial is a real study in human relations. Also, I was always frustrated as a lawyer by the feeling that I was falling behind on what was happening in the law, and I thought being a judge would give me more time to read up on the law, to come to know the law really well. (Alberta Court of Queen's Bench judge)

> I always liked criminal law, and enjoyed trial work as a lawyer; I saw the job as a challenge, and I thought I could make a contribution to the provincial bench in terms of improving its credibility and the rigour of its process, the more so as less than half the bench was legally trained at the time that I accepted the appointment. (Alberta Court of Queen's Bench judge)

> One day when I was a lawyer, my secretary said to me at the bar one evening, "You've lost your zest for the law, and

you don't enjoy your practice like you used to." That really made me stop and think. She was right, you know, but I hadn't been conscious of it before. My practice had become routine. There was no challenge left, and I needed a challenge. One of my colleagues told me I was being considered for a judicial appointment, and that I should talk to the chief judge. I talked to the chief judge, and he encouraged me, but I explained to him that I was a Tory and I didn't think I'd get an appointment from a Liberal government. The chief judge said politics weren't so important any more, so I sent in my application. (Ontario District Court judge)

To be sure, this type of response can blur into the Type I answer; the new challenge might tempt because the old challenge has lost its attraction. However, the distinct wording that the judges used — "I thought it was about time to try something different" as against "I couldn't take it any more" — and the difference in tone are such that assigning a judge's response to one or the other category is neither arbitrary nor difficult.

More than one–third of the judges in both provinces indicated the idea of a "new challenge" as the primary reason for their acceptance of judicial appointment. The proportion was fairly constant for all levels of court.

Type IV: "Culmination of Legal Career"
[strong motivation/idealistic reasons]
A quarter of the Alberta judges and an eighth of the Ontario judges said they accepted their appointments because a position on the bench represented the crowning pinnacle of a legal career, reflecting an aspiration that is a natural impulse for all lawyers. (Again, there is a striking difference in terminology between this group of judges and those who spoke in terms of a "new challenge.")

We have divided these responses into two sub–groups: those who emphasized that a judgeship was the pinnacle of the profession, the normal outcome of a legal career of competence beyond a certain level; and those who emphasized the honour of being appointed a judge, as an extraordinary opportunity to be welcomed with surprise rather than anticipated and expected.

appointed a judge, as an extraordinary opportunity to be welcomed with surprise rather than anticipated and expected.

Type IVa: "Pinnacle of Profession"

A lawyer should move through the profession; after a certain amount of maturity, a certain level of accomplishment, a lawyer should serve as a judge. It is a normal professional career evolution for lawyers of a certain level of ability. (Alberta Court of Appeal judge)

I always considered a judge to have the most important role within the legal system, and I always had the view that if it was offered to me and I could afford it, I would accept it. It would not have occurred to me to turn it down, although I admit that I would have turned down an appointment to the Provincial Court, because the breadth and type of work are not my cup of tea. (Alberta Court of Appeal judge)

In my day, every young lawyer thought that a judgeship was the goal; that idea was built into the profession, and I was no exception. (Alberta Court of Queen's Bench judge)

I'm old–fashioned enough to believe that the judiciary at the senior levels is an important enough job that if someone thinks I'm good enough to do it, I'm obligated to accept. It is also nice to have the notion that you are having a say in the operation of the administration of justice. (Alberta Court of Queen's Bench judge)

Every trial lawyer, even those who say otherwise, aspires to a high judicial office. It is the combination of the independence and the responsibility, along with the great divergence of problems to which you are exposed. It is a satisfying and interesting life. (Ontario Supreme Court judge)

I agree with the late chief justice Cartwright; he said that all he ever wanted to become when he was a lawyer was a judge. It is the culmination of a legal career. To be honest, the prestige was part of it. (Ontario District Court judge)

Several of the judges stressed the extent to which they felt "flattered" by the offer of a judicial appointment. These responses are included under category IV (honour) on the grounds that people are flattered more by elevation to a pinnacle than by a chance to escape or even by the offer of a new opportunity.

Type IVb: "Flattering Honour"

One of the reasons that I accepted the appointment is, I suppose, simply ego; you're always flattered to be asked, and that makes it hard to say no. (Alberta Court of Appeal judge)

I have to admit that it was a bit of an ego trip to be appointed, especially at an unusually young age, and I thought it useful to have a younger person on the bench. (Alberta Provincial Court judge)

Part of the reason that I accepted the appointment was just that it was flattering to be asked. (Alberta Court of Queen's Bench judge)

It's an honour to be asked to be a judge. But there are other things you have to consider as well. You wonder how long you can take the pace in court. On the other hand, the phone won't ring off the hook any more, and you can do one case at a time. (Ontario Supreme Court judge)

Again, the differences between the levels of the court are striking. Over half of the Alberta Court of Appeal judges, barely one–third of the Court of Queen's Bench judges, and only two of the responding Provincial Court judges described their appointment as the pinnacle of their career or a flattering honour. Given the lingering notion that the three levels of court constitute a hierarchy of status and prestige, it makes sense that the higher the level of the court a lawyer is asked to join, the greater the honour associated with the suggestion.

The proportion of Alberta judges mentioning the honour of attaining a judicial appointment was double that in Ontario. A comment from an Ontario judge suggests an explanation for this difference:

> Years ago, just about every lawyer wanted to become a judge as the culmination of his career. But now things have changed. Toronto is so big that nobody knows who the judges are any more. Judges aren't honoured and respected like they used to be. I think that nowadays lawyers become judges for other reasons — to avoid stress or for a new challenge. (Ontario Court of Appeal judge)

It may be that the change in social values has been greater in Ontario than in Alberta. Because Alberta has no metropolitan centre comparable to Toronto — in which the millions of residents can become faceless and impersonal — Alberta judges may feel that they are better known and recognized and therefore more respected by the members of a more cohesive legal profession and by the broader community. This implies, however, that it is a question of time–lag rather than of absolute difference, and therefore that the honorific pull of a judgeship may be on the decline with the impersonality caused by urbanization.

Satisfaction with the Job on the Bench

Most judges indicated that they were happy about their decision to accept a position on the bench; two–thirds of the Alberta judges and two–fifths of the Ontario judges said that they never had any second thoughts and never considered returning to the practice of law. Several spoke enthusiastically about their work on the bench, although others made more nuanced and shaded comments. We were, of course, speaking to the survivors; any individual sufficiently disappointed or discouraged to leave the bench within a few years of appointment (and such individuals do exist) would, by the very nature of this study, not appear on any interview lists.

> I have never had any second thoughts; I am damn glad I became a judge. I thoroughly enjoy it, because I feel I am contributing something worthwhile. (Alberta Provincial Court judge)

> I wasn't overjoyed at the idea of becoming a judge, but I saw it as a challenge and now I really enjoy the work, I am delighted that I was appointed. (Alberta Court of Queen's Bench judge)

> I haven't been on the bench long enough to burn out, and I have no desire to return to private practice, although I do see some evidence of a "second burnout" phenomenon in other judges. (Alberta Court of Queen's Bench judge)

> I miss some of my clients that I had as a lawyer, but I'm happy I'm a judge because I don't have to hustle for the money. (Ontario Supreme Court judge)

> As a judge, I'm usually less driven by events than I was as a lawyer. As a lawyer, I used to go to the office after a trial and there would be 40 phone messages — no kidding. Now, the only person who phones me is my wife, and that's great. (Ontario District Court judge)

About a quarter of both the Alberta and Ontario judges indicated that they had experienced second thoughts about taking the position. One–third linked this only to the transition period, the early months or years of being a judge, and another third said that they had only occasional second thoughts and had never seriously considered leaving the bench.

> I went through the usual first–week syndrome, waking up in a cold sweat thinking, "What have I done?" And I have had the occasional bad day since, but nothing serious, and I have

Huron County Library

--- Currently checked out ---
Title: John J. Robinette :
peerless mentor : an apprecia
Date due: 31/3/2009,23:59

Library name: Goderich Branch
Library
User ID: 06492001475816

Title: Judges and judging :
inside the Canadian judicial
Date due: 1/4/2009,23:59

Visit us on-line @
www.huroncounty.ca/library

never seriously considered returning to practice. (Alberta Court of Queen's Bench judge)

I had some second thoughts when I was first appointed. All judges miss the association with clients, and the hustle–bustle of practice. (Alberta Court of Appeal judge)

I had second thoughts for the first couple of years, mainly for economic reasons, but I really enjoyed the work and the relative lack of pressure. (Alberta Court of Appeal judge)

After more than 15 years on bench, I still have some second thoughts; basically I still feel that judges should be appointed in their mid–30s to make a profession or a career out of being a judge, as opposed to thinking of it as an adjunct or a footnote to a career, but there should be something like sabbaticals to keep judges from going stale and burning out. (Alberta Provincial Court judge)

I think I enjoyed life most during the first few years of practice as a lawyer, when everything was challenging. Being a new lawyer is more challenging than being a judge. But I'd never go back to the bar; it would be too dull now. Being a judge is fascinating. (Ontario District Court judge)

I enjoy being a judge more than being a lawyer. But it depends on what you're like — a hockey player or a referee. Some guys like being out in the arena, but I'm more of a referee–type. (Ontario Provincial Court judge)

Only a handful of Alberta judges gave any indication of serious second thoughts, of having regretted the decision. In these cases, the answers referred to immediately personal circumstances.

For Ontario judges, the most common reason for not being entirely satisfied with a judicial appointment was that the stress of the judgeship turned out to be no less than the stress of private practice; the "escape to the bench" turned out to be illusory.

I accepted a judgeship because in my practice I had gotten
to the stage of having 200 open files. My clients were calling
me on weekends and evenings and I had no time left for my
family. I thought that being a judge would give me more
time for my family, but now I'm working just as hard as I
did before. There is such a backlog in this court — and I'm
determined to get rid of it — that I find myself taking my
work home with me most days. But at least the telephone
doesn't ring like it did before. (Ontario District Court judge)

The judges who indicated having had some second thoughts about
appointment included judges from all levels of court in similar
proportions. The reasons for accepting appointment do seem to
have a connection to reservations about the position; for example,
six of fifteen Alberta judges who took appointment to escape
some aspect of private practice indicated having had second
thoughts, including three of the four who had serious second
thoughts or even regrets about accepting appointment. Of the
eighteen Alberta judges motivated by the idea of a new challenge,
only one spoke of any reservations apart from those involved in
the transition, and of the five judges drawn by more pragmatic
considerations, only one mentioned even transitional doubts.

Summary: Why Do Judges Become Judges?
About one–third of the Alberta judges and almost half of the
Ontario judges indicated *negative* factors as a major reason for
accepting appointment, typically stress or boredom with the practice of law. The rest indicated more *positive* incentives, including
those who spoke of a "new challenge" and those who saw a
judgeship as the "pinnacle of the profession" and the offer of such
a position as "flattering."

The "new challenge" responses were more common, especially
in Ontario. The proportion of the two types of response is to some
extent a function of the level of the bench involved; the proportion
of those citing negative factors falls, and the proportion of those
citing positive factors rises, as the level of analysis shifts from the
Provincial Court through the superior trial courts to the Court of
Appeal. Only one judge in ten spoke of more practical considera-

tions, such as security or independence. A majority of judges indicated real satisfaction with the judicial position, with only one–quarter revealing second thoughts about being a judge. The judges with second thoughts came disproportionately from the ranks of those citing negative factors for having accepted judicial appointment.

Not one judge in either province mentioned becoming a judge for the salary; at the same time, few of the judges who indicated having second thoughts mentioned financial considerations. Although judicial salaries may seem exorbitant to many Canadians, they are lower — and often substantially lower — than what an ambitious lawyer earns as a partner in a major law firm. Even though a number of judges mentioned that they certainly had not accepted a judgeship for financial reasons, when the Ontario judges were asked whether their salaries were adequate, only two–fifths responded with a definite "no." One–fifth said they were inadequate but not too bad, and two–fifths said that the salaries were adequate. Interestingly, this range of responses is not significantly different from the responses given by crown attorneys about the adequacy of their salaries.

For many judges, the advantages of a less stressful and more challenging job — and one carrying with it a substantial pension and disability benefits — outweigh any potential salary loss, at least at a certain point in their career. As one Ontario High Court judge put it: "I became a lawyer to make money. I made a lot of money. I thought that there must be more to life than that, so the challenge of a judgeship appealed to me."

To many Canadians, the attractions of a position on the bench must seem sufficiently obvious that there is an element of irony in talking about "second thoughts." Judges are reasonably well paid compared to most occupation groups in our society; their working conditions are pleasant; their hours (at least that portion involving contact with the public) are not unreasonable; and they are subject to little in the way of direct supervision or discipline. However, there is a down–side to the judicial profession. One part of this is the stress of constantly making decisions that carry a major, and often irreversible, impact on other individuals; another is the extent to which public expectations regarding the behaviour of judges off the bench as well as on it impose restrictions on judges that are shared by few other occupations.

Coping with Judicial Isolation

The late chief justice Bora Laskin (2) once wrote that judges "can guard their judicial independence if they remain aloof from ... social or political controversy." The case of former B.C. Supreme Court judge Thomas Berger illustrates some of the ambiguities and problems that surround this important point or principle.

If the core of the special limitations on judges is a set of actions (like direct political commentary) subject to formal sanction, the penumbra is a range of activities open to most citizens but deemed inappropriate for judges. Does the aloofness thereby associated with judicial office lead to a feeling of isolation? Some 70 per cent of the judges in Ontario and Alberta agreed that it did. They felt that at least some isolation from the larger community is an unavoidable side–effect of being a judge. Some 40 per cent said that being a judge results in a great deal of isolation, not only for themselves but also for their families.

Most lawyers make many of their friends within the legal profession, and becoming a judge puts a strain on these friendships, the more so for judges who frequently have lawyers appearing before them who were close friends in law practice days. As well, lawyers are often active in community organizations and service clubs and feel that once they are on the bench it is not appropriate to maintain a high profile, especially if fundraising or lobbying government is involved. Finally, lawyers tend to be active within political parties, and these relationships must be attenuated, if not severed, after a judicial appointment. As the average age of judicial appointment comes down, the impact of appointment on the families of judges becomes more significant as well.

The sense of isolation was stronger for Alberta judges than Ontario judges, with half of the Alberta judges reporting a "great deal" of isolation, compared with a quarter of the Ontario judges. In addition, some judges felt that the "aloofness" they were supposed to maintain included a public expectation that they would live up to an image of perfection. The following comments are typical:

Judges have to maintain high social standards. I am a "father figure." Many people come to me for advice about their personal lives. (Ontario Provincial Court judge)

Judges should never be seen dressed casually in public. This might destroy the respect that people have for judges and the legal system. (Ontario District Court judge)

Judges can't be seen in licensed premises or a liquor store. I didn't realize this until my clerk saw me go into the liquor store the day after I was appointed, and sat me down and gave me a lecture about what the public expects of us. (Ontario High Court judge)

The smaller the community, the more the judge must watch the reputation. My family tells me it's like living in a glass house. (Ontario District Court judge)

Many judges feel they are expected to demonstrate that they are above the petty pleasures and inclinations of ordinary mortals. How do they cope with this expectation? Some admitted to us that they were not coping well. To appear impartial they had cut off their friendships with members of the bar but had made few other friends. Some judges said that the isolation had led to alcoholism for some of the judges they knew (but not, of course, in public; most judges feel it is inappropriate to be seen in a pub or a beer parlour). Others said that they saw judicial isolation as a problem that could only be dealt with through a conscious strategy. One judge, for example, made a point of taking his family on regular visits to see friends in other communities, since he felt it would not be proper for the judge to make many friends in the community where he sat.

For judges in the larger centres, there is the very practical consequence that they tend to make their friends and conduct their social relationships within the circle of their fellow judges, certainly on their own bench and possibly (but not invariably) on the other benches as well. This solves the problem at the personal level, but at the price of creating a vicious circle of rather disturbing proportions, as judges test out their reactions to their world and their feeling about specific issues with other judges and virtually no one else.

Almost 90 per cent of the judges thought that their personalities changed after they became judges. Two–fifths of the judges (and three–fifths of trial lawyers and crown attorneys) reported that judges tended to develop "swelled egos" after appointment, while one–fifth of these respondents thought that a judgeship brought out the judge's good qualities. It would be difficult for anyone, given the power and independence of a judge, not to suffer from some sort of swelled ego from time to time, and certainly judges should not be singled out for this weakness — we freely admit that university professors tend to have the same problem. Some of the judges that we talked to volunteered that their families helped them to "stay down to earth." A Provincial Court judge in Northern Ontario reported to us that he invited his teenaged son to watch him in court one day. When the court recessed the son visited his father in the judge's chambers and said, "Dad, at home you're a really nice guy. But in there you threw your weight around too much. Why can't you be polite to those people?" The judge said that in the end he was grateful to his son for the reprimand.

Admired Qualities

It is one thing to ask why a person becomes a judge; it is quite another to ask what it is that judges believe they become in the process. One way to approach this is to ask them about the qualities they think are most important to being a good judge, or about the attributes of their fellow judges that they most admire.

To determine the judges' subjective perceptions of the most important dimensions of the judicial role, we posed a question to all the Alberta judges: "In your view, what are the qualities which cause a judge to gain the respect of his fellow judges, the bar, and the community at large?"

It was clear from their answers that almost all of the judges focused on the first of the three reference groups — their fellow judges — as opposed to the wider communities of the bar or the general public; this spontaneous narrowing of the topic is itself

Table 4.3 Admired Qualities: Alberta Judges

Qualities Mentioned by Judges (multiple responses recorded)	Level of Court			
	All Judges	Court of Queen's Bench	Court of Appeal	Provincial Court
Industry, diligence	21	5	10	6
Courtesy	13	3	5	5
Empathy	13	2	4	7
Patience	12	3	5	4
Knowledge of the law	11	2	5	4
Intelligence	10	4	5	1
Sense of fair play	10	1	3	6
Makes difficult decisions	9	3	3	3
Write/express ideas clearly	7	1	5	1
Common sense	6	–	6	–
(10 Most Common Responses)	(112)	(24)	(51)	(37)
Other Responses:(50)(10)(22)(18)				
Seize important issues	5	1	4	–
Sense of humour	5	–	3	2
Control of courtroom	4	1	1	2
Helps other judges	4	–	4	–
Consistency	3	–	1	2
Humility	3	1	–	2?
Open mind	3	2	–	1
Impartiality	2	2	–	–
Competence	2	–	1	1
Faith/love fellow man	2	–	1	1
Intellectually sound	2	–	2	–
Dignity and decorum	2	–	1	1
Flexibility	2	1	1	–
Innate ability	1	1	–	–
Reasonableness	1	–	–	1
Explains to people	1	–	–	1
Sincerity	1	–	–	1
Honesty	1	–	1	–
Social Conscience	1	–	1	–
Draws line re private life	1	–	–	1
Independence	1	1	–	–
Good in pre–trial conference	1	–	1	–
Clear sense own values	1	–	–	1
Objectivity	1	–	–	1

revealing. Our follow–up question was: "Among your fellow judges, there are probably some that you admire, that you think of as examples of what a good judge ought to be; we are not interested in the names of these specific judges, but rather in the qualities that you particularly admire and respect in them."

The question was intentionally open ended, in that we asked judges to apply their own labels and priorities rather than choose admired qualities from some previously generated list. It follows from this that if a judge did not indicate a specific quality, this does not necessarily mean explicit rejection of that quality, but only that it did not spring to mind as one of the most important qualities of a judge. We intended that this open–ended questioning would reduce the extent to which judges would generate an extensive list of conventional values and elicit instead a short list of qualities that they spontaneously feel to be pre–emptively important.

The judges indicated a wide variety of qualities, which to some extent group themselves logically. "Industry", "diligence", "hard–working", "conscientious" and "get the work done" are five different ways of saying the same thing; we call this quality *industry*. Similarly, terms such as "sensitive", "empathy", "humane", and "sympathy for people appearing before him" all point to a single quality; we refer to it as *empathy*. Even after such consolidation, we were left with 33 different items. Only one of these items was indicated by as many as one–third of the judges; and one–third of them were mentioned only by a single judge. Table 4.3 illustrates these figures, including a breakdown by level of court.

Valued Quality: Industry

The most frequently mentioned quality was industry, a willingness to work; the proposition that would elicit the highest support from Alberta judges is that a good judge is a judge who gets the work done and who puts the time in to make sure that it gets done. Of the 51 judges interviewed, 21 volunteered this factor as one of the most important in earning respect on the bench. Several explicitly made it the most important and one said it was the only important quality. Some of the representative comments are:

I don't like the nine to fivers; a judge must be conscientious and hard–working. Unfortunately, this quality is rare in judges; most of them can get by being pretty casual about their work. (Provincial Court judge)

A judge gains respect for his work habits; he must be some-one who works hard at it, who puts the time and effort in, who takes it seriously. This is more important than whether or not he is terribly learned. (Provincial Court judge)

A judge gains respect for his willingness to work, the work-load he is willing to accept, the extent to which he gets his work done promptly. There is no getting around it, some judges are just lazy. (Court of Queen's Bench judge)

The consistency of this priority across all three levels of the bench is striking; for both Section 96 benches it was the most often mentioned quality, and for the provincial bench it was a close second. (It is at first glance mildly curious that the high volume pure provincial court should be the one accorded the slightly lower priority; one third of Provincial Court judges as against half of Section 96 judges mentioned it.)

Several of the judges, especially the longer–sitting judges, con-nected the importance of this quality to recent developments within the judiciary. They said that their own appointments had come "at the end of an era" when one could take a rather leisurely approach to being a judge because the workload was moderate and there was excess capacity in the court system, and they con-trasted this with the heavy workloads and high pressure that now exist. The implication is that industry and a willingness to tackle the workload expeditiously have become more important now that the caseload is just barely under control than it would have been a couple of decades ago.

Valued Quality: Courtesy

Thirteen judges (three from the Court of Appeal and five from each of the trial courts) identified courtesy — simple politeness to counsel, to the parties to the case, and to witnesses — as one of the qualities of a good judge; for one judge this was the only quality bearing on the respect of colleagues. A number of judges identified this quality as "being a gentleman," and more than one spoke of consciously trying not to be like some of the heavy–handed judges before whom they themselves had practised. Many felt that this quality tended to be eroded simply by length of service, in that judges tend to become hardened and impersonal and arrogant as the number of cases they have heard multiplies. They thought the quality was also threatened by the caseload pressures that had built up through the 1970s and 1980s, so that it now often took time to be polite and time is always at a premium.

A judge has to be a gentleman, he has to be courteous; as a lawyer, I ran into some real tough judges, and I have always felt the need to behave differently myself. (Court of Appeal judge)

To earn respect, a judge must be a gentleman, courteous in his conduct toward other judges, the bar, and the public. (Court of Appeal Judge)

I look for a guy who remains steady, civil, and polite, who treats people as if they were of worth, although this sometimes gets hard to do after you've been on the bench a few years. (Provincial Court judge)

What is most important is, quite simply, a judge's qualities as a gentleman, both in the courtroom and out of it. There is just no excuse for bad manners in the courtroom, and I have no respect for a judge who behaves that way. (Court of Queen's Bench judge)

The judge who is respected is the judge who has the characteristics of a gentleman in the way he treats others: treat everyone with dignity and respect, don't bully people. (Provincial Court judge)

Valued Quality: Empathy

Thirteen judges (two from the Court of Appeal, four from the Queen's Bench, and seven from Provincial Court) spoke approvingly of the qualities of "humaneness", "humanity", "compassion," and "sensitivity." They felt that neither the sordidness of many cases nor the repetitiveness of routine should cut the judge off from holding a sympathetic feeling for the parties to the case. They said that the balance is hard to maintain, and it is precisely for this reason that judges who accomplish it are admired. More than one judge (especially in Provincial Court) spoke of being exposed to values and attitudes and lifestyles that they had never dreamed existed, and that they did not particular approve of; this exposure made empathy more difficult but not less important or desirable.

> It is important that judges be tolerant, that they be understanding of the pressures that people who appear in court are under. (Provincial Court judge)

> A judge must have empathy for the people who appear in his court. (Provincial Court judge)

> As a judge, you need compassion, a feeling for people in front of you. (Court of Queen's Bench judge)

> I admire a judge for the sympathy he shows for people who appear before him. (Court of Queen's Bench judge)

Valued Quality: Patience

Twelve judges (three from the Court of Appeal, five from the Court of Queen's Bench, and four from Provincial Court) indicated that one of the critical qualities for earning the respect of fellow judges is patience, the willingness to hear people out and not to hurry things through. It was conceded that the quality of patience, like that of courtesy, tended to be eroded both by length of service and by caseload pressures, but even more than courtesy its absence in a judge could get in the way of the effective performance of duties; the judge who cuts things short and hurries things along runs the risk of appearing to work to a schedule and a destination that have been decided beforehand.

> There is an awful tendency for judges in court to be quick as against being right; it is important to have a judge who is ready to listen. (Provincial Court judge)

> The qualities which cause a judge to gain the respect of his fellow judges [include]: the ability to listen; the ability to be patient even with the most exasperating people, and you get lots of them in court. (Court of Queen's Bench judge)

> A judge has to understand people, and has to be able to sit; to put it inelegantly, to be a judge you have to have a hard ass. (Court of Appeal judge)

> A willingness to listen and not to force the pace is important. (Court of Queen's Bench judge)

Valued Quality: Knowledge of Law

Eleven judges (two from the Court of Appeal, five from the Queen's Bench, and four from Provincial Court) said that a knowledge of law was important. This quality was sufficiently straightforward that most judges indicated it by simply using the three–word phrase, and only a few felt any need to elaborate on it, as in the following example:

> One of the most important qualities is a knowledge of the law, which doesn't necessarily mean that I have to agree with the conclusions that the judge is reaching about the law, but I have to respect the extent to which a judge is thorough and knowledgeable. (Provincial Court judge)

Indeed, at first glance the only surprise is that this quality was not mentioned by more judges, or even by all judges. However, several judges went out of their way to stress that this was *not* the most important quality, that it took a back seat to other values that were pre–emptively important or that it was valuable only if linked to some other quality. Several cited with approval the classic cliché, "If he knows a little law, so much the better," and others spoke of "flexibility" or of "not sticking by the letter of the law in the light of specific circumstances" in ways that suggested a conscious antithesis. Only one other valued quality (intelligence or brilliance) elicited a comparable polarity. We are not, of course, trying to suggest that these judges would approve of a colleague who was ignorant of the law; the point is the smaller, but still significant one, that encyclopedic technical expertise in the law is not the bull's–eye on their target of judicial performance.

Valued Quality: Intelligence

Ten judges (four from the Court of Appeal, five from the Court of Queen's Bench, and one from the Provincial Court) spoke of intelligence as earning respect for a judge. They spoke approvingly of a judge's "qualities of mind," or of brilliance, or of scholastic or academic qualities.

> General intelligence is one of the qualities which cause a judge to gain the respect of his fellow judges. (Court of Queen's Bench judge)

> I respect a judge for having a good mind, for how close he comes to being a real back–room lawyer. (Court of Queen's Bench judge)

> An important quality for all judges, trial and appeal alike, is intelligence without arrogance. (Court of Appeal judge)

> What earns respect is a combination of academic excellence and common sense; many judges have one or the other, but some judges (very few) have both, and these are respected by both bench and bar. (Court of Queen's Bench judge)

> The critical qualities for a judge are industry, impartiality, and intelligence (in no particular order). (Court of Appeal judge)

We found it striking, however, that most of the judges who spoke of intelligence or brilliance as an admired quality qualified it as not being the most important quality, or as being valuable only if it was offset by or paired with some other specified quality. One judge added that it is good to have academically inclined, brilliant judges "as long as there are not too many of them," surely an unusual and grudging way to praise an attribute. Indeed, three judges (one Provincial, two Queen's Bench) explicitly excluded brilliance or an "academic mind" from the qualities they admired in a judge; it was not only not a prerequisite to being a good judge, but something of a handicap. At the extreme, the general judgment could be taken to indicate something of an anti–intellectual bias within the legal profession. More moderately, it could be read as a stress on the practical dimensions of the judicial process, with intelligence *simpliciter* carrying overtones of an impractical perfectionism.

Valued Quality: Fairness

Ten judges (one on the Court of Appeal, three on the Court of Queen's Bench, and six on the Provincial Court) spoke of fairness, or even–handedness, or a sense of fair play as an important characteristic of a good judge; one judge saw it as the *only* critical quality. Two spoke not just of being fair but of appearing to be fair, in the sense of giving the participants in the case a firm sense that their arguments had been heard and considered, as the central dimension of this attribute.

> What I admire is basically, just a judge that tries to be a judge; someone who is fair. (Provincial Court judge)

> A judge must have a sense of fair play. (Provincial Court judge)

> A judge must be fair and square about things. (Provincial Court judge)

Again, such a quality seems sufficiently straightforward that if anything is surprising, it is that more judges did not mention it. A partial explanation may lie in the fact, mentioned in a variety of contexts by many judges, that a large number — even a majority — of the cases that they hear are cut–and–dried situations where one party is clearly in the right and the other is clearly in the wrong. In the case of such a mismatch, too punctilious a concern with fairness can turn the judge into a handicapper and get in the way of an expeditious and just resolution of the case.

Other Valued Qualities

Smaller numbers of judges mentioned other qualities. Nine judges (three from each of the three benches) said they admired fellow judges who were *decisive*, who made decisions expeditiously, including and especially the hard decisions, the ones that courted misunderstanding rather than popularity. "A judge must not be afraid to be wrong," one judge said. For most trial court judges, this included the idea of making the "tough" decisions without constantly looking over their shoulders and worrying about what the Court of Appeal might say. (This suggests some interesting tensions with the doctrine of *stare decisis*, a point we will explore further in chapter 8.)

Seven judges (five from the Court of Queen's Bench and one from each of the other two benches) gave high respect to the capacity for *writing* lucidly and incisively, for expressing legal concepts and ideas clearly in writing. They spoke of this as a straightforward and pragmatic talent, distinguishing it explicitly from the more suspect quality of "brilliance." Some saw this as a fading attribute of the judiciary — "A lot of judges just can't write well any more." — while others spoke approvingly of the available courses in legal writing. Six judges, all on the Court of Queen's Bench, spoke highly of the quality of *common sense*, again explicitly distinguishing it from brilliance. All the judges who suggested this were trial judges although, somewhat surprisingly, none of them were from the Provincial Court.

> What earns respect is a combination of academic excellence and common sense; many judges have one or the other, but some judges (very few) have both, and these are respected by both bench and bar. (Court of Queen's Bench judge)

Five judges (one from the Court of Appeal and one from the Court of Queen's Bench) respected colleagues for their *analytic capacity*, for the ability to penetrate a trial or a legal problem quickly to seize upon the central questions or issues at stake.

> The most important quality is the ability to analyse problems and to get to the heart of the matter; a good judge is one who can bring counsel right to the key problem right away, which saves a lot of time and time is always at a premium. This ability is largely a question of confidence and experience. (Court of Queen's Bench judge)

Obviously, the relationship between this quality and patience is problematic; one person's incisiveness is another's impatience. If a single judge had mentioned both qualities, we could see it as a question of balance, of an Aristotelian mean; in fact, no judge mentioned both, and the twelve judges mentioning patience and five citing incisiveness are seventeen different individuals. This suggests two differing conceptions of the judicial role in contemporary circumstances, one work–oriented and the other client–oriented.

Five trial judges (three from Court of Queen's Bench and two from Provincial Court) thought judges had to have a *sense of humour*, not in the sense of being stand–up comics (this would violate dignity and decorum and imply disrespect for the parties) but more as an inward and personal quality allowing them to maintain perspective by being able to laugh at themselves. As Table 4.3 shows, other qualities were indicated by still smaller numbers of judges.

This catalogue, not to mention the number and diversity of valued qualities, is perhaps more overwhelming than informative. It seems to us, however, that it is possible to group the list into larger packages that illustrate how specific groups of judges see and react to their world. Basically, the characteristics indicated by judges as relevant to their admiration and respect for colleagues can be gathered into three general categories, each highlighting a different dimension of judicial behaviour.

The first set, *professional/legal values*, includes such factors as knowledge of the law, intelligence or brilliance, ability to write ideas clearly, ability to seize the important issues, impartiality, intellectual soundness, innate ability, and independence. This set highlights the technical and procedural side of law, understood as a coherent framework of principles and concepts to be understood in themselves. In a phrase, it is a preoccupation with technical or "black letter law." The focus of this group of values is the profession itself, and the qualities indicated mesh well with the conventional list of ideals of the legal profession generally.

The second set, *personal/interactive values*, includes humaneness and sensitivity, patience, courtesy, sense of fair play, common sense, a sense of humour, humility, faith in and love of fellow human beings, flexibility, the ability to offer clear explanations, sincerity, honesty, social conscience, and a clear sense of personal values. The image of the law implied is less technical (the law in itself) and more pragmatic (the law as it impacts upon specific individuals). The focus of this group of values is the clientele, the individuals actually appearing in court, and the qualities indicated mesh with a view of justice that is less abstract and book–oriented and more personal and people–oriented.

The third set, *procedural/work–oriented values*, includes industry, diligence, decisiveness, control of the courtroom, a willingness to help other judges, consistency, competence, dignity and decorum, reasonableness, an ability to draw the line between private and public life, and an ability to work well in pre–trial conferences. The concern here is more with the managerial and collegial aspects of performing the judicial role, rather than with textbook characterizations of the law. The focus of this group of values is the workload and caseload, and the set meshes with an approach more oriented to tasks and efficiency.

Because both the number of judges interviewed and the number of responses per judge differ for each of the three benches, we will make the comparison by expressing a specific value as a percentage of total responses; for example, of the 32 value–responses given by the 10 Court of Appeal judges, 11 (or 34 per cent) refer to elements of what we have identified as the professional/legal list — and so on for the other benches and the other sets of values. Thus collected, the voluminous list from Table 4.3 can be presented more compactly in Table 4.4.

Table 4.4 Percentage of Judges' Responses Indicating What They Value in Other Judges, by Kind of Court (Alberta)

What judges admire in other judges	Court of Appeal	Court of Queen's Bench	Provincial Court	All Courts
Professional/legal values	34%	29%	11%	24%
Personal/interactive values	38%	40%	57%	45%
Procedural/work–oriented values	28%	31%	32%	31%

Alberta judges as a group stress personal/interactive values most highly, procedural/work–oriented values next, and professional/ legal values slightly below that; the same rank–ordering is true of both trial courts, although the order of the last two is reversed for the Court of Appeal. Professional/legal values are ranked more highly by the judges on the Court of Appeal than by other judges, with the percentage of judges mentioning such values dropping off sharply as we move through the Court of Queen's Bench to the Provincial Court. This seems consistent with the greater stress on professional qualifications in appointments to the Section 96 courts and especially the appeal courts.

Conversely, judges on the Court of Appeal mentioned personal/interactive values less often than trial judges, and judges on the Provincial Court mentioned such values significantly more often than Section 96 judges. Judges on all three benches mentioned procedural/work–oriented values with comparable frequency, although to the extent that there is a variation among the three it is a systematic one with the high volume courts stressing such values slightly more.

The patterns confirm the characterizations that many of the judges we spoke to made of their own and other courts. The Provincial Court is a "people's court," and the judges on that court respect judges for their ability to interact with the people appearing before them, for their interpersonal skills. The Court of Appeal is much more a "lawyer's court," and the judges on that court respect judges (in their court and other courts) for those skills and abilities that are more directly connected to the legal profession. The Court of Queen's Bench falls in between, more people–oriented than the Court of Appeal but placing a higher stress on legal and professional skills than the Provincial Court. The similarity in the proportion of judges on all three benches who mentioned more explicitly task–oriented skills reflects the perception of a caseload that is now being barely coped with and threatens to create a serious back–log problem in all courts.

What Do Judges Strive To Be Like?

A clear pattern emerges of the qualities that Alberta judges as a group regard as characteristic of those judges who deserve the respect of their peers, and from these attributes we can derive an outline of the prevailing notion of the role of the judge.

As a group, Alberta judges value the qualities of diligence and industry, of humaneness, of patience and courtesy, of a knowledge of the law and intelligence, of a sense of fair play and decisiveness. At a somewhat lower level, they attach importance to clear writing, common sense, grasping the central elements of a case, and a sense of humour. The composite picture is, however, somewhat misleading, because the judges in question are divided among three different benches, and the prevailing picture is somewhat different for each of the three in both content and priorities.

Judges on the Court of Appeal value industry, intelligence, courtesy, patience, and decisiveness; knowledge of the law, humaneness, and impartiality remain important but rank slightly lower. They mentioned legal/professional skills more often, and personal/interactive skills less often, than was the case for the other benches; they made references to specifically work–oriented skills in the same proportion as other judges. This seems consistent with the general image of an academically inclined appeal court that is feeling caseload pressures. Perhaps the only surprise is that only two judges of the ten interviewed specifically mentioned knowledge of the law; but as we've noted, it would be an error to read too much into this omission, which might only indicate how much such a quality is taken for granted.

Judges on the Provincial Court admire the qualities of humaneness, industry, fair play, courtesy, and patience; marginally less important are a knowledge of the law and decisiveness. They mentioned personal/interactive skills more often, and specifically legal/professional skills less often, than was the case for the other benches. This seems consistent with the image of the Provincial Court as a high–volume court that must interact directly with people who know little of the law and its nuances, and who are frequently unrepresented by counsel. In the terms that several of the judges used, it is a "people's court" rather than a "lawyer's court," although the rising frequency of representation by counsel means that the contrast cannot be pushed too far.

Judges on the Court of Queen's Bench respect their colleagues for industry, common sense, knowledge of the law, patience, intelligence, and the ability to write clearly; also important are the ability to seize the critical issues, courtesy, cooperation with fellow judges, and humaneness. Apart from the priority placed on diligence, which is pervasive through the court system, this ranking of admired qualities makes the judges on the Court of Queen's Bench an interesting midway point between Provincial Court judges and Appeal Court judges — more impressed with legal knowledge, intelligence, and writing ability than provincial judges, but giving a higher priority to such human values as common sense than appeal court judges. Most intriguing is the importance several judges attached to a judge's willingness to cooperate with fellow judges — the only specific reference to collegial values that emerged from the interviews, and a value that might have been more readily anticipated from a panel court than from a functionally dispersed trial court.

To Be a Judge

To become a judge involves a good deal more than simply becoming immersed in a new job. It means adapting to a new way of life.

Most lawyers who seek a judicial appointment do so either because, as high–achievers, they like to be challenged and have "outgrown" their law practice, or because they want to "escape" the stress or the boredom of their practice. Most are ready for the changes that await them, but few can cope without encountering at least a few problems along the way. First they have to face the problem of adjusting to the power and prestige that judges have, without succumbing to an inflated ego. Next there is the sense of isolation created by the goal of impartiality and the community's expectations about judges' behaviour. It is perhaps helpful that most judges enjoy an informal collegial atmosphere with their colleagues and can try to live up to the qualities they admire most in these other judges. Because they are high–achievers in a context of heavy and possibly growing workloads, it is not surprising that judges would admire the quality of industry in their colleagues.

But we are struck by the extent to which judges also stress empathy and humanity, and patience and courtesy, even above knowledge of the law and intelligence. It seems to us that this tendency is something the authorities responsible for judicial recruitment appointment should bear in mind. Moreover, as we look more closely at the judicial decision–making process, first in trial courts, then in appeal courts, and finally in the apex of the judicial hierarchy — the Supreme Court of Canada — it will become clearer why the judges have stressed these qualities above all others.

5

Judicial Decision–Making: Trial Courts

The workload of trial courts is made up predominantly of cases being heard for the first time. Trial judges spend little (if any) of their time reviewing the decisions of other courts or judges, although occasionally appeals from municipal by–law cases such as convictions for illegal parking will be heard in a Provincial Court, or appeals from convictions for minor offences in a Provincial Court will be heard in a section 96 trial court.

There are two levels of provincial trial courts in Canada. The first is the basic workhorse court, usually known as the Provincial Court, which has judges appointed and paid by the provincial government and handles 90 to 95 per cent of all the cases processed by the Canadian court system each year. The second is the provincial superior, county, and district trial courts, which have federally appointed (and paid) judges even though the courts themselves are established and maintained by the provinces. Judges in these courts always sit alone when hearing trials, and not in panels, unlike the continental European courts — in France, for example — where most trials are conducted by a panel of three judges. Jury trials are rare in Canada (although not so rare as they were 10 or 20 years ago), and take place only in the superior, county, and district courts.

Clearly the decision is the core of the judicial process. It is the logical focus of the court proceedings and of the human drama that is so awkwardly crammed into them. Small wonder that movies and television programs so often build themselves around this stark motif, effective even when it is melodramatically misrepresented — the robed figure behind the bench, the bang of the gavel, the stern "objection overruled," the grim conclusion "I find the defendant guilty as charged." It is both revealing and significant that "the judge" represents one of our society's last officials who routinely wears a special garb of office and is addressed by an honorific title rather than by a specific name. The highly formal routine of the court contrasts starkly and effectively with an increasingly breezy and informal society. We compare this, for instance, to our own roles as professors; we cannot help but be struck by how often our students, even in first–year classes, call us by our first names, and by how stuffy and inappropriate we often feel when we are referred to by a more formal title.

On the one hand, we acknowledge and respect judges for their rigorous professional training, for their personal experience in a demanding profession, for their selection from the ranks of the profession for elevation to the responsibilities of the bench. On the other hand, we insist that beneath the robes judges are people much like the rest of us. They have to struggle to keep their minds from wandering during repetitive technical evidence. They must avoid being distracted by idiosyncratic human detail from the real legal issues involved. They must grasp the nettle of making — without perfect certainty — decisions that will change the lives of those who, usually involuntarily, appear before them.

The essence of this activity is the phenomenon of judicial power. To an individual caught up in the judicial process, *power* is an obvious and oppressive reality; to be in court is to hand control of events over to others, to the lawyer who will present your case but above all to the judge who will pronounce the decision that can only be appealed to other judges. But we know from our interviews that most judges are extremely uncomfortable with the notion of judicial power, and we know as students of the law that much of the trappings of the legal process exists precisely to remove the judges from the appearance of exercising an individual arbitrary power.

Models of Judicial Decision–Making

The process of making a judicial decision is at one and the same time straightforward and mysterious, obvious and inscrutable.

What a judge thinks he or she is doing in reaching a decision is the inner reality of the judicial process. Like riding a bicycle, rendering a judicial decision is something that cannot be completely reduced to an exhaustive verbal description, although it can certainly be performed without such a reduction. However, understanding it is essential for such purposes as evaluating judicial performance, reforming court procedures, or reforming the judicial appointment process.

Everyone knows that when judges are hearing cases, lawyers present them with evidence, legal arguments, and precedents that the judges carefully consider before they reach a decision. But knowing that is no more useful than being told that Wayne Gretzky is a great hockey player because he skates and shoots the puck. Academic theorists have suggested a variety of models for conceptualizing this process, although these are based more on impressions and abstract theory than on systematic empirical research. (See Champagne and Nagel, Mitchell Klein, and Weiler.) Some of these models are:

- the judge as computer (the mechanical application of rules to factual situations)
- the judge as umpire (making snap judgment calls to permit the routine in the courts to continue with a minimum of delay)
- the judge as King Solomon (creatively devising a just solution to a given problem and manipulating the law to reach that result)
- the judge as plain dispute–resolver (providing case–by–case decisions for the parties involved in specific disputes), and
- the judge as policy–maker (providing future–oriented assessments of the implications of a legal issue or government policy).

These different models may seem mutually incompatible. However, each is thought by its proponents to be appropriate to specific courts and certain kinds of cases. The "policy–making" model is thought by some to be the approach that the Supreme Court of

Canada ought to follow, while others feel that the "plain dispute–resolver" model is more appropriate. Some would apply the "computer" model to the trial courts, while others would prefer the "umpire" or "King Solomon" model, depending on the kind of case, the court's workload, and the qualities that judges are thought to possess. This lack of consensus about how judges ought to behave merely underlines the complexity of the judicial decision–making process. All of the models attempt to penetrate the important formal rituals in court to identify how judges do (or ought to) perceive and carry out the central part of the judicial process.

However, in our interviews with trial judges in Alberta we found that individual judges themselves did not often consider the decision–making process to be either mysterious or complex. When we asked the trial judges to describe how they reached their decisions, most answered first by saying that all judges followed pretty much the same approach, and that "everyone knew" what judges did and how they did it. More than one concluded by saying, "I suppose that the other judges told you exactly the same thing," an assumption so patently incorrect that it was hard for us not to be drawn into discussion.

Beyond some obvious and important common ground — the need to approach a case without bias, not to judge litigants by their appearance, to listen carefully and patiently, and to postpone a decision until as late in the proceedings as possible — there was a considerable degree of diversity. A number of distinct ways of conceptualizing and relating to the process of making a decision emerged. These did not connect in any simply way to the level of court involved; we did not find one mind–set typical of Provincial Court judges and another of federally appointed judges. Judges tend to underestimate the diversity that exists within their own ranks in terms of the processes used to reach a judicial decision.

We asked each judge the same question: "From your own experience, is there a general process by which you reach a decision on a particular case?" In some cases, when the judges asked us to explain this question in more detail, we followed with: "When you as a judge first begin hearing a case, you have no idea which party has the right of it, and yet at the end of the case you as a judge must give a decision for one party or the other. How would you describe, how would you put into words, the process whereby you move from the first point to the second?"

Again, the question was explicitly and intentionally open–ended so that we would not force judges to choose from among a set of preconceived models; rather, we hoped to derive a set of models from the judges' spontaneous descriptions.

After sorting responses into "similar" and "dissimilar" groups from various perspectives, it became clear to us that the responses could be distinguished on two different dimensions, which we call "formalism" and "discretion." By *formalism* we mean the extent to which the judges had developed an understanding of their decision–making that could be articulated as a specific and discrete rational process, as opposed to one that was automatic or intuitive or artistic. By *discretion* we mean the extent to which the judges saw the process as requiring a significant degree of arbitrary personal choice or judgment, as opposed to a mechanical process in which the answer simply presents itself when the right buttons are pushed.

From this sorting out process, we created a four–part figure, each cell of which can be seen as a distinct "model" of the decision–making process, as Figure 5.1 indicates.

The 41 trial judges were divided into groups according to whether they described the decision–making process in terms of high or low levels of formalism, and according to high and low levels of discretion. The four possible combinations of these factors result in four basic models of judicial decision–making in the trial courts.

There were "typical" responses associated with each model (see Figure 5.2), although the high–discretion models can be

---

Figure 5.1 Models of Judicial Decision–Making in Trial Courts

		Formalism	
		Low	High
	Low	I improvisers	II strict formalists
Discretion			
	High	IV intuitivists	III pragmatic formalists

**Figure 5.2   Typical Responses Associated with the Four
Decision–Making Models**

Model I: "improvisers" (low formalism, low discretion)
typical response: "There is no single process of making a decision because
cases present too much variety; nevertheless, different judges would usually come to the same decision about the same case."

Model II: "strict formalists" (high formalism, low discretion)
typical response: "The making of judicial decisions often revolves around
highly technical and objective questions requiring little in the way of a
conscious formal intellectual process for their application."

Model III: "pragmatic formalists" (high formalism, high discretion)
typical response: "There is a conscious, understandable process that all
judges should follow in reaching a judicial decision. This process can be
formulated in terms of a "check list" of items, or a "shifting balance"
between the two sides, or "water rising" to a specific level.

Model IV: "intuitivists" (low formalism, high discretion)
typical response: "The process of a judicial decision is best described in
terms of a "gut–feeling" about the trial as a whole, a "key moment" in a
trial around which everything revolves, or arriving at a feeling of what the
most fair outcome should be, and then putting together the rationale that
justifies reaching the outcome."

---

further subdivided according to the specific way that the judges
described the process.

Model I: "Improvisers"
[low formalism, low discretion]
The improvisers typically said that there was simply too much
variety in the types of cases and the kinds of situations arising in
court to attempt to describe any one decision–making process.
Rather, a judge had to have a repertoire of decision–making models, picking and choosing among them as the situation demanded.

> Such dramatically different cases come before my court, that
> there is really no general rule or process that I can describe.
> (Provincial Court judge)

I have no rigid or general process because the cases are all so different; the only really basic rule is that you can't allow yourself any ideas until you hear all the evidence. (Court of Queen's Bench judge)

For some judges, it was the types of cases that created the variety: for example, the many different kinds of offenses with which individuals were charged. For others, it was the multiplicity of the human dramas played out in the courtroom: even if the types of lawsuits or criminal charges were finite, the human elements specific to each case created too many variables to be reducible to any set of forms. For both, however, judicial decision–making required not a single rational process but a wide variety of strategies or approaches that defied generalization.

Four judges, two from each of the two trial benches, saw decision–making exclusively in terms of the "improviser" model. Three others, also representing both benches, made some comments in this vein as part of a more complex response. It is interesting that this answer was as likely to be given by a Queen's Bench judge as by a Provincial Court judge, despite the fact that many judges thought the judicial role differed for the two trial courts because the caseload of a Provincial judge was more narrowly specialized and therefore more routine, while that of a Queen's Bench trial judge was more varied and therefore more complex.

This type of response might be seen as evading a candid analysis of the decision–making process. We did not get this impression, and we do not intend to imply it; we believe that these responses should be taken at face value. The casual, matter–of–fact tone typical of these responses suggests that neither the selection of an appropriate strategy for a given case nor dealing with that case once the strategy has been selected should be seen as an intellectual puzzle. Nor do these responses convey any feeling that different judges would be likely to come to different conclusions about the outcome of the same case. The responsibilities of a trial judge reduce to a commonsensical response to an incredible range of situations, based on professional experience and expertise;

however significant the consequences may be for the parties, the process itself is non–problematic.

Model II: "Strict Formalists"
[high formalism, low discretion]

Some other judges agreed that talking about an intellectual process of decision–making was too grand a language for the sorts of cases that they were called upon to decide, but their reasons for feeling so were rather different. These judges stressed that the work of a trial judge is focused more around findings of fact — what really happened, who really did what — than around any complex question of law. They felt that in a large number of cases the facts are not difficult to establish, and the facts are all that is needed to reach a decision.

> It is very seldom that I have to make decisions of any complexity or difficulty; the cases that come before Provincial Court are just not of that kind. (Provincial Court judge)

> Decision–making is pretty straightforward in Provincial Court; you just find the facts and then apply the law, and neither is usually very difficult or complicated. (Provincial Court judge)

> As a trial judge, my primary duty is to be a finder of fact; I must see that the trial is conducted according to the rules of evidence and procedure, and I must take the facts and apply them to the law. It is usually not difficult; I am able to make most decisions from the bench, and less than 10 per cent present such difficulty or complexity that I have to reserve judgment. (Court of Queen's Bench judge)

These judges often suggested that a judge's job could be (and often was) made to sound more complex and mysterious than it is, and they resisted such dramatization. It was not that the cases lacked interest or that their reduction to a routine either constituted or caused "judicial burnout"; these were not the overtones. Rather, although idiosyncratic detail abounds in the cases that they hear and they could appreciate as much as anyone the drama of human life as it appears in the courtroom, these judges felt that much of this detail was beside the legal point. Once the irrelevant particulars were cleared away, the matching of fact to law to generate the appropriate outcome was a simple and routine process. The difficulty, such as it was, was in the clearing away, not in the process that followed.

Again, it may be surprising to some that this type of response was no more frequent among provincial judges than Section 96 trial judges; five provincial judges and four Queen's Bench judges characterized their decision–making exclusively in terms of this "strict formalist" approach, while four provincial judges and three Court of Queen's Bench judges said that this approach was true of many cases while describing in different terms the way they reached their decisions on other cases.

This second model, that cases are so straightforward or routine as to suggest no major intellectual problem and no large role for discretion, suggests judges who identify cases and legal issues in terms of one or more frequently repeating types, each of which is routine. This description of the process bears some similarity to the ideal decision–making process prescribed by a group of legal theorists known as "judicial positivists." According to a broadly Austinian theory of positivism, most judicial decisions can be made mechanically, and there is rarely any room for judicial discretion.

Model III: "Pragmatic Formalists"
[high formalism, high discretion]
The judges that we label "pragmatic formalists" described a conscious and explicit process by which they moved from an uncommitted state of mind at the start of a trial to a firm decision at or before the end of the trial. They stressed, however, that even if the proper procedures were followed, the result is not always obvious; there remains an important and irreducible place for judicial discretion.

Even those who thought many of their cases were routine often told about how they reached decisions on a rare case that raised more difficult questions. As well, many stressed that they had to "go through the motions" even in easier cases to "keep themselves in practice" for the tough cases, or to avoid overlooking them.

There were three conceptually distinct metaphors that different judges employed to describe the process that we have labelled "pragmatic formalist."

Decision by Means of "the Check List"

The most common metaphor employed by the "pragmatic formalist" judges to describe their decision–making process was the "check list": drawing up, in a more or less formal way, a list of the things that have to be proved, and then considering everything that happened at the trial according to where and how it related to that check list. More than one judge mentioned the importance of reminding oneself over and over of something so simple as which side carried the onus of proof, that is, the onus for putting the check marks in place; losing sight of it, which could easily be done, caused unnecessary confusion and delay.

Some, using "onus" in a less technical sense, thought of the check list method as "switching the spotlight" from one side to the other; once the Crown has made a point, the onus swings to the defence to answer it, and so on. This whole process was explicitly connected to the notion of linear thinking central to the whole process of legal reasoning: establish A before you can go on to B, which in turn has to be established before you even look at C. In the end, using this approach, many decisions become straightforward, although some require a certain amount of discretion.

> You write down what plaintiff or Crown has to prove, then listen to the evidence and assess the credibility of the witnesses to see if the points have been met. You keep in mind sort of a mental check list, with the plaintiff or Crown letting you put checks beside them, then the defendant making you erase some of them. (Court of Queen's Bench judge)

> I have developed my own system of actually physically "charting" the facts as they emerge, especially in long trials, in a kind of diagrammatic form, and then toward the end of

the trial I start working up a rough draft of the factual story as a focus to keep an eye on the major questions. Although in many trials on simpler questions this usually doesn't involve very much, it is still a useful device to keep myself on track. (Provincial Court judge)

Decision by the "Shifting Balance"

Other judges used a second metaphor, that of "the shifting balance." These judges stressed the importance of "staying loose," of holding back from letting themselves make even a provisional decision, until all the evidence had been presented. They saw each piece of evidence or each witness or each argument by counsel as swinging the balance from one side to the other, with the decision to be reached on the basis of the direction the balance pointed at the very end of the trial.

Some judges spoke of sometimes not knowing even at the end of the trial which way to go, and only being able to reach a final determination by sitting in chambers, reviewing the evidence and rethinking through the notes of the trial. The responses of these judges indicated that a certain amount of intuition was sometimes required to make the final decision.

The most important principle is the obvious one: you just get yourself in a neutral frame of mind, then sit there and listen, listen and concentrate, all the way through; you find yourself changing back and forth throughout, and your impressions can swing from one side to the other and back again throughout the trial. (Court of Queen's Bench judge)

Especially in a long trial, you have to weigh everything continuously; your views constantly swing back and forth, and you have to weigh the total evidence at the end of each day's proceedings to stay on top of it; I seldom find myself reaching a conclusion part–way through the trial, because I have had too much experience with how solid one side can look until you hear the other side. (Provincial Court judge)

The difference between the first two metaphors in the "pragmatic formalist" category seems more than simply different words used to describe a single process. The first (the check list) breaks the process of judicial decision–making down into a finite series of steps that lead and contribute to an ultimate conclusion. The shifting balance, on the other hand, stresses a suspension of judgment until the final moment, at which point all the evidence is assembled into a package to generate the outcome. Where the first approach fragments the process of decision–making over several points in time, the second explicitly focuses it at a single such point, although that point need not be the same for all trials or for all judges. What these approaches have in common is the combination of structure and intuition.

Decision by Cumulative Process
Several judges spoke of a cumulative process, of conceptualizing a trial as a process of piling one fact upon another or one element upon another until the foundation is sufficiently solid to justify a decision as to guilt or liability.

> I believe that everyone is entitled to have their day in court. No matter how solid the case looks, you have to wait, have to suspend judgment until you've heard the evidence. The judge has to keep a focus on the facts, and I summarize the facts each evening after the trial, so after a lengthy trial I will still have at my fingertips who said what when and how convincingly. Decision–making is a cumulative process: just keep piling things up and making notes until something firm emerges. (Court of Queen's Bench judge)

> In criminal cases, it is just a question of proving the charge beyond a reasonable doubt, like the water level rising to a bench mark. In civil cases, it is just a question of the balance of probabilities as directed by law, or by the preponderance of evidence, and these phrases mean just what they say, so it is simply a straightforward question of applying them. (Court of Queen's Bench judge)

Again, the difference in metaphor suggests more than a superficial variation in the approach. The "rising level" suggests a decision–making process that is both fragmented like the check list and focused like the shifting balance. Whereas the balance presumably could keep shifting until the last moment of the trial, the level could become high enough at almost any point within the trial. Further, where the check list suggests a single route that must be followed to a judicial conclusion, the rising level carries no such built–in assumption.

The "pragmatic formalist" responses (including in a single category those judges who spoke of a check list, those who spoke of a shifting balance, and those who spoke of a cumulative process) comprise just under half of the trial judges interviewed, including just under half from each bench. Nine judges (two–thirds from the pure provincial bench) spoke in terms of a check list, seven (four from Court of Queen's Bench) of a shifting balance, and three judges (all Court of Queen's Bench) of a rising water level. In general, these judges see many or all of the cases appearing before them as presenting an intellectual problem and have developed an articulable formal process for dealing with them. Unlike the strict formalist judges, however, the judges in the pragmatic formalist camp did not describe the decision–making process as cut and dried. Although they felt judges ought to follow structured processes, they thought that the facts or the law were sometimes not entirely clear, so that judicial discretion sometimes played a role.

This description of the decision–making process bears some similarity to the realist school of jurisprudence. According to realist theorists such as Jerome Frank or Karl Llewellyn, in some difficult cases equally intelligent and diligent judges may come to different conclusions about how the case ought to be decided, even if they follow all of the correct legal procedures. This is because the law and the rules of legal reasoning can never be clear enough to cover all possibilities unambiguously. Most realist theorists think that judges ought to apply the law impartially, and they would agree that for routine cases, the results should almost always be the same. It is the hard cases, such as constitutional cases, in which the law cannot be applied mechanically to produce "one correct result." In these cases the individual judge's personality determines the result, and not the legal rules.

Model IV: "Intuitivists"
[low formalism, high discretion]
A number of judges spoke of decision–making less as a rational process than as a matter of intuition — of something that was simply known rather than deduced or concluded. To use the obvious polarity, judging is an art rather than a science, the product of character and experience rather than focused learning. Judges expressed this process of intuiting in three different ways.

Decision by Gestalt or "Gut Feeling"
For some judges, reaching a judicial decision is at least partly a question of an instinct or a "gut feeling" (a phrase specifically employed by several judges) that grows over the course of the trial until the judge simply knows the best way to decide the case.

The development of this instinct, the ability to arrive at a gut feeling about the case as a whole, is very much a matter of experience with the law, and some judges spoke either of not yet having fully developed it, or of having reached decisions only with real trepidation until they had gained the necessary experience to rely on those intuitive feelings. Assessing the credibility of witnesses was one, but not the only, sort of judgment that was seen in terms of an intuition that could not be broken down into a series of rational steps, but which simply accrue to an experienced and trained mind.

> I see the courtroom as a laboratory of human behaviour. I watch the mannerisms of witnesses, of the parties, of the lawyers. There is a kind of psychology operating that the judge must be aware of, must take into consideration, must use to get the best understanding of the situation. Instinct and experience must play a big role: it is not and cannot be just a question of the technical weighing of evidence. (Provincial Court judge)

Sometimes part–way through the trial you just know where you want to go and it is just a question of finding the best way to get there. Like the old lawyer's maxim has it, just make the judge want to find in your favour, and he'll find a way; that isn't a bad way of describing the process. (Provincial Court judge)

I have been a judge too long to make any quick assessments; rather, I have learned just to watch, to listen, to get a general feeling for the case. I often find toward the end of the trial that I know which way I'm going, but I don't know yet what I'm going to say to explain how I got there. (Court of Queen's Bench judge)

Both Provincial Court judges and Court of Queen's Bench judges were represented among the seven judges who spoke of decision–making this way, and both civil and criminal trials were included in their comments and examples.

Identifying the "Key Witness" or "Key Moment"

For some judges, the process of reaching a judicial decision fitted better with the standard Hollywood format, with a single pivotal moment when everything clicked into place, when uncertainty became certainty. Some of the judges who offered this description did so almost apologetically, saying that they were constantly surprised by how often things worked out so neatly, even with trials that had initially seemed very complex; but they said their experience over time tended to confirm the generalization rather than to make it exceptional or unusual.

To be sure, this approach was not suggested as making the job of the judge easy or effortless, because they still had to follow the evidence closely to be able to identify the key moment, and because sometimes the neat resolution never occurred and they had to muddle through by more prosaic methods. But despite its melodramatic overtones the approach was volunteered and staunchly defended by three Court of Queen's Bench judges.

Often the whole thing will revolve around the credibility of a single witness or of several witnesses, or around a single piece of evidence, and you find yourself working away on that one thing, sometimes one way and sometimes the other, until it comes clear, and then the decision is easy. (Court of Queen's Bench judge)

Criminal cases almost always turn on one element of the crime or one part of the evidence. It sometimes takes a while to work out what the critical element is going to be in any case, sometimes you don't know what it is until well into the trial, but once you've got it, you know what to focus on, and everything falls into place. (Court of Queen's Bench judge)

The Judge as "Seeker of Justice"

Some judges said they make a decision by arriving at a feeling of the outcome that is the most fair or the most just, and then they put together the rationale that allowed them to reach that outcome. For them, the central point of law is not simply uniformity or conformity with a rule or standard, but the seeking of justice or fairness, and because case is unique the search for fairness might well lead them to an outcome that is not a simple replication of the outcome in generally similar cases.

It is always the case that certain priorities and premises exist in the legislation; therefore the judge must focus on the questions that the legislation presents to him, questions such as: What are the options? What are the legal principles involved? What are the facts? Then the judge has to look at the decision he seems to be moving toward in terms of these questions: Is it just? Is it fair? What will it accomplish? (Provincial Court judge)

Sometimes the law is the issue, for example when there is nothing as yet from the Alberta Court of Appeal, and the appeal courts of the other provinces have gone different ways; this is not infrequent in Canada. This requires a great

deal of detailed work from the judge, and at that stage, your
own attitude determines the result. It is really a question of
the way that you want to go. Personally I am always aware
of being anxious that the decision not be gratuitously hurtful,
of wanting to do justice. (Queen's Bench judge)

Certainly it is not our intention to characterize as eccentric or
unusual the identification of law in terms of justice, or to suggest
that these two judges represent the only ones interviewed who see
justice as a critical part of what they do in reaching a decision.
However, the relationship between law and justice is both complex and problematic. Mr. Justice Devlin, for example, speaks of
the need for a judge to overcome the "bias in favour of the justice
of the case and against any law that seems to deny it." Certainly,
to stress the misfit between law and justice is to cast doubt upon
the direct relevance of formal legal training and experience, and
thereby upon the legal profession's monopoly of judicial office.
For these reasons, it is worth identifying as a separate category
those judges whose description of their own decision–making
gave a priority to "fairness" and "justice" over "law" and "procedure."

This fourth general set of responses, including in a single category those judges who spoke of a gut feeling, those who spoke of
a key moment in a trial, and those who spoke of seeking justice,
characterize judges who see the resolution of a legal issue as less
an intellectual process than a decision that is intuited rather than
deduced, in which both experience and feeling are key elements.
For some judges, what is known intuitively is a gut feeling for
assessing credibility or culpability; for others, it is the just or fair
outcome of a specific case; for others, it is the critical moment or
the key piece of evidence in a trial that permits everything to fall
into place and the answer to become obvious. We have labelled
the judges giving these responses as "intuitivists."

Tables 5.1 and 5.2 summarize the responses of all judges as to
how they reach decisions. Some judges did give a second and
differing response, but we have categorized them in Table 5.1 only
in terms of their major or strongest response. Table 5.2 "double

counts" these multiple response judges by including them in both primary and secondary categories.

Table 5.1 Decision–Making Styles of Alberta Judges (Major Responses Only)		
Formalism		
low	high	Total
Discretion		
low improvisers 10% (n= 4) (2 PC 2 QB)	strict formalists 22% (n = 9) (5 PC 4 QB)	32% (n = 13) (7 PC 6 QB)
high intuitivists 24% (n = 10) (4 PC 6 QB)	pragmatic formalists 44% (n = 18) (9 PC 9 QB)	68% (n = 28) (13 PC 15 QB)
Total 34% (n = 14) (6 PC 8 QB)	66% (n = 27) (14 PC 13 QB)	100% (n = 41) (20 PC 21 QB)

The 41 trial judges were divided into groups according to whether they described the decision–making process in terms of high or low levels of formalism, and according to high and low levels of discretion.

PC = Provincial Court Judge   QB = Court of Queen's Bench Judge

Although there are some differences between the two benches, the pattern generally suggests a roughly similar diversity in the styles of judicial decision–making between the two trial benches. Taking both benches together, high discretion responses outnumber low discretion responses by about two to one, and high formalism responses outnumber low formalism responses by about the same margin. Compared with Queen's Bench judges, Provincial Court judges describe their decision–making processes in terms that put less stress on discretion and more on following regular procedures, which is what we would expect from the greater specialization (and hence the higher levels of routine cases) of the Provincial Court. It may be surprising to some that the two benches are not more sharply differentiated on the basis of their perception of the role of discretion, given the popular conception of the Provincial Court as dispensing assembly–line justice to routine cases, while cases requiring discretion flow upward to provincial superior courts such as Alberta's Queen's Bench.

Table 5.2 Decision–Making Styles of Alberta Judges (Multiple Responses)			
	Formalism		
Discretion	low	high	Total
low	improvisers 17% (n = 7) (3 PC 4 QB)	strict formalists 39% (n = 16) (9 PC 7 QB)	56% (n = 23) (12 PC 11 QB)
high	intuitivists 27% (n = 11) (5 PC 6 QB)	pragmatic formalists 46% (n = 19) (9 PC 10 QB)	73% (n = 30) (14 PC 16 QB)
Total	44% (n = 18) (6 PC 8 QB)	85% (n = 35) (14 PC 13 QB)	129% (n = 53 responses from 41 judges) (26 PC 27 QB)

The 41 trial judges were divided into groups according to whether they described the decision–making process in terms of high or low levels of formalism, and according to high and low levels of discretion.

PC = Provincial Court Judge   QB = Court of Queen's Bench Judge

In their study, Cornelius M. Kerwin, Thomas Henderson, and Carl Baar suggest that judicial decisions can be categorized according to how cases are processed. They have suggested three categories: "procedural" (complex factual issues, adversarial and low–volume cases), "decisional" (high–volume, routine cases and parties frequently unrepresented), or "diagnostic" (diagnosing a problem in legal interpretation or social interaction and prescribing a solution). Any court may oscillate between all three types, although certain types of decisions may be more frequent in some courts than in others. Applying the above categories to the Alberta courts, the Court of Queen's Bench would best represent the procedural model. The Provincial Court has three divisions: criminal, youth, and small claims. The criminal and small claims divisions would best fit the decisional model, and the youth court the diagnostic model.

The Kerwin–Henderson–Baar model, however, does not help to explain how the judges of the various courts describe their decision–making processes. From the perspective of these authors, we would expect the judges of the procedural courts to congregate toward the pragmatic formalist category, the judges of the Provincial Court (criminal and small claims divisions) to gravitate toward the strict formalist position, and the judges of the family and juvenile division to tend toward categories I and IV (low formalism). That this is not the case might indicate that the kind of court in which judges serve may not have much impact on their decision–making style, which may be more directly related to the judges' personal qualities, randomly distributed among the judges of the various courts.

Table 5.3 Decision–Making Styles of Alberta Trial Judges by type of court

Decision–Making Process			procedural (QB)	decisional (PC Cr&Sm)	diagnostic (PC F&J)	Total
				Type of Court		
	1 Improvisers	n	10% 2	8% 1	14% 1	10% 4
High Pro-ceduralism	2 Strict formalists	n	19% 4	23% 3	29% 2	22% 9
High Discretion	3 Pragmatic formalists	n	43% 9	54% 7	29% 2	44% 18
	4 Intuitivists	n	29% 6	15% 2	29% 2	24% 10
	Total	n	100% 21	100% 13	100% 7	100% 41

QB = Court of Queen's Bench Court, PC F&J = Provincial Court, Family and Juvenile Division, PC Cr & Sm = Provincial, Criminal and Small Claims divisions

Summary: Trial Court Decision–Making Strategies

It has often been assumed that because of the strict procedures that judges must follow, the decision–making process allowed for little discretion on the part of judges. The decision–making process was basically mechanical, albeit so complex and so frequently saturated with technical legal issues that judges could never be replaced by computers or lay people. It was also conventional wisdom that the decision–making process in the superior courts was more intricate and sophisticated than that in the inferior courts because of the greater "importance" (in terms of the seriousness of the crime or the monetary value of a civil action) of cases in the superior courts.

Our research questions both of these assumptions. By classifying the judges' actual descriptions of the decision–making process, we identified two common themes, which we labelled "degree of formalism" and "degree of discretion." We can only make sense of the judges' responses by treating these as two *different* factors, rather than as the opposing ends of a single continuum. In other words, it is possible for judges to stress conformity to what they consider as the "correct" decision–making procedures (although the description of "correctness" varied considerably) and to emphasize how much discretion they had within the rules. In fact, the largest group of judges (44 per cent) described the decision–making process in these terms, and we labelled them *pragmatic formalists*. We were able to divide about half of the judges into two more or less equal groups: *strict formalists* (high formalism, low discretion), and *intuitivists* (low formalism, high discretion). The remaining one–tenth of the judges we called *improvisers* (low formalism, low discretion). The proportion of judges in both the Provincial Court and the superior court who fell into these four groups was comparable.

Jury Trials

Jury trials take place only before provincial superior and district court trial judges (in Alberta, Court of Queen's Bench). They constitute a special category, because in a sense the judge has little to decide: the jury determines guilt in a criminal trial, or liability and/or damages in a civil case. The judge's duty is to preside over the court and to summarize the trial for the jury before it deliberates to reach a decision.

Early in Canada's history jury trials were the norm in both criminal and civil trials. Nowadays, jury trials constitute only about 2 per cent of the criminal cases involving indictable offences (and none involving summary conviction offences), and at the most 6 per cent of the civil cases in the superior and district courts, according to Russell (6). There are some indications that jury trials are becoming less unusual than they were 20 years ago, but they are still very rare, much more so than (for example) in the United States.

The principle behind jury trials is a democratic one: citizens should have the right to be judged by their peers, and citizen participation in the justice system will help to ensure its fairness and accountability. Jury trials are on the wane partly because juries are often perceived to be incompetent by lawyers, judges, and legislators, and partly because many lawyers think they are likely to get a better deal for their clients in a trial conducted by a judge sitting alone. Another factor may be that prospective jurors are often not treated with much consideration by the justice system, and therefore fewer and fewer citizens willingly give their time for jury duty.

All Canadian citizens 18 years of age and over are eligible for jury duty and must serve on a jury if called. Each year, court officials choose prospective jurors at random from lists of residents, although members of certain groups — lawyers, the police, and their spouses (because of possible conflicts of interest), medical doctors, veterinarians, persons with disabilities, and persons who would suffer undue financial hardship — may be exempted. Some of those on the initial roster are called up for jury duty, depending on the number of jury trials scheduled. For example, in Metropolitan Toronto nearly 30,000 persons are initially selected from lists of residents. After screening out those who are exempted, about 500 persons are called to the courthouse every second week from September through June; at any one time, there are usually four jury trials proceeding which include both civil (six–person panels) and criminal (twelve–person panels) trials.

Persons called to the court house must sit in a waiting room to be on hand for ten working days in case they are needed. When a jury panel needs to be struck, some of those in the waiting room are questioned (under a judge's supervision) by the lawyers for both sides; the lawyers challenge and attempt to dismiss anyone who they think might be biased against their client and accept others until the six–person or twelve–person jury is complete. Most of those on hand for jury trials are never selected; a few may serve two or three times during the two–week period. A person actually selected for a jury must sit with other jurors until the completion of the trial they are selected for, regardless of how long that takes.

For their efforts, jurors usually receive little compensation. In Ontario, for example, they are paid $2.75 a day to cover their expenses, although if they become involved in a long trial and must serve beyond ten days, they receive $42.50 a day after the tenth day and about $100 a day after the fiftieth day. For some jurors, however, their employers are kind enough to continue their regular salary during the two–week jury duty period.

The judges we interviewed thought that jury trials were a small but important part of the system, and that there was a special knack to presiding over them that not all judges possessed in equal measure. They conceded that jury trials were less stressful by placing the determination of guilt or liability with the jury rather than the judge, but thought this was offset by the need to be much more careful about procedure and by the difficulties of walking the tightrope of the jury charge at the end of the trial — technical enough to please a possible court of appeal, but matter–of–fact enough to help the jury. They thought jury trials took longer than trial by judge alone (partly because of the time spent parading the jury in and out of the courtroom while lawyers argued about the admissibility of evidence or lines of questioning) and they seldom disagreed with the jury's findings except for some reservations about the tendency of juries to be too easily impressed with eye–witness testimony.

Consultation and Collegiality

We also asked judges about the extent to which they consulted with their fellow judges in making judicial decisions or in dealing with administrative arrangements: "Do you consult with other judges or your chief justice/judge in making determinations concerning a) judicial decision–making (for example, advice as to a point of law or of evidence); and/or b) administrative arrangements (for example, advice or assistance with respect to scheduling or other matters of that nature)?"

Only two judges spoke of consultation on a regular basis with a chief or associate chief justice or judge. For most judges on both trial benches, the rare consultations with their chief were initiated from above, and they related either to administrative arrangements or (more rarely) to some aspect of decision–making (usually sentencing) — in which case, the contact was usually understood by the judge as a first (albeit mild) level of judicial discipline. This suggests that the collegiality of a "first among equals" chief justice of a small appeal court cannot be transferred in any simple or direct way to a large and geographically dispersed trial court.

Discussion relating to administrative arrangements is rare, except as it relates to a "baby judge" (the judges' term for a newly appointed member of the bench). Only two of the judges interviewed spoke of committees of judges meeting occasionally to consider administrative matters.

Table 5.4   Styles of Consultation and Decision–Making Alberta Trial Judges

	Bench		
Approach to Consultation	Provincial Court	Court of Queen's Bench	All Trial Judges
solo judge	20% n 4	29% 6	24% 10
collegial judge	60% n 12	71% 15	66% 27
organized bench	20% n 4	– 0	10% 4
Total Judges	100% 20	100% 21	100% 41

The way that judges discussed consultation with their colleagues created three distinct identifiable groups: the "solo judge," the "collegial judge" and the "organized bench judge." The solo judge model focuses on the concrete decision in the specific case in terms of a responsibility that is compromised by any consultation save the most formal and specific; the role of the judge is played out within a single courtroom. The collegial judge model values informal and ongoing consultation ("shop talk") either for pooling experience or for contributing to consistency in outlook and performance; the role of judge is a cooperative one, but the interchange is voluntary and informal. The organized bench judge model assumes a formal (basically hierarchical) organization, and the structuring of interchange so as to compromise individuality and discretion.

The "Solo Judge"

The "solo judges" denied that consultation was a useful or significant part of the way they carried out their duties, except for the temporary context of a newly appointed judge adjusting to the details of transition to the bench. Some judges linked this to the non–problematic nature of the decision–making in their own court, but others saw it as a matter of principle, a duty to the disputants or the accused. They spoke of not being willing to abdicate full responsibility for making their own decisions, and saw any extensive consultation as the first step toward that abdication.

> I consult only minimally with other judges. The decision is my responsibility, and I'm the only one who has all the details. I used to consult more often when first appointed, mostly on procedural matters, but I just thought of this as a transitional thing. Once I got a better feel for things, I felt that I should go it on my own. (Provincial Court judge)

> I wouldn't want feedback before I make the decision for fear it would influence me unduly. (Provincial Court judge)

I don't usually consult with my fellow judges. I would if I thought it appropriate, but I don't often feel that way. I rarely just kick things around with my colleagues. Sentencing is the only area where I wind up talking shop. (Court of Queen's Bench Judge)

Another group of solo judges spoke of "consultation" in a very specific and focused sense; they would seek out other judges on a one–to–one basis to ask advice on specific problems or issues, often while the trial was still in process or after they had reserved decision. This practice is most pronounced on the Court of Queen's Bench, and often justified on the grounds that although judges on that bench do not formally specialize, many are especially experienced and informed in a specific area of law.

If I have a problem, such as a question about the admissibility of evidence, I will seek out the judge who is the best informed in that area; asking advice in this way is not a regular or a routine thing, but it is something that I do if and when a difficult question comes up. (Court of Queen's Bench judge)

For both groups of solo judges the physical layout of the courtroom, with the trial judge sitting alone on the raised bench presiding over the proceedings, provides appropriate symbolic representation of the judge's role as well. For these judges, the phrase "the decision is mine alone" accurately describes the responsibility and role of the judge.

Seven judges (four from the Provincial Court bench) minimized or explicitly denied the desirability of consultation with colleagues. Five others, all from Queen's Bench, spoke of consultation only in terms of approaching a specific colleague one–on–one for focused advice in unusual situations. The solo judge style is the exclusive self–characterization of about one–quarter of the judges interviewed.

The "Collegial Judge"

For most trial judges, however, ongoing consultation with their colleagues is an important part of how they carry out their responsibilities. Although the trial judge is necessarily a solo performer, presiding alone over the courtroom and fully and personally responsible for the decisions reached, judges usually value the opinions and ideas of their colleagues. For these judges, consultation is a matter of "shop talk," taking place casually in informal surroundings (over the lunch table or over coffee in the lounge) and usually limited to general terms or principles or ideas.

> I consult with my colleagues a lot. I think that is a real advantage of living in a city like this where all the judges are on one floor and have their own dining room. It gives you a lot of opportunities to talk things over, sound people out, see how other people feel about things. The Court of Queen's Bench is a good court, we talk things over a lot, especially sentencing, which is often the trickiest part of a criminal case. (Court of Queen's Bench judge)

> One of the beauties of having a number of judges in the same centre ... is the whole idea of consultation. I consult frequently with other judges, both talking over general ideas, and (more rarely) seeking specific advice, more on the basis of general respect for an individual than specific specialization or expertise. (Provincial Court judge)

A number of judges said they consulted with their colleagues occasionally or rarely, but only because of a lack of opportunity to do so. For these judges, consultation is a value but not a practice. For obvious reasons, this response tended to be given by provincial judges on rural circuits who were residents in smaller centres.

> I occasionally consult with other judges, ask them "what would you do?" sorts of questions. I like to talk about general ideas with other judges. I suspect I might do it quite

a bit more if I were in more frequent contact with other judges on my court. (Provincial Court judge)

Judges speaking favourably of consultation in the form of casual, unfocused, ongoing exchanges exemplify a second approach to the role of the judge, that of the collegial court. (This situation is, of course, realized more fully by the appellate courts. In the trial courts it is modified by the fact that interaction is limited to out–of–court situations, tangential to the judicial process rather than a formally integrated part of it.) The give–and–take, the sharing of ideas, the spreading of a common style or repertoire of styles among a finite group by osmosis through informal interaction, is the hall–mark of this second group.

A total of 27 trial judges -- almost two thirds of those interviewed -- fit the "collegial judge" model, identifying informal consultation or "shop talk" with colleagues as an important component of judicial decision–making.

The "Organized Bench Judge"

Six judges (four Provincial and two Queen's Bench) mentioned regular formal sessions when all or most of the judges in their court in their city made a point of getting together to talk over specific issues or problems for the purpose of working out a common way of dealing with them. Some spoke about a formal agenda for such get–togethers, and some about regular and scheduled meetings. This constitutes an approach to consultation between judges and a conceptualization of the judicial role that is significantly different from casual chats over the coffee table or one–to–one requests for advice in another judge's chambers.

All the judges in my court in this city meet every second Wednesday for two hours on a regular basis to talk over things that are coming up, and to consider possible problems. This, of course, is in addition to the more frequent and less formal chats. (Provincial Court judge)

There is a certain degree of formalized consultation on administrative matters through service on committees, the rotation of supervising judges and the like. (Court of Queen's Bench judge)

Those judges who see consultation as important, and who discuss it in terms of regular formal meetings with most of the judges in their court in their area, exemplify what we call the "organized bench" approach. It is usually assumed that the relatively recent innovation of designating chief and associate chief judges/justices for all trial courts resulted from the need to designate specific responsibility for onerous administrative tasks, implying that there are important central organizational responsibilities for the activities and direction of each court. The assumption would perhaps be fully realized if the formal meetings took place in all parts of the province, were chaired by associate chief justices and if these conferences had some kind of formal decision–making powers. This is clearly an overstatement of existing practice on all three counts.

The Implications of the Three Approaches to Consultation

What is the significance of the existence of these three models of consultation? It seems to us that these three approaches can be related to the massive changes that the provincial court structure has undergone both in Alberta and other parts of Canada in the past 20 or 25 years.

Some 20 years ago the court system was clearly built around two contrasting models. The first was that of the solo judge. Magistrates (now Provincial Court judges) and District Court judges (now merged with the superior trial court) were the masters of their own judicial realm. They were usually the only legally trained professionals connected with a specific courtroom on a permanent basis, and often for geographical reasons they were severely limited in contact with other judges who were similarly engaged.

The second model was the collegial court in the form of the provincial courts of appeal, which existed since at least the 1920s in every province outside the Maritimes and over the last two decades has expanded into those provinces as well, and which always sit in panels — now usually three, rarely five, almost never seven. In the early years the numbers on these courts were small enough so that it was not unusual for the full court to decide important cases. The old–style superior trial courts (before they were merged with the district courts) were in a sense caught between the two models. The relatively small number of judges in these courts (often not more than a dozen) and the close physical proximity to each other and to the appeal division contributed to a situation in which the superior trial court could approximate the immediate personal ties and ongoing personal interaction of a collegial court, even though the judges presided alone in their courtrooms and did not sit in panels.

The "organized bench" model can be seen as a more recent innovation which results both from the increased numbers of judges and the resultant need to coordinate their activities to promote efficiency, and from increased workloads. A Queen's Bench judge told us that 20 years ago the courts worked at a leisurely pace with "a lot of slack in the system." In contrast, the new Court of Queen's Bench suffers the caseload problems endemic to the mass–volume trial courts of modern Western countries. This caseload pressure has led to a need for greater formal coordination and organization of judicial work. The new Provincial Court, established in 1975 with higher professional standards and procedures than the magistrate's courts it replaced, also expanded considerably in size. Working under even greater caseload pressures than the Queen's Bench, the Provincial Court is similarly pulled between the courtroom logic of the solo judge, and the efficiency–oriented hierarchical organization described by the organized bench.

Given these important changes in numbers of judges and caseload, it is surprising that only 10 per cent of the judges we interviewed described consultation with other judges in any way that corresponded even roughly with what we have termed the organized bench approach. The concept of "role lag" may help to explain this phenomenon. According to the role lag theory described by Beverly Blair Cook, judges tend to view court operations from the perspective of the practice and expectations in place when they joined the court, and try to fit any subsequent changes into that model. This explanation would seem to indicate that we should expect longer–serving trial judges to incline to the solo judge model and recently appointed judges to reflect more the values of the collegial or organized bench.

To test this approach, we divided the judges into three groups according to the "stage of career" divisions for judges suggested by Lenore Alpert, Burton M. Atkins, and Robert C. Ziller. These are initiation and resolution (the first five years); establishment (years six through fifteen); and commitment (more than fifteen years). Using the concept of role lag, we would expect the solo judge or collegial judge model to be adopted more by the established or committed judges, and the organized bench model more by the newer judges. As Table 5.5 shows, however, this explanation does not appear to work.

Table 5.5 Styles of Consultation and Stage of Career				
	Consultative Model			
Stage of Career		solo judge	collegial judge	organized bench	Total
initiation & resolution		31%	69%	–	100%
	n	5	11	0	16
establishment		17%	71%	12%	100%
	n	3	12	2	17
commitment		25%	50%	25%	100%
	n	2	4	2	8
Total		24%	66%	10%	100%
	n	10	27	4	41

Another way of explaining why few judges have embraced the organized bench approach is to suggest that the consultative approach adopted by judges depends primarily on whether judges sit in a procedural, decisional, or diagnostic court — the typology proposed by Kerwin, Henderson, and Baar. As we've seen, the Court of Queen's Bench is primarily a procedural court because it deals with cases involving more intricate factual or legal questions. The criminal and small claims divisions of the Provincial Court are basically decisional because they process high volumes of more routine cases. The youth court division of the Provincial

Court is diagnostic because of its concern with finding innovative means of promoting the rehabilitation of young offenders.

It seems logical that judges in diagnostic courts would tend to adopt a collegial type of approach. This is because they deal with such a mixture of routine and complex, subtly nuanced issues that informal ongoing consultation with colleagues may help. The solo judge model may be more compatible with procedural courts because of the extent to which judges in those courts become immersed in the details and intricacies of extended trials. Finally, the organized bench approach seems more likely to be appropriate to judges in decisional courts, which deal with large volumes of cases that are frequently highly similar in nature and must be dealt with by multi–judge courts (that is, multiple courtrooms within a single location, each presided over by a single judge) with a high caseload pressure.

As Table 5.6 shows, however, these expectations are *not* borne out. The collegial approach is strongest in the decisional courts, and the organized bench approach is strongest in the diagnostic courts. This suggests that a combination of leadership and the identification of judges with conceptual models stressing judicial autonomy, rather than the situational logic of the specific court's caseload, are the key explanatory factors.

Table 5.6 Styles of Consultation and Type of Court				
	Consultative Model			
Type of Court	solo judge	collegial judge	organized bench	Total
procedural (Queen'sBench) n	30% 6	70% 14	– 0	100% 20
decisional (Provincial Court, Crim. Division & Small Claims) n	8% 1	85% 11	8% 1	100% 13
diagnostic (Youth Court) n	38% 3	25% 2	38% 3	100% 8
Total n	24% 10	66% 27	10% 4	100% 41

Although an organized bench approach may be the most logical one for large multi–judge courts experiencing caseload problems, the chief justice of the Queen's Bench and chief judge of the Provincial Court, as well as many of the senior Provincial Court judges, may have chosen — by design or by default — not to institute such an approach. This may be because they realize the difficulties of persuading a group of individualistic judges to cooperate with an organized bench initiative. The interviews with judges in Ontario revealed that when it comes to their case–flow management responsibilities, three–fifths of them preferred little or no supervision from their chief judge or justice, or from the relevant senior judge. As well, three–quarters of the sample of trial lawyers interviewed in Ontario and Alberta said that autonomy in their work was "very important" to them.

Judges, as former practising lawyers, are used to working independently, and the solo judge approach would come naturally to them once appointed to the bench. If they consult each other (the collegial model), it must be at their own initiative and on their own terms; they resist having collegiality (let alone a more hierarchical form of authority) imposed on them. On the other hand, the three youth court judges who spoke the language of the organized bench model were members of a local court with a strong senior judge who believed in the utility of a collective approach to problem–solving; the prestige of seniority could start the practice, and experiences of success maintain it, without any implication that it could or would be generalized to other components of the court.

Summary: Decision–Making and Consultation

The dominant conception of the judicial role in Alberta is the collegial model — for Provincial and Court of Queen's Bench judges, both for newly appointed and established judges. This model stresses the value of ongoing informal interaction among judges, either as a means of benefiting from wider experience or as an ongoing personal performance check. These findings contrast markedly with the U.S. study of Robert Carp and Russell Wheeler, who suggest, "All the interviewed [federal district] judges, including those in multi–judge cities, expressed reluctance in bothering other judges with routine problems."

A smaller but substantial number of judges, more so in Court of Queen's Bench than in Provincial Court, identify with the solo judge model. This model stresses the responsibility of the individual judge within the trial setting, and either rejects consultation altogether or limits it to specific focused advice. The smallest group of judges, mainly in Provincial Court (especially the youth division, which is diagnostic or treatment–oriented) articulates a notion that we have labelled the "organized bench" — using formal ongoing interaction to coordinate responses to situations or problems.

Although there may be sound logical and efficiency–related reasons for an organized bench approach to replace the others in the multi–judge and backlogged courts, it appears that judges — like many professionals who value their autonomy (including doctors and university professors) — are unlikely to jump at the opportunity. If the U.S. experience is any indication, we can think in terms of an evolution from solo judge through collegial bench to organized bench; all indications, however, suggest that in both Alberta and Ontario neither the self–images of judges nor their self–description of the decision–making process have moved very far along this continuum.

Sentencing

In criminal cases where the trial decision is "guilty," the judge must pronounce the sentence. This is in many ways the most dramatic display of the judge's discretion, judicial power at its starkest. Sometimes (not very often in Canada) the decision of guilt or innocence is assigned to a jury, but the sentencing decision always belongs to the judge alone, who receives but is not bound by the recommendations of counsel. The most extreme of the sentencing options vanished with the abolition of capital punishment, but the range of punishments that Canadian judges can and do hand out every day remains extremely broad, and on the upper end they are not to be taken lightly.

Considered in the abstract and starting from first principles, it is by no means inevitable that the same person who finds guilt should be the one to set the sentence, or even that judges should be the ones to make the sentencing decision at all, but in Canada they have been given this responsibility. At one time in our history, when there were no criminologists and no specialists in rehabilitation, it made perfectly good sense for judges to do sentencing. Today, with the emergence of the social sciences and the shift in emphasis from retribution to rehabilitation, it is no longer self–evident that judges are necessarily the most sensible choice for this important responsibility. Few criminal court judges have had any exposure to the literature on criminology or rehabilitation, apart from the occasional seminar they might have attended; nothing in the selection process requires that their legal training or practice should have included anything that would give them special insight into this important area.

Some critics have suggested that to increase the chances that the sentence chosen will be the most likely to rehabilitate the offender, it might be useful to replace judges with sentencing boards composed of criminologists and other specialists. This issue — of who is to set the sentence — will be prominent from time to time on the justice system reform agenda, so it is worth keeping it in mind as we consider how judges tell us they go about making the sentencing decision.

Obviously, the determination of the appropriate sentence must be based on a set of factors that overlaps but is not identical with those that drove the decision about guilt or innocence. While the trial decision centres on whether there is enough evidence to convict, and on the precise meaning of the law under which the conviction is sought, the sentencing decision is directed at one or more of five goals: maximizing the potential for the rehabilitation of the offender, deterring other potential offenders through example, deterring the particular offender from committing other offences, incapacitating the offender to protect society, and handing out the appropriate amount of punishment so that society can "get even" with the offender.

In his study of magistrates (now Provincial Court judges) in Ontario, John Hogarth has shown that all five goals influence most judges, but that some judges tend to stress one of the goals over the others, depending on their personalities, their experience, or the range of options they consider available to them. Hogarth found that 55 per cent of the judges he interviewed rated reformation as a "very important" goal of sentencing. The proportions for the other sentencing goals were: general deterrence, 37 per cent; individual deterrence, 23 per cent; incapacitation, 13 per cent; and punishment, 9 per cent. (Hogarth, p.71) Martin Friedland has shown how the sentencing philosophies of judges have tended to swing back and forth between the extremes of reformation and punishment according to societal views and research trends.

The Criminal Code of Canada, a federal statute, presents judges with a range of options for pronouncing sentences for particular offenses. Most often this range is very broad. For example, a person convicted of manslaughter could receive a suspended sentence — meaning no time in jail is served — or could be sent to prison for up to ten years. Someone convicted of ordinary assault could receive a suspended sentence, a fine of up to $500, a six–month jail sentence, or a combination of these sentences.

Although the possible range of sentence is often great, trial judges do not have a completely free hand. They are constrained by the law and also by provincial court of appeal decisions about sentencing. By increasing sentences that are considered too lenient and decreasing those that are too harsh, the appeal courts set more narrow practical limits on the discretion of trial court judges than the Criminal Code itself; from time to time, appeal courts will hand down a bench–mark decision on sentencing, laying down the "tariff" for a particular offence and the criteria relevant to assessing a higher or lower sentence.

In one case about ten years ago, an Alberta appeal panel stirred a furious public reaction by concluding a sentence appeal with the statement that "On a scale of one to ten, I'd say this rape is about a four." The terminology was inappropriate and the crime was particularly heinous, but the incident indicates exactly what appeal courts try to accomplish when they make guideline decisions to help trial judges set sentences. It is noteworthy that sentences cannot be appealed beyond the provincial appeals courts to the Supreme Court of Canada.

During the past five years, 60 to 80 per cent of the criminal appeals in Ontario and Alberta were sentence appeals or included a sentence appeal, a proportion significantly higher than in the other provinces. Some lawyers and judges we talked to in those provinces suggested possible reasons for the high number of sentence appeals. It may result from the trial judges in these provinces handing down harsher sentences, or it may be the result of a program by these appeal courts of guideline judgments on sentencing, or it may be because these courts of appeal are perceived to be "tinkerers" willing to make modest adjustments to sentences even in the absence of major error. However, it is always the case that by watching the run of sentence appeal decisions a trial judge can get a rough feeling of what to do to minimize the chance of being reversed on appeal (and therefore of being appealed in the first place).

If there are significant differences between Alberta trial judges in the way they approach the making of a judicial decision about guilt or liability, there is comparable diversity in the way they approach the problem of sentencing. We have organized our analysis of the sentencing decision around four issues: (1) the perceived difficulty of the decision, (2) the importance of consultation, (3) the separation or melding of the trial decision and the sentencing decision, and (4) the importance of consistency in sentencing decisions.

Is Sentencing Difficult or Straightforward?

For many judges the sentencing decision is difficult, often more so than the decision about guilt or innocence. This may seem a strange comment until we remember how many trials are routine or revolve around fairly simple matters of fact; as well, if the accused pleads guilty to the charge, the judge does not have to worry about the determination of guilt but only the problem of sentencing. Although they frequently insisted that legislation and guideline decisions from the court of appeal narrowed the judge's range of choice more than many people assume, most judges found the selection of the appropriate sentence difficult even within this relatively confined zone.

Sentencing is often the most difficult part of the job, no question about it. Sometimes you just sweat blood over it....

Sometimes, however, it is very easy; it is always a relief when it turns out that way. (Court of Queen's Bench Judge)

Sentencing is excruciating; it is just a son of a bitch to have to sentence someone. I think it is even harder for me because I don't believe that jail has any reformatory influence, and although there is a deterrent effect it is entirely on people who would not commit the crimes anyway, not on the people that do. (Court of Queen's Bench judge)

Sentencing is always difficult, because your decision is going to have a great impact on the defendant, and it is impossible ever to know for sure whether you hit it right or not. It is all the more difficult because the judge's personality is always a factor in sentencing. (Court of Queen's Bench judge)

However, other judges do not find sentencing at all difficult. For them the sentencing is a straightforward part of the criminal trial process; sometimes they find it easier, but certainly never any harder, than the determination of guilt.

The statutes and the Court of Appeal guideline decisions lay down a schedule and I simply apply it in a routine way. The range of choice for the trial judge is not as wide open as a lot of people assume. I don't worry about the rationale for punishment — I am not convinced by the deterrence argument, and we all know rehabilitation doesn't work very well — but it is not my job to worry about it, just to apply it. (Court of Queen's Bench judge)

I have no special difficulties with sentencing. Most cases are pretty easy, pretty routine — for example, I tend to get lots of drinking and driving cases. (Provincial Court judge)

Fifteen of the judges we interviewed thought that the *trial decision* tended to be routine and mechanical, and fifteen found the *sentencing decision* to be straightforward, but the overlap between these groups was surprisingly small; only seven judges (five Provincial Court, two Court of Queen's Bench) appear on both lists.

There are pronounced differences between the two trial benches. Court of Queen's Bench judges are twice as likely as Provincial Court judges (71 per cent compared to 35 per cent) to find sentencing difficult. This is not surprising, given that many of the cases heard in Provincial Court involve less serious crimes than those heard in Court of Queen's Bench. This suggests both a smaller range of possible sentences and a lower maximum sentence, and therefore a lower level of stress in making the appropriate choice. However, one should not push the contrast too far; Peter Russell (6) points out that the Canadian judicial system is unusual for the very high proportion of serious crimes that are in fact decided by the lowest level of trial courts. This means that Provincial Court judges can and frequently do hand down very heavy sentences, and in these cases the burden of choice could be expected to weight as heavily upon their shoulders as upon those of any superior court judge.

Judges are aware when they make a sentencing decision that the public (in the form of the media) is watching, and is always ready to criticize, but by convention judges never defend themselves and suffer the criticism in silence. Several mentioned that they had become resigned to the fact that every 18 months or so the media went on a crusade about disparities in sentencing, and all judges could do was wait until things died down again. After all, if Parliament has created a wide range of possible punishment for a specific crime, then there must be examples of that crime that deserve the least serious punishment, and other examples of the same crime that deserve the most serious punishment, and the judge's responsibility is not simply to identify the crime but to locate it within that spectrum — but, the judges said, sensational headlines are easier.

Away from the anonymity of the larger centres, the pressure is even more pronounced, as the judge has to face neighbours and acquaintances who read the headlines and may agree that a malefactor got off much too lightly. Judges also complained that they often "take the flak" for decisions that are completely out of their hands, such as probation or early release or mandatory supervision. The public also tends to overestimate the power of a judge to require that an individual be incarcerated in a particular institution, or to mandate a specific course of treatment.

Judges on both trial courts worry about the many factors that differentiate them from the bulk of the people who appear before them, many of whom are from minorities or sub–cultures with which the judges can have no direct identification, and of whose lifestyles and conditions they have no immediate experience. Serving on the bench can be an eye–opener about people and practices that the average citizen — and the average judge before elevation to the bench — has no idea of. "You spend the whole first year waiting for your eyebrows to come back down," one judge said. As another one put it: "Most of the time, we are enforcing middle class values on people who will never have the slightest idea what middle class life is all about. Frankly, it just worries the hell out of me sometimes."

Do Judges Consult with Colleagues or Make Sentencing Decisions on their Own?

Most judges consult with their colleagues about sentencing issues, just as they tend to consult about issues concerning other aspects of trial court decision–making, but with the added concern of seeking some degree of uniformity in sentencing.

> The other judges in my court and I get together frequently to discuss problem cases, especially concerning sentencing. (Provincial Court judge)

> I think I have to be aware of what other courts are doing in similar cases, to know what the 'going rate' is and to a certain extent this is the purpose of reading case law and of 'shop talk.' (Court of Queen's Bench judge)

For other judges, sentencing is a matter on which they do not consult, sometimes from lack of opportunity (many provincial judges in rural areas seldom interact casually or routinely with fellow judges), and sometimes because they think consultation is desirable but not very important. For some, however, the lack of consultation is a question of principle; they believe they have a duty to the defendant before them to make their own decision about the appropriate disposition following the determination of guilt.

> Sentencing is pretty straightforward, and the standards are pretty clear; there isn't much to talk over. (Provincial Court judge)

> I find it useful to keep track of the way that sentencing is being handled in other jurisdictions, but I tend to rely on the arguments and presentations of counsel for this. (Court of Queen's Bench judge)

We might expect that those judges who consult other judges about trial issues would be the ones who consult each other about sentencing problems, but this was not the case. Some judges consult with fellow judges on other trial questions but not on sentencing; others seek feedback from colleagues on sentencing but not on anything else. What remains striking is the degree of diversity, the lack of a single standard answer, even on such apparently straightforward questions. This is especially surprising given the firmness with which many of them spoke about the matter. "Of course; you couldn't do this job any other way," one judge might say — but many of their colleagues do.

In general, the judges we interviewed are twice as likely to consult with their colleagues about sentencing as they are not to consult, even more so for Court of Queen's Bench judges (four–fifths) than for Provincial Court (less than half). This difference would seem partly attributable to need — the wider range of sentences on more serious crimes makes consistency more important and more difficult for Court of Queen's Bench judges — though we should remember Peter Russell's caution: nowhere in the world do judges in the lowest level of court handle as large a percentage of the major criminal cases. Opportunity is also relevant; Court of Queen's Bench judges are more likely to be resident in one of the two major urban centres, or to spend time in one of those centres on circuit. Provincial Court judges, in comparison, are more often isolated in smaller centres with no regular opportunity to consult with their colleagues.

Intriguingly, there is no strong connection between the perceived difficulty of a sentencing decision and the likelihood of consultation with colleagues. Three–quarters of those who found sentencing difficult, compared with three–fifths of those who did not, indicated that they consult with their fellow judges. Court of Queen's Bench judges formed a large majority of those who answered "yes" to both difficulty and consultation, while Provincial Court judges were by far the largest part of those judges answering "no" to both.

Is the Sentence Decision Distinct from the Determination of Guilt?

For two–thirds of the judges, determination of *guilt* and determination of *sentence* are clearly separate. They think it is at least unwise, and at most improper, to yield to the temptation of running over alternative punishments in their minds while the trial is still in progress, before all evidence has been presented and counsel has summed up their case. For some it is a matter of principle, a component of the trial process whose recognition is of real value:

> Sentencing is never in my mind during the trial. First the finding of guilt, and then the sentence: that is a very basic principle of the trial process. (Court of Queen's Bench judge)

> You can get awfully angry with the accused sometimes, and you have to learn to keep your emotional distance. That is why I often adjourn for a while to 'cool off' before imposing the sentence. (Court of Queen's Bench judge)

Others see it in much more practical terms, more as a matter of common sense:

> I make a total separation between trial and sentencing.... There is no point in wasting time wondering "If I found him

guilty now, how would I sentence him?" when I (or the jury) might still wind up finding him not guilty. (Court of Queen's bench judge)

Sentencing is a completely separate matter, because during the trial itself I have no knowledge, and should have no knowledge, of a number of factors that are relevant to sentencing, such as whether the accused has a criminal record or not. (Court of Queen's Bench judge)

But if a majority of judges consider the two matters as sharply separate, there is a substantial minority of judges who think that the two matters necessarily and unavoidably run into each other. If some were rather apologetic about it ("I shouldn't but I do"), others thought this combined approach was simply common sense.

I try never to think about sentencing until guilt has been decided, but often, even though I know I shouldn't, it is hard not to have it ticking over in the back of my mind. (Court of Queen's Bench judge)

Usually ideas about sentencing are running through my mind throughout trial. I usually know by the time I have decided about guilt what I am going to do about sentencing. (Court of Queen's Bench judge)

As you listen to the trial, especially as it starts to wind up, you start thinking about the sentence. Many of the elements relevant to sentencing (such as mitigating circumstances and the like) are very clearly emerging during the trial. (Court of Queen's Bench judge)

The judges' views about whether sentencing is considered separately do not seem to be connected to their views about the difficulty of sentencing. Three-quarters of the judges who find sentencing difficult, as against two–thirds of the judges who do not, consider the two matters separately.

The breakdown in level of court turned out to be quite different from what we had expected. Because of the greater volume of cases and faster trials in the Provincial Court, we thought that these judges would be more likely to intermingle the sentencing with the trial decision than Queen's Bench judges, who can work at a somewhat less pressured pace, and who often have the luxury of being able to adjourn the sentencing decision until a later day. But our expectations were not met; only a quarter of the Provincial Court judges mixed the two kinds of decision–making, as compared to more than one–third of the Queen's Bench judges. Perhaps the slower pace of decision–making in the Court of Queen's Bench gives judges more opportunity to begin to think about sentencing during the trial.

Do Judges Keep Sentencing in Line with Other Judges?

This is in many ways almost a trick question, and we felt a little uneasy about impaling the interviewees on the horns of the dilemma it presents. On the one hand we might have a judge who denies any preoccupation with consistency with others and insists that no one else heard the details of the trial, no one else is as qualified to select the precise point on the sanctioned continuum of available punishments. Such a judge seems indifferent to the notion that justice means treating equals equally and not having so much ride on the good or bad luck of which judge an accused draws to preside over the trial.

On the other hand is a judge who assiduously follows the sentencing patterns of colleagues and tries never to stray away from them, who carefully walks in the footsteps of the rest of the judiciary. Such a judge seems to be denying any role for the combination of acumen, personal wisdom, professional experience, and legal expertise that alone could deserve the prestige and the responsibilities of the bench. In other words, this is very close to being a question that has no right answer, just two wrong ones, and we appreciate the candour and honesty of our interviewees. Certainly, none of them backed away from the dilemma we so casually presented them.

Most of the judges — two–thirds — attached considerable importance to knowing what other judges are doing about sentencing, for the explicit purpose of ensuring that their sentencing is following a similar pattern. (There was no difference between Provincial and Queen's Bench judges on this question.) Precisely because there is a degree of judicial discretion in sentencing, they want to be sure they are using that discretion in much the same way as other judges in similar conditions. One of the principles of our legal–judicial system is that the accused is being made subject to the law, not to the will of the person sitting on the bench; from this it follows that it should make as little difference as possible which individual judge decides the case. Most judges conceded that one could never make that difference disappear, but it was their duty to make it as small as possible.

The judge's personality is always a factor in sentencing, you just can't avoid it, although I try to keep the impact of the personality factor as small as possible by keeping in touch with other judges and their feelings, through reading and 'shop talk'. (Court of Queen's Bench judge)

It is important to avoid your own personal preferences, personal feelings in sentencing; to do that, you have to be aware of what other courts are doing in similar cases. (Court of Queen's Bench judge)

Lawyers keep track of trends in sentencing, so a judge really has to stay on top of it if he is going to keep his credibility. (Provincial Court judge)

About one–third of the judges, however, saw sentencing differently. They saw it as their responsibility to match the statute and the individual case in front of them to the very best of their ability. While an awareness of the kinds of sentencing decisions made by their colleagues might be useful, they felt that it was an improper abdication of responsibility simply to follow that pattern and to suspend their own personal judgment.

> You have to keep a number of questions in mind about the decision about sentencing: Is it just? Is it fair? What will it accomplish? Questions like this are much more important than worrying about staying in line with what others are doing. (Provincial Court judge)

There seems to be a connection between the difficulty and discretion; of the ten judges who attached importance to exercising their discretion independently, eight also indicated that they found the sentencing decision difficult. This seems understandable: judges aware of an irreducible element of personal discretion in their sentencing will tend to find the decision difficult, while judges who narrow the discretion by closely following their judicial colleagues will find sentencing somewhat easier.

Summary: Sentencing and Trial Judges

Judges in criminal cases must go through a second decision–making process if an accused person is found guilty: the sentencing decision. According to the judges, the decision–making process for sentencing is quite different from that for the determination of guilt. Two–thirds of the judges report keeping the two processes separate in their minds, while the rest state that the two processes are so closely connected that they cannot be separated. It is with regard to sentencing that there are some sharp differences between the Provincial Court judges and the superior court judges. More than two–thirds of the superior court judges found sentencing difficult, compared with only a third of the Provincial Court judges. This difference makes sense, given that the superior court judges are often able to impose harsher sentences. What must be kept in mind, however, is that both groups of judges find the trial decisions themselves to contain about the same degree of difficulty, regardless of the seriousness of the charge in criminal cases.

Because of the degree of judicial discretion often involved in the sentencing decision, two–thirds of the judges stressed the importance of consulting with each other about sentencing issues so as to minimize the unfairness that might result from abuse of the judges' discretion. One wonders, however, whether this informal safeguard is enough, or whether it may be more appropriate for the sentencing decision to be made by sentencing boards whose members — unlike the judges — are trained in the relation between sentencing and the rehabilitation of the offender. Another approach, which has been implemented with some success in the state of Washington, is the establishment of sentencing tribunals to set more specific ranges for sentences for particular offences than those established by legislation; such a process would replace the parameter–setting role of the provincial court of appeal.

It seemed to us the four elements of difficulty, consultation, distinctness, and discretion were both objective and relevant components of the sentencing decision. It had been our expectation that judicial responses would fall into identifiable patterns, and that judges would cluster and group themselves in coherent ways — most plausibly, by the level of court and the type of jurisdiction that they exercised. This expectation was not borne out by the results, which instead present the sentencing decision as a highly nuanced and highly individualized process, an art rather than a science, and one whose diversity was underestimated by the judges themselves.

Conclusion

What is striking about our findings concerning the judges' approaches to decision–making is the different degrees to which the judges stress conformity to correct procedures, the different descriptions about what the correct procedures are, and the different amounts of discretion they think they have and are willing to exercise. The *process* of judicial decision–making is certainly *not* mechanical, although for straightforward cases judges may well come to the same conclusions via different routes. The chances of judges making the best possible decisions in the difficult cases will depend on a combination of their intellectual abilities, their character, the quality of their training, and their grasp of the social milieux out of which the cases they hear arise — qualities that are most likely to receive the greatest consideration in judicial selection procedures which are non–partisan.

Given the variety of the different approaches that judges apply to decision–making, it seems that judges could enrich each other

by sharing their different perspectives in formal or informal discussions. We found that this fairly frequent sharing of ideas and
perspectives does occur informally for two–thirds of the judges.
Few judges reported that the exchange of ideas and viewpoints
tended to take place mostly through organized meetings of the
judges. We found this result surprising, given the tremendous
expansion in size of the trial courts and the resultant need for more
coordination among the judges. Our explanation is that judges, the
great majority of whom are former practising lawyers, are used to
working independently. They like to consult with each other, but
only on their own terms. A more organized approach to judicial
consultation is likely to work only as a result of the strong leadership of the senior or chief judges.

The approaches described by the Provincial Court judges con-
trasted the most with those described by the section 96 judges with
regard to sentencing. Most Queen's Bench judges said the sentencing decision was difficult, while most Provincial Court judges
did not. Outside of this difference, we found a great variation in
the approaches to the sentencing decision described by the judges.
Criminological research, as Hogarth shows, has confirmed over
and over again that the sentences meted out by judges for the same
offences and the same kinds of individuals can vary considerably
from one judge to another. Perhaps the widely different approaches to the sentencing decision are part of the explanation for
this phenomenon.

The change to professional sentencing boards is unlikely to
occur in our very conservative legal system; moreover, there is
little evidence to indicate that the sentences established by other
professionals would benefit both society and offenders more than
those set by judges. It makes more sense, as both Hogarth and
Russell (6) believe, to concentrate reform efforts on providing
judges with more information about the effects of various and
different kinds of sentences, and to take into account the skills
required for effective sentencing when choosing judges in the first
place.

Earlier in this chapter we referred to the paradox that the trial
court decision–making process is both complex and straightforward. When one considers the variety in approaches to decision–

making among the judges, and the elaborate strategies that some have worked out to assist them, the process appears complex indeed; to individual judges, however, who have spent an average of ten years making adjudicative decisions, the process often appears straightforward. It is no wonder, then, that some eventually tire of the trial court process and hope for a promotion to an appeal court where the approach to making decisions in three–judge panels presents new challenges.

6

Judicial Decision–Making: Courts of Appeal

B ecause provincial appeal courts sit in panels, the dynamics of the decision–making process are somewhat different from the single–judge trial courts. Most of the appeal judges have been elevated from the trial court, so they probably go through the same mental processes when they hear a case as they did on the trial bench. But at the conclusion of the hearing, they typically leave the courtroom and confer with each other before returning to announce the decision.

Every province in Canada now has a separate provincial superior court (staffed by federally appointed judges) whose full–time and exclusive responsibility is the consideration of appeals from decisions of the lower courts; these are judges who never conduct trials and who rarely concern themselves with examining witnesses, but devote themselves to the consideration of arguments alleging error in the conduct or the outcome of a trial. Ontario and Quebec have had full–time specialized courts of appeal since Confederation (although the Quebec Court of Appeal, formerly named the Court of Queen's Bench, retained a vestigial trial jurisdiction as well); Manitoba and British Columbia acquired their courts of appeal in the first decade of the twentieth century, and Alberta and Saskatchewan followed suit in the 1920s. The Atlantic provinces were the last to develop this specialized apex of the provincial court structure, New Brunswick and Nova Scotia in the 1960s, Newfoundland in 1974, and Prince Edward Island in 1987. In these provinces before this, appeals would have been heard by superior court trial judges sitting as a panel.

Provincial courts of appeal vary in numbers from twenty–four judges in Quebec (six of them supernumerary) to three in Prince Edward Island. (Table 1.1 shows the number of judges in the other appeal courts.) The judges almost always hear cases in panels of three, but for cases that raise extraordinary legal or constitutional issues, they will sometimes sit in panels of five or, even more rarely, of seven. For the smaller appeal courts, this means that the entire court may hear some cases; for the larger appeal courts, it means that even the most significant and unusual cases are considered by only a portion of the full membership.

The decision of provincial appeal courts is almost always unanimous. In Ontario, for example, there are dissenting opinions in only about 2 per cent of the cases heard, according to a study by Carl Baar, Ian Greene, Peter McCormick, and Martin Thomas. Comparable information is not available for the other provincial courts of appeal except for the *reported* decisions, meaning the 15 to 40 per cent (depending upon the province) of all appeal court decisions for which the judges provide written reasons that are reported in the law reporter for the province or region. The rate of dissents for reported decisions varies from about 4 per cent in Ontario and the Maritime provinces, to about 14 per cent in Quebec and Manitoba.

After the panel decides whether an appeal will be upheld or dismissed, the judges re–enter the courtroom. The presiding judge — usually the senior non–supernumerary judge, with trial bench experience included for the determination of seniority — announces the decision. In Ontario — the only province for which extensive data are available — the appeal is dismissed in about three–quarters of the cases.

In five–sixths of the criminal cases and three–quarters of the civil cases in Ontario, judgments are given orally in court (meaning they are almost never reported in the case reporters), almost always on the day the appeal is heard. About half of the remaining cases result in written decisions, and the rest are decisions that the judges dictate into a tape–recorder, later to be transcribed. With regard to the written or taped decisions, the judges will often announce the "bottom line" in the courtroom, and the written judgment or transcription of the tape is released several days, weeks, or months later. The limited figures that are available for Alberta suggest similar proportions. It should be noted, however, that the Ontario and Alberta courts of appeal process more cases per year than any other, and far more than most other provincial Courts of Appeal, and it would be unwise to assume that the practice in other provinces necessarily parallels those two provinces. For appeal courts with a smaller caseload, it may well be that every case generates a set of written reasons for the decision.

In most provinces, about half of the appeals involve criminal cases, and the other half involve civil or private law cases, as shown in Table 6.1. Provincial appeal courts hear criminal appeals primarily with regard to *indictable* offences; these are the more serious offences in the Canadian Criminal Code. The appeals for less serious federal and provincial offences, known as *summary conviction offences*, are appeals from the Provincial Court and are heard by single judges in the province's superior or district trial court, although they can be appealed higher by leave of the court of appeal itself. (Typically, the application for leave and the appeal

Table 6.1 Caseload and Civil/Criminal Breakdown: Canadian Provincial Courts of Appeal 1987			
Province	Civil Cases	Criminal Cases	Total Cases	% Civil
B.C.	399	265	664	60.1%
Alberta	360	840	1200	30.0%
Saskatchewan	224	297	521	43.0%
Manitoba	161	245	406	39.7%
Ontario	265	1211	1476	18.0%*
Quebec	955	316	1271	75.1%
New Brunswick	103	58	161	64.0%
P.E.I.	45	24	69	65.2%
Nova Scotia	101	146	247	40.5%
Newfoundland	38	40	78	48.7%
Total:	2651	3442	6093	43.5%

Note: Figures for calendar 1987, except N.B. [fiscal 1988], and P.E.I. & Nfld. [calendar 1988].
* This low percentage of civil cases in Ontario is partly a result of the fact that there is a special section of the superior trial court known as the "Divisional Court" that hears administrative law appeals that are heard in the appeal courts in the other provinces.

itself are heard and resolved at the same time.) The general principle for Canadian courts in both civil and criminal cases is that
the first appeal is a matter of right; subsequent appeals are a matter
of leave.

Each year the larger appeal courts — those in Ontario, Quebec,
British Columbia, and Alberta — decide about one thousand
cases. (It is difficult to compare the caseloads of the various courts
because they all define "case" differently.) Because the judges sit
in panels, and because every third week or so is a "judgment
week" during which the judges attend to their written decisions,
this means on most sitting days they hear three or four cases. Some
unusually complex cases, however, take several weeks for legal
argument, and more time again as the members of the panel
deliberate and draft their written judgment.

This means that the "typical" appeal case is disposed of rather
quickly. In Ontario, for example, we found that the *average* hearing time (from the time that the lawyers begin their arguments to
the time the senior judge announces the decision) is an hour for
criminal cases and one and a half hours for civil cases. But the
most common hearing time is 20 minutes for both criminal and
civil cases. (Baar, Greene, McCormick, and Thomas) In these
"typical" appeal court cases, the lawyer for the appellant will
speak for ten to fifteen minutes. If the appellant's lawyer has a
weak case — which is not uncommon — the judges do not call
on the lawyer for the respondent to speak. If the lawyer for the
respondent is called on, he or she will speak for only two or three
minutes. The judges will go out of the courtroom, decide on the
outcome, re–enter the courtroom, and announce the verdict within
five minutes.

These are the most common, run–of–the–mill cases, which
make up most of the appellate workload; although most people
would be surprised to hear it described this way, much of the work
of the appeal judges (like much of the work of trial judges) is
consumed by repetitious and almost mind–numbing routine.
There are more complex cases, lasting hours, days or weeks, and
for them the procedure is very different — but by their very nature
these cases are unusual, atypical.

Almost half of Ontario's criminal cases involve offences against property (theft, fraud, and break–and–enter, for example). Offences against persons (assault, robbery, manslaughter) make up about a third of the caseload, and the rest of the cases involve other wrongful acts (traffic violations, tax evasion, and drug possession or trafficking, for example). The overwhelming majority of appellants (over 90 per cent) are male. In Canada, unlike the United States, appeals can be brought both by accused persons and the Crown. (Most U.S. jurists consider it unfair for the government to have the power to appeal a trial decision.) About 15 per cent of criminal appeals are brought by the Crown in Ontario; the rest are brought by accused persons convicted at trial. About 40 per cent of the criminal appeals are abandoned by the appellants before the appeal hearing occurs, either because they realize their case is weak, or in the case of accused persons, because they have already served most of their sentence before the appeal is heard.

In Ontario, about 80 per cent of the criminal appeals from 1983 to 1987 were appeals of the trial judge's sentence; in Alberta, the figure is about 60 per cent. (Because of the large number of sentence appeals, the proportion of criminal cases in these two courts is much higher than — indeed, almost double — the 40 per cent average in most provinces.) The proportion of sentence appeals in the other provincial courts of appeal is much lower, although exact figures are not available. It may be that the reason for the high rate of sentence appeals in Ontario and Alberta is that the appeal court judges in these two provinces are willing to vary sentences by relatively small amounts. If this is the case, it would encourage sentence appeals, in that appellants have a reasonable chance of having their sentence reduced. In the years for which figures are available, the numbers showed a 33 per cent or better chance of success in both Ontario and Alberta. In the other provinces, appeal judges are more reluctant to change the trial judge's sentencing decision unless they consider it to be grossly unfair, and this attitude seems to discourage sentence appeals both from accused persons and the Crown.

Our sample of Ontario Court of Appeal records from 1983 to 1987 indicated that almost half of Ontario's civil appeals are brought by individuals, a third by corporations, and a sixth by government agencies or departments. Of the individuals, two–thirds are male. Although the records are not complete with regard to the type of case, it appears that about half of the civil cases involve business law (contracts, business property, bankruptcy), one–third concern family law, about one–sixth relate to torts (private wrongs such as suits for damages), and one–twentieth concern labour law.

The elapsed time between the trial and the appeal is much longer for civil cases than criminal cases. In Ontario, there is typically a nine–month delay between the trial and the appeal, whereas in civil cases there is about a sixteen–month delay on average. This discrepancy results partly from the desire of appeal court judges to bring criminal appeals on quickly to minimize the unfairness that results if innocent people are kept in jail waiting for their appeal. As well, lawyers in civil cases try to settle out–of–court if possible, and the courts welcome and encourage such negotiated settlements; in fact, more than half of the civil appeals filed never get to trial, often because a settlement has been reached by the parties involved. Because of the negotiations going on between the lawyers for the parties, the lawyers are sometimes not overly anxious to have the case go to trial early.

For most Canadians who appeal a trial court decision, the provincial court of appeal decision represents their final appeal. Except for criminal cases where one of the judges on the panel dissents, or where the appeal court and trial court come to different conclusions, appeals to the Supreme Court of Canada require the permission of the Supreme Court to proceed. The Supreme Court receives some 400 applications for "leave" (permission) to appeal each year, and grants only about 100 of them; by comparison, the provincial courts of appeal taken together decide more than 6,000 cases per year. Thus, the highest courts of the various provinces are gaining in prominence as the Supreme Court puts the brakes on the number of appeals it can hear.

Background Experience

Most of the judges on the Alberta Court of Appeal had previously been trial judges. Both at the time our interviews were conducted (in 1983), and at the time of writing (1990), judges elevated from the trial bench tended to outnumber judges appointed "from the street" (as the elegant but somewhat misleading phrase would have it) by about two to one. This puts Alberta (with British Columbia) toward the high end of the spectrum of provincial courts of appeal; Manitoba, with less than half, is toward the low end. In general and over a reasonably long haul, there tends to be a rough balance between appeal judges with and appeal judges without trial bench experience; we do not know whether this is by policy or by chance.

It nonetheless remains the case that somewhere between 55 and 60 per cent of all provincial appeal judges appointed in this century were elevated from the trial benches. What happens is that judges elevated from a trial court tend to be older. Therefore they serve on the appeal bench for a shorter time than judges first appointed directly to the appeal bench.

We asked the judges if anything in their personal backgrounds or experiences had particularly contributed to their style or behaviour on the bench, and many of them volunteered their own experience as a trial judge. They felt this experience gave them a more realistic and balanced feeling for what went on inside the trial courtroom and reined in their temptation to second–guess the trial judge. We had the impression that this question was the subject, if not of argument and analysis, then at least of good–natured ribbing within the court; the judges who had been appointed "off the street" were defensive, almost defiant, in tone when they suggested that it was an advantage as an appeal judge to have had no trial experience, because the others tended to be too understanding, even soft, on the performance of trial judges. The trial judges we interviewed did not indicate observing any such tendency; if anything, they felt that elevated judges were too ready during an appeal to feel they could put themselves in the position of the trial judge and do the job better.

The only other natural grouping that many judges spoke of was the division between "hawks" and "doves" on sentencing; one also mentioned the difference between "academically inclined" judges who like "law in the abstract," as opposed to "pragmatic and practical" judges. All of the judges rejected a "liberal/conservative" dichotomy as too facile, with or without capital letters.

Judges saw the differences within their ranks primarily as a matter of individual personalities, not of past experience, because "It's such a funny business that you never know what a guy's going to be like on the bench". They said that some former defence lawyers are the hardest sentencers while former prosecutors rank high among the doves.

Some of the judges who had been both trial judges and appeal judges said they were "amazed to discover how much of a difference there is" between the two, with the trial judge's sole concern the "happy resolution of the case in front of him" but the appellate judge's concern the law itself and trends in the law. On the appellate court, "you have to be conscious that what you do on any given day may become the law in Alberta for one hundred years" while the trial judge "binds nobody, not even himself." There was some comment, and some concern, about the fact that the Supreme Court of Canada seemed to be "firming up the idea" that in some areas of law "that are far from negligible" it would not grant leave to appeal, and so in a growing number of areas "we are really becoming the final court." They saw this as a rather sobering thought ("We'll have to be just that more careful") and as being in many ways a more important development in the role of appeal courts than the Charter itself.

Court of Appeal judges were aware of being "part of a team" and therefore lacking "the glorious independence of a trial judge." At the same time, several judges thought that it was important not to overstate the differences between appeal courts and trial courts. "The same objectives prevail regardless of court. The object is to be right, and the vehicle is to be careful — this is true of any court, and how you go about this job depends on your jurisdiction and the nature of the case."

One judge even thought that although there was a difference in role, the implications clearly cut both ways: "The trial judge has to find the facts, and so he must be aware of his prejudices and fight to overcome them. On an appeal court, you cannot distort the facts because they have already been established, so there is not the same leeway for giving vent to prejudices. In this respect, the trial judge's role is more demanding, because it requires more effort to be aware of biases, although for any judge not to be aware of his own biases is dangerous." Another judge pointed out, "We on the court of appeal don't usually see the litigants, just the lawyers arguing about the details, so we can tend to lose touch with what is really going on in the law suit or criminal trial, and this can be a dangerous kind of isolation."

Collegiality

All judges stressed both the frequency and importance of interaction with their fellow judges. The Alberta Court of Appeal is a "very chummy court, and we're bouncing ideas off each other all the time." As evidence of the "chumminess," one judge pointed out that everyone was on a first–name basis, something which he said was not the case for all appeal courts. The extent to which there is consultation on any specific case varies according to the case. Many cases are straightforward enough that they "don't need any real consultation," but for all save the most routine cases there is "extensive verbal discussion" within the particular panel. Others will be the occasion for either informal shop talk in the lunchroom or lounge, or for more focused advice from respected colleagues with special knowledge of a relevant field, although usually, "If you don't reserve a judgment, there is very little interchange except inside the panel." Cases involving larger questions of law (or, according to one judge, any civil case where there is not unanimity on the panel) will be reserved, and usually discussed at length as widely as possible before resolution.

The situation of the court's members being physically divided between Edmonton and Calgary is seen as a serious nuisance that limits ongoing communication and exchange. (Only in Alberta and Quebec are the appeal courts divided between two cities; in Quebec part of the court sits in Montreal and the other in Quebec City.) "It would be a lot nicer without the geographical split, but it is not a major problem," one Alberta judge commented. The logistically complicated but generally satisfactory solution is to have the entire court sit in each centre in alternate months, and to rotate the panel memberships as randomly as possible. In general, consultations with justices of the Court of Queen's Bench (except for the person on rotation sitting as an ad hoc appeal judge) are very infrequent, despite the fact that the offices and facilities of courts were at the time of the interviews (but no longer) shared in both cities. One judge did stand out in the importance he attached to "keeping in touch with the experiences and viewpoint of the trial judges" and in the fact that he mentioned trial judges seeking him out to "throw ideas around."

Procedure

Three–Judge Panels

One of the ways in which the Alberta Court of Appeal adjusted to the caseload problem was by hearing the vast majority of cases in three–judge panels, a practice one judge spoke of as being relatively recent and having started "just after I came on the court." Five–judge panels are used occasionally, seven–judge panels extremely rarely. The days when all the judges of the Court of Appeal would sit together to decide cases are gone forever in Alberta as in most other provinces. Panels are drawn up by the chief justice (with occasional last minute shuffles), but are not announced far enough ahead of time to give lawyers any opportunity for "panel–shopping."

Some of the judges thought there might be some limited scope for "panel–avoidance," for lawyers trying to delay consideration of the case when they saw what panel they had drawn, but certainly not to the extent of causing any great problems. The panels are by no means permanent; on the contrary, their composition is changed "quite frequently and with very short notice." Judges rotate among the panels, not just within but between the two centres in which appeal judges are resident, to reduce the potential for panels developing their own fixed but divergent patterns.

Coordination and continuity between such shifting panels and within a court divided between two centres was a problem the judges were fully aware of. They employed a variety of means to deal with it: frequent consultation outside the panels; circulating written judgments through the entire court for comment; a reluctance to reverse or depart from decisions of their own court ("otherwise the law gets confused"); and fairly frequent full–court meetings to work out a common approach to specific problematic questions of law. Several of the trial judges interviewed assumed that because of the panel problem appeal court judges made a major effort to come up with a unanimous decision within each panel, taking the extra time to work out the common ground that this implied, but no appeal court judge referred to anything like this. ("We try to talk it out, but it really comes down to a question of how strongly you feel about it; you don't cover up or ignore a genuine feeling just to give a unanimous panel.")

A regular feature of Alberta appeal court panels, and one that distinguishes it from all the other provinces, is "pulling up" a Court of Queen's Bench judge to serve as an *ad hoc* appeal judge for a month, after which the judge returns to the trial bench. This is especially so for sentence appeals, which are normally heard by three–judge panels of whom two are *ad hoc*. On principle, this opportunity is rotated among the judges of the Court of Queen's Bench, so mathematically any given judge could expect to sit with appeal judges once every four years or so, but in practice more than a few of the trial judges decline the invitation. The appeal judges thought that it is an excellent practice that works out well for both sets of judges involved. It "helps to keep the Court of Appeal judges in touch with the reality of trials and trial courts" and at the same time helps some of the trial judges understand why things sometimes look so different from the appeal court side. They thought most of the Queen's Bench judges caught on quickly and by no means weakened the panel.

Process

With some minor variations, the general procedure described by Alberta appeal court judges was straightforward and built around a simple recurrent theme: you have to be prepared to do a lot of reading. First, the judges read the factums — the briefs submitted by the appellant and respondent that cover their arguments and sometimes include supporting evidence in the form of case law or social science research. They read the appellant's factum first, the respondent's factum second. Next they read the trial court judgment, then the pleadings (what the appellant is asking for), followed by the transcripts of the specific part or parts of the trial decision that gave rise to the arguments. Finally, they do personal reading and research on points of law. A couple of the judges interviewed read the judgment before the factums; some tried to read up on a critical authority or authorities in the general area of law before moving on from the factums to the judgment.

To be sure, this was the "full treatment" that applied only to "serious" cases, and not a routine that was followed through for every single case. It was also the ideal, which could not always be achieved given the time and caseload pressures of real life. In practice, as one judge said, it is "simply impossible to read every-thing because the volume of stuff is just terrific; every session I get a stack up to five feet high." How far judges work through the ideal list depends on how they feel the appeal case is shaping up and "how serious the questions really are." Some judges usually had a "pretty good idea of how they would go" after reading the appellant's factum alone ("That is usually enough to flag an ill–advised appeal"), and would only read much further if something made them curious. Although as a principle they tried not to reach a firm conclusion until they heard all the arguments, and some-times they changed their minds as the case went along, several said they "usually" knew which way they were going "by half–time": that is, by the time the appellant's lawyer had finished presenting his case.

As a rule of thumb, it was suggested that about one–third of all appeals actually boiled down to an invitation to retry the case, which the appeal judges rejected on principle. Another one–third revolved around specific questions or details of the trial or the law; and at most one–third raised more general issues or questions of law. One judge said, "I generally find that about 90 per cent of appeals can be handled mechanically and routinely; only a minor-ity of them raise major questions of law." None of the judges interviewed personally kept or were aware of firm figures on the success rate of appeals in the province, but one said: "I used to think that the appellant had about a 35 per cent chance of success; now I think that is probably wrong, probably on the high side, but I wouldn't want to put any specific number to it, and I don't keep track myself of how often the judgment of trial court is varied."

Two judges said, "There is no real rule as to presumption," that they "tried not to go into it with any firm rule as to which side has the onus of proof [because] this is an appeal, not a trial, so the standard rules about presumptions applied at trial don't get extra weight again." Five others, however, said that "the general rule is that the appellant must demonstrate error, so the appellant's counsel has the burden of giving you reasons to feel otherwise." Indeed, this is the principle that seems to be built into the normal procedures of the Court of Appeal: the respondent's lawyer is only called on if the panel feels that the appellant has made out a plausible case to be answered, and often they do not. As a rule, "You don't reverse a trial judge's decision unless you are really sure that he is in error," that "he made a clear mistake on the way to his decision."

For one judge the presumption was more limited: "I like judges to give convincing reasons for what they have done, so for me the presumption doesn't reach very far." Most said there was no difference in this regard between civil and criminal cases; the defendant had the benefit of presumption of innocence in the trial, and does not enjoy the same advantage on appeal.

A "Hot" Court

When appeal judges talk about "hot" and "cold" courts, they are not talking about the quality of the air conditioning or the mood that characterizes argument. For them, a hot court is an appeal court that begins research, reading, and consultation among the judges on the appeal before hearing arguments from counsel; a cold court is an appeal court that as a matter of principle starts with the oral arguments ("goes in cold") and moves on to the reading or intra–court debate on the basis of the issues raised orally in court. As one judge said, "All Alberta judges believe in the principle of the "hot" court, and have started to do research even before the hearings start." Another judge objected to the way the panel process was handled, and especially the way judges were rotated between the two major centres, because this practice served to undercut the principle of the hot court. The members of such a panel tended to read ahead of time but to come together physically only for the actual oral hearings, and therefore to come at things "colder" than he would have liked.

Difficult Questions of Law

On the question of whether they had enough time to consider difficult questions of law, the appeal judges were split right down the middle. Five thought that they did have time, that "We can always take as long as we need." One said, "I am satisfied with the time and attention we can give to any difficult question; I think we do a good job." However, a couple of judges had a feeling of a looming caseload crisis, and one added rather wistfully that he was generally satisfied but "often it would really be nice to have a little more time."

Five other judges were flatly dissatisfied with the time spent on difficult questions, with one speaking of an "unseemly haste" to push cases through. Two thought the situation was one of a real trade–off: they could stay ahead of the caseload problem only by consciously taking a little less time for difficult questions, with every indication that the purchase would become progressively more expensive. One judge saw the trade–off as "a kind of coercion on the judges" that annoyed him, but another commented more philosophically that it is only in a perfect world that you would expect no trade–off of this sort at all.

Citations

In the work of finding and using citations Alberta appellate judges saw themselves as bound by decisions of the Supreme Court of Canada, an opinion heavily qualified by one judge who complained, "The Supreme Court has no time for decent judgments." They also felt bound by (or at least very reluctant to depart from) decisions of their own court. For most of them, "If you find such a precedent, that's it." If not, you looked elsewhere, but all other precedents were persuasive rather than binding; "We can disagree with anyone else [so] it depends on the judge who writes it, and on how persuasive and solid the argument is." Most of them looked next to other Canadian appeal courts, four mentioning Ontario but with qualifications: for one, Ontario precedents were strong only on jury trials; for others, it depended on the panel or the individual judge rather than the court itself. One judge said he preferred to follow the Court of Appeal of British Columbia. Another said he paid attention to appeal courts "from the Ontario border west." Two judges said they were especially anxious not to disagree casually with other provincial courts of appeal on law common to both jurisdictions because, as one of them put it, "It is an important principle to try to keep the law of Canada unified."

All of the judges like to look as well at the higher English courts, typically the English Court of Appeal and (less frequently perhaps) the House of Lords, just after the Canadian Supreme Court. The higher English courts enjoy respect because of the high quality of their judgments, especially in fields such as tort and contract.

Precedents from U.S. courts were also mentioned, but with a more qualified acceptance. Such sources were consulted "rarely" or "to a lesser extent" or "almost never" or "not very often." One judge said he consulted U.S. precedents "only if there are no Canadian or English cases" that were comparable, and another said "only if I know of a particularly good American judge." They also said they consulted U.S. cases only in specific fields (different judges spoke of insurance law, petroleum law, and aviation law). Four judges also mentioned the courts of New Zealand and Australia (one added South Africa as well) as something to "include in the canvas on a major or new point of law."

More than half of the judges also talked about the special problems that the Charter was posing, and indicated special reading and canvases to prepare for anticipated Charter cases. As they pointed out, the U.S. experience is a little daunting, in that one case in three in the United States involves some aspect of the Bill of Rights. One mentioned the importance of "starting with the academics: they get into print fast, whereas cases are taking time to move up through the system." They saw U.S. case law as clearly relevant, but with qualifications. They tended to read it only for preliminary guidance or a background on problems and things that have to be considered. Judges said they were reluctant to follow U.S. cases too closely and were not ready to assume that Canadian doctrine should simply parallel the U.S. law. Three judges found the European Covenant useful because of wording similar to the Charter, and one said the European Court "had some very interesting cases that are most instructive."

At the same time, many stressed that (except for binding precedents) they were looking for guidance and ideas so they could avoid feeling locked in to parroting or slavishly following another judge. They certainly felt that they were not limited to cases cited by counsel. One said, "I read all the cases that the lawyers put before me, but then I go on to read ones I find on my own, and I go anywhere I have to go." Another added, "My general attitude is that I am searching around for the best way to resolve the question, so I try to look at everything, wherever I might get help." One judge was particularly candid: "I look for decisions that accord with my own instinct of the case and its impact."

When we looked systematically at reported decisions in 1987, we found that the judges of the Alberta Court of Appeal used an average of four judicial citations per judgment. Of these citations, 30 per cent were drawn from the Supreme Court of Canada, and 20 per cent from prior decisions of the Alberta Court of Appeal itself. One–fifth of the citations were from other provincial courts of appeal (half of them from Ontario), and one–tenth were from Canadian trial courts. The judges drew 15.2 per cent of all citations from English courts (including the pre–1949 Judicial Committee of the Privy Council, then the highest court of appeal for Canadian law) and only 1.2 per cent were drawn from U.S. sources. Except for the very low numbers for U.S. cites, this finding matched reasonably well the self–description of the judges in 1983.

The patterns do vary from province to province. For example, Saskatchewan judges tend to cite the Supreme Court more often; British Columbia judges make more frequent reference to English decisions; Ontario judges are the most likely to consult U.S. sources; and Quebec judges draw an unusually high proportion of their citations from decisions of Quebec courts (both trial and appeal). What these figures cannot answer, of course, is the "chicken and egg" problem: Do judges cite these cases because lawyers use them in argument before them, or do lawyers use these authorities in argument because they know the judges are more likely to be persuaded by them?

Sentencing

Except when they were consciously setting down a bench–mark case to "establish the tariffs" on sentencing, the judges in general felt that sentencing appeals should be handled carefully. One judge said he would not vary a sentence if his own feelings were "within a third (either way)" of the trial judge's sentence, and another said that sentencing review panels always strove for unanimity. Other judges complained, as one of them put it, that some of their colleagues "seemed to feel that on sentences they are entitled to treat it as if it was *de novo*" rather than "just ask whether it is in the ball park, whether there is some real error."

This self–perception of restraint contrasts strikingly with the frequency with which Alberta trial judges complained about the tendency of the Court of Appeal to "tinker" with sentencing. The statistics show that in Alberta (as in Ontario), the appeal judges are willing to give some ground to one–third or more of the appellants who approach them, which represents quite a considerable rate of success.

Drafts of Written Judgments

Drafts of written decisions are circulated, not just within the panel but to all judges on the court. All the judges think it is important to read all written judgments, and to respond to or at least to comment on as many of the decisions as time and caseload pressures permit. One judge stated: "This is a very high priority with us, and it is one of the last practices we will drop under pressure of workload, because it is very important that the decisions of the various panels be consistent with each other. This is the big reason why this court cannot grow any larger, why we cannot simply generate more panels to handle more cases."

Although circulation for thoughtful comment might be desirable, it would seem to be very much the potential victim of sheer numbers. There are about 150 reserved decisions in Alberta each year; some of the reasons for judgment will be brief (the length of the average reported decision in 1982 and again in 1987 was in the neighbourhood of five pages), but many are longer, and most are tightly argued. One suspects that a rising caseload (with or without additions to the appeal bench) will over time make the process of circulation more perfunctory and formal than many judges would like.

More than one judge spoke with concern of the obvious problem that can arise from circulation: What would happen if it became clear that a majority of the court strongly disagreed with a majority of the panel? At that point, the court would be impaled firmly on the horns of a dilemma. On the one hand, it is unacceptable that judges who did not hear the argument or have the opportunity to direct questions should decide a case; on the other hand, it is unacceptable that a panel of the Court of Appeal should deliver a decision with written reasons whose precedential value is entirely illusory. In their experience, such a problem had not occurred on questions of any real significance, but they were unsure how such a problem would be dealt with when it did arise.

At least one such case did occur in Quebec, when the Quebec Court of Appeal reconvened a case for rehearing before a much larger panel, giving as its reason for doing so the fact that the circulation of written drafts had revealed a major division within the court on several relevant issues. We have no idea how widespread or how frequent such a practice might be across the country, but in Alberta we were told of only two similar cases that had occurred in the last decade.

The Role of the Chief Justice

The chief justice was described by all in the classic and predictable phrase as a "first among equals," as "a leader but by no means a boss." He has a considerable administrative burden, but the appeal judges thought it was very important that he should continue to sit as a judge rather than devoting his time exclusively to administration, as happens in some other provinces. (Administrative duties also include not only those on the Court, but also those as second in command to the Lieutenant-Governor.) The chief assigns panels (both the size of the panels and the specific judges who will serve on each), and all the judges thought that he constantly tried to mix up known types ("hawks" and "doves" on each panel) and to make sure that every judge regularly serves on panels with every other judge. Some trading around of assignments can take place, but it is not to be done casually or without a pressing reason. During the "fairly frequent" meetings of the entire court, the chief justice is in the chair, but tends to look for a consensus, or at least a measure of general agreement, among the members of the court rather than simply "laying down his own line for others to follow."

On any panel the senior judge always presides from the centre seat (with the most junior judge on the left), and this is always the chief justice when he serves on a panel. But when it comes to the panel reaching conclusions, the chief justice is only one individual who "can't just pull rank" but must try to persuade the others. The chief justice "has some influence on the conduct, not on outcome, of the case," and "tries to shape the direction of the court, but more in terms of image than substance." On the less formal and more personal side, he is also seen as being responsible for the happiness of his judges, for "smoothing down ruffled feathers and making sure members are getting along."

What was explicitly denied, however, was that the chief justice had any major role regarding case-flow or the processing of cases. The constant refrain was that "we take as long as we need to" and "case–flow is a matter for the individual panel, not for the chief." The senior judges in each centre, including the chief justice, were involved in case–flow to some extent in deciding how cases that were ready to proceed would be divided among panels, but not to the extent of it being appropriate to put pressure on a panel to get a case done at other than its own pace. Only one judge wondered if this might have to change if the caseload continues to increase; at the time of the interviews in 1983 the appellate caseload was in the middle of a sharp rise, but indications later in the decade were that it might have levelled off.

Although the panel situation put "some kind of onus on a judge" to work at the pace of the others and not to slow them down, this was more a matter of courtesy to colleagues than a responsibility to any specific person, including the chief justice. It was even suggested (not grimly and seriously, but not casually and frivolously either) that it was at least a technical violation of the notion of judicial independence to have the chief justice "riding people" because he wanted decisions, "especially dissenting ones," written up very quickly.

All these details suggest that the phrase "first among equals," however tired the cliché, is in fact the best description. The chief justice is not a sergeant–major, not a boss, not a task–master with disciplinary powers to punish or reward; however, he (at time of writing no woman had ever served as chief justice of a province) is an individual who deserves respect for the office and usually for having earned the respect of appellate colleagues (chief justices are more often elevated from the present bench than appointed from outside).

Delay

None of the judges on the Court of Appeal saw any problem with delay in their own court. Several commented that some trials seemed to take a long time working their way up the system to the Court of Appeal, and sometimes they wondered why, because, as one judge put it "When some cases that started in 1977 are just reaching the Court of Appeal in 1984, this is just too long." This sort of delay clearly indicated, the judge said, that "there is some problem elsewhere in the system, but I don't have any real knowledge as to where that might be." The one bottleneck judges were aware of was frequent delays in receiving transcripts. However, none saw any delay that was caused by their court, and all insisted, as one of them said, that "Whenever the case is ready to go, this court can put it on the list right away for hearing next month; there is no delay." Another added, "It is never the case that something is ready to go ahead but is held up because of this court." One stated proudly, "The Alberta Court of Appeal has the best timing of any Court of Appeal in Canada," and only one judge worried that sometimes they seemed to take longer than was really necessary to get their own judgments written and published.

One factor in preventing the build–up of a back–log was the fact that, as compared with trial courts, the Court of Appeal has a relatively easy time with scheduling. Fewer individuals need to be contacted, there is no trouble with witnesses, and the Court of Appeal generally enjoys a high priority in the competition for the time of busy lawyers. The lists are drawn up by the judges themselves, with one judge in each centre having responsibility for the criminal list and (apparently) another the responsibility for the civil list on a long–term basis.

However, their pride was by no means tinged with complacency, and only two judges did not wonder out loud how much longer they would be able to stay on top of things. A few noted both the horrendous increases in the caseload of the Court of Queen's Bench and the fact that their own caselist had trebled in a decade. One told of how in the last year or so they had started "to feel that we are about to be swamped with cases; it is not a serious problem yet but it could get to be." Some spoke of "starting to feel the pressure" or of "not having the time we used to have" or of being "just too busy now, just too many silly days." One said, "We are gradually getting to the point where the court may be overwhelmed, where overload may begin forcing delays." Several commented that although the caseload pressures started building up with Alberta's economic boom, the recession by no means reversed the trend; the courts were seeing different kinds of cases, but not by any means in smaller numbers. However, none thought that an intermediate court of appeal (even along the lines of the Ontario Divisional Court that was established in the superior trial court to hear administrative law appeals) was a viable option for Alberta, except possibly for sentencing appeals exclusively.

Overview

Anyone who has sat in on an appeal court hearing will have been struck by how different the atmosphere is from that in a trial court. Often the hearings are in large courtrooms populated only by the three judges, a clerk, an orderly, and the two lawyers arguing a case. Unlike a trial, the parties involved in the litigation (other than their lawyers) are usually not present, and there are no crowds of witnesses or other parties waiting for their trial. The judges do not limit themselves to rules of order and questions of follow–up detail of witnesses; instead, they actively question the lawyers and engage in protracted exchanges with them, sometimes in rather combative terms. The judges often appear unpressured, as if they would be content to listen to the arguments of the lawyers all day, if necessary.

This impression belies what is really going on. By the time of the trial, the judges have done a great deal of reading about the case before them. Some have already made up their minds about how the case should be decided, and may secretly be anxious to get on to other, possibly more difficult, cases so that a backlog of unheard cases will not develop. Should the sitting day be completed early, the judges will go to their offices to write judgments, read the case law from other jurisdictions, and pore through the factums that have piled up on their desks. Most judges will take unread material home with them for evening and weekend reading.

We are struck with the carefully honed skills of appeal court judges to digest enormous volumes of written materials quickly, and to pick out what they consider to be the central issues for more careful consideration. This is a skill that they begin to develop as private lawyers and then (for most of them) as trial judges. It is small wonder that the retirement age for these judges is set at 75; few could have developed these skills by society's usual retirement age of 65. But most enjoy their work, in spite of all the pressures involved. Not only do they appreciate being able to serve their society by helping to resolve contentious issues as fairly as possible, but they also enjoy the unique insights into the nature of human beings which they gain through the more interesting cases that come their way, and the intellectual challenge of resolving difficult questions of law.

But for every unique and complex case heard by a court of appeal judge, there are at least four or five routine ones. Most of the appeals heard by provincial courts of appeal are appeals by right; if a person wants to present a case, he or she has every right to do so, no matter how trivial, stereotypical, farfetched, or weakly grounded the arguments might be. This is definitely not the situation in the Supreme Court of Canada, where since 1975 cases are selected for hearing by the judges themselves because they represent difficult and important issues of legal interpretation.

7

The Supreme Court
of Canada

The Supreme Court — the highest court of appeal in Canada, and the one that establishes the precedents that bind all the courts below — is the most visible court in the country. And because the judges can choose most of the cases the court hears, its procedures are quite different from those of the other courts of appeal. There are few easy cases, and almost all of the decisions for which the court has granted leave to appeal result in lengthy written judgments. The average Supreme Court decision takes up about 20 pages in the *Supreme Court Reports*, the official case reporter for the court; the decisions in major cases, of course, run much longer. This is in sharp contrast to most reported decisions of the provincial courts of appeal, which usually run to five pages or less; and it is also in contrast to the Supreme Court's own decisions of 20 or 30 years ago, which tended to be considerably shorter.

History

Today the Supreme Court of Canada plays a major role in national politics, its members frequently appear on the covers of national news magazines, and its pronouncements on human rights and constitutional procedures are eagerly awaited and rigorously examined. But it was not always so; the prominence, status, and high profile of the Supreme Court have taken decades to develop, and even 25 years ago people would have scoffed (sometimes rather regretfully) at the suggestion that it would one day enjoy its present role and importance.

According to James Snell and Frederick Vaughan, there are four key dates in the history of the Supreme Court's rise to its current prominence and stature. The first date is 1875, when Alexander Mackenzie's Liberal government introduced and passed the Supreme Court Act — some eight years after section 101 of the Constitution Act 1867 had contemplated the creation of "a general court of appeal for Canada." The eight–year hiatus between Confederation and the Supreme Court Act created the highly anomalous constitutional status of the Supreme Court itself: the referee of Canadian federalism is not entrenched in the Constitution as is the Senate but is rather the creature of unilateral federal legislation. Consequently, several of the critical events of Supreme Court history are themselves the product of unilateral federal initiative, not of formal constitutional resolution.

Sir John A. Macdonald's Conservatives introduced legislation to establish a Supreme Court in 1869 and again in 1870, but both bills were withdrawn, and it fell to the Liberals to create Canada's first federal courts. The legislation created an Exchequer Court at the same time, using single judges from the Supreme Court to exercise original jurisdiction. There were initially six members of the Court, two of whom were required to be from the bar of the province of Quebec; this number was increased to seven members in 1927, and to nine members (three from Quebec) in 1949. The Supreme Court did not, however, receive a permanent home until 1882, when it moved into a renovated stable shared with the National Art Gallery. Contemporary accounts indicate that on warm days, an occupant's nose provided a constant reminder of the original use of the structure. The Court did not move into its present building until 1946, and until 1949 it shared the space with a federal government department. Today the Supreme Court shares its building only with the Federal Court of Canada.

The early Supreme Court laboured under a number of handicaps, some fortuitous and others structural. For 20 years a quorum of the court was only one less than its total complement of judges, which created recurrent problems in convening a panel, especially when one or more judges suffered from poor health. (The solution, in 1896, was to reduce quorum to four.) Personality clashes between judges, extreme tardiness in releasing decisions, and the mediocre quality of many of its judicial opinions also contributed to the Court's poor reputation and disappointing performance. These characteristics were especially pronounced during the period of the Strong Court (1892–1902) — the implicit pun is not apt — when the Court's chief justice was widely considered to be bad–tempered, chronically ill, and intellectually lazy. Nor did things improve with Chief Justice Sir Henry Strong's departure, when a series of weak appointments clearly motivated by political patronage further undermined the Court's reputation. The close personal friendship between Mr. Justice Sir Lyman Duff (1906 to 1944; chief justice from 1933) and Prime Minister W.L. Mackenzie King, recounted by Duff's biographer David Williams, did little to improve the stature or independence of the Court.

The second important date, 1949, saw the abolition of appeals beyond the Supreme Court to the Judicial Committee of the Privy Council of Great Britain (J.C.P.C.), which had served as the ultimate court of appeal for Canada as for other parts of the British Empire. This subordinate status was completely outside the Court's control and devastating to any attempt to build its credibility. It was bad enough that any decision of the Supreme Court itself could be appealed higher, to a British committee that often showed scant respect or consideration for the principles or arguments within the Supreme Court's judgments; even more serious was the possibility of appeals proceeding directly from a provincial court of appeal to the Judicial Committee, bypassing the Supreme Court altogether. These direct appeals are known as "per saltum" appeals. Peter Russell (6) indicates that roughly one–half of the significant decisions of the Judicial Committee took this per saltum form, leaving the Supreme Court a helpless bystander to the development of important parts of Canadian law. The net effect was to leave the Supreme Court very much in the shadow of its imperial counterpart, and unable to do much to redress the balance.

Successful attempts to overcome this problem on the Court's behalf were long in coming. Initial suggestions in 1875 to cut off Judicial Committee appeals were, for all practical purposes, ignored. The Criminal Code was amended in 1888 to make the Supreme Court the final court of appeal, but in 1926 this amend-

ment was declared by the J.C.P.C to be invalid because it con-
flicted with imperial statutes.[13] After the Statute of Westminster
in 1931 (in which the British Parliament officially declared
Canada to be an independent state), the criminal code amendment
was re–enacted in 1933 and upheld as valid in 1935.[6] Civil and
per saltum appeals were abolished by an amendment to the Supreme Court Act in 1949, after a 1947 reference case had confirmed in advance the constitutional validity of the enactment.[2]
Only in 1949, just before its own seventy–fifth birthday, did the
Court become supreme in law as well as in name, after an exceptionally lengthy adolescence. The amendment applied only to
cases initiated after 1949; cases begun before that date continued
to wend their way to London, and the last Canadian appeal was
decided by the Judicial Committee in 1959 (*Ponoka–Calmar Oils
v. Wakefield*,[15]), although the last decision of significant constitutional import was decided in 1954 (*A–G Ontario v. Winner*,[3]).

The abolition of Privy Council appeals gave the Supreme Court
the opportunity to create a bold new role for itself, but its early
performance fell far short of the optimistic expectations that had
welcomed the "truly Supreme Court." The court's first constitutional law case after coming of age (*Johanesson v. West St. Paul,
1952*[11]) was a vigorous affirmation of federal jurisdiction over
aeronautics and of the "peace order and good government" clause,
but the case was one of a kind rather than the beginning of a solid
line of interpretation. Similarly, a string of cases from Quebec
involving the Jehovah's Witnesses [4,5,7,12,24,25,28] generated
outcomes that delighted civil libertarians, but the jurisprudence
that justified the decisions was confused and disappointing, opportunistic rather than firmly principled.

The general trend of decisions in division of power cases was
mildly in favour of the federal Parliament (inspiring articles such
as Peter Hogg's "Is the Supreme Court of Canada Biased in
Federalism Cases?" which concluded that it was not), but without
a clarity of purpose or doctrine. The hopes raised by these cases
were dashed by an extremely restrained and legalistic application
of the 1960 Bill of Rights, with only a single vigorous Bill of
Rights decision (*R. v. Drybones 1969*,[20]) to mar the general
pattern of acquiescence. Out of a total of thirty–four Bill of Rights

cases, the Supreme Court upheld the rights claim in only five. (Russell [6]) On the positive side of the ledger, there was a general improvement in the quality of appointments, the better ones including Ivan Rand (1943–59) and Roy Kellock (1944–58).

One appointment, that of Justice Bora Laskin, proved to be so significant that it is tempting to make the appointment itself an additional key date in the history of the Supreme Court. Laskin's scholarly reputation was considerable when he was appointed to the Ontario Court of Appeal in 1965 and elevated to the Supreme Court of Canada in 1970, becoming chief justice in 1973. In addition, he brought to the Court a strong vision of the constitution and the major role it provides for the national government, and a firm determination to persuade the other judges to follow him, although for several years he made some of his most vigorous arguments on the Supreme Court, as he had on the Ontario Court of Appeal — in dissent.

Under Laskin's leadership, the Court tried to meet in larger panels, as often as possible as a full Court, to hear and decide cases, a move that logically tends as well to greater consistency in decisions. He was without question one of the most controversial and influential of Canada's Supreme Court justices, as well as one of its most scholarly and respected. It is mildly ironic that Laskin, Canada's great dissenter on the Supreme Court, was succeeded as chief justice by the judge who had dissented the most firmly from some of Laskin's decisions in federalism cases, Manitoba's Brian Dickson. (In civil liberties cases, however, Laskin and Dickson were more often in agreement.)

The third important date was 1975, when an amendment to the Supreme Court Act sharply reduced the scope of appeals by right, and dramatically increased the Court's control of its own docket. (The relevant legislation was passed late in 1974, and came into effect early in 1975.) An appeal by right, as the term implies, is one that the Court has no right to refuse, but to which it must assign hearing and decision time. For much of the Court's existence, an appeal by right has existed for any capital criminal case, and for any civil suit involving more than $10,000. By the 1970s "nearly all" of the Court's caseload was made up of appeals by right (Russell [6]) and according to some estimates, up to 70 per cent of the justices' time was spent on routine matters. (Snell and Vaughan) The pressure of business obliged the Court to give most of its decisions from the bench upon conclusion of oral argument, without even adjourning for a brief conference.

After the 1974 amendment there was an appeal by right for many fewer cases (such as an appeal court decision on a Crown appeal reversing an acquittal; or an appeal court decision for which there is a dissent on a question of law), and according to S.I. Bushnell some 80 per cent of the cases were heard by leave of the Court. From a Court that was obliged to take all comers, the Supreme Court became to a very large extent its own gatekeeper.

The change was an extremely important one, not least because judicial person–hours for hearing arguments, researching cases, and writing decisions are a finite resource. The more cases the Supreme Court is obliged to hear because of appeals by right, the less time and effort it can spend on any of its cases, including those that it has selected to hear because of the national importance of the legal issues they raise. The expansion of leave jurisdiction, by contrast, allows the Court to limit the number of cases it will hear, and therefore to deal with them more thoroughly — for example, by relaxing the restrictions on the granting of intervenor status. (An intervenor is a person or an organization — not a party to the original case, but likely to be affected by the outcome — who is allowed to present a legal brief indicating the aspects of the case that affect it and arguing the position it thinks the Court should take. The federal and provincial governments have a right to intervene; other groups, such as the Canadian Civil Liberties Association, may apply for the Court's permission to intervene.)

The Court can limit its pronouncements to cases that raise legal questions of national importance, or to situations in which a diversity of interpretations among the various provincial courts of appeal calls for the enunciation of a uniform national doctrine. As well, the Court can decide when it wants to deal with controversial or complex questions, allowing lower court decisions to accumulate until the issues can be dealt with comprehensively, or giving controversial questions the time to "cool" politically to the point where a judicial determination will be accepted. Control over its own docket does not just guarantee more "bang" for the judicial "buck"; it also allows the Court considerable discretion as to when and where things go "bang."

A major exception to this discretionary power is "reference cases" (also called "advisory opinions"), which are the product of the federal government's power to ask the Supreme Court a hypothetical question of law. The Court had usually considered itself obliged to answer, although there is some question about a right to refuse. Over the last hundred years, one provincial government after another has given itself the same power with respect to its own court of appeal, and those decisions can be appealed to the Supreme Court. Reference cases tend to be few in number, but often very important in their content and impact. Technically, an advisory opinion does not constitute a binding precedent, but in practice the distinction is of little importance.

It was widely expected that the 1974 changes were only a first step, and that subsequent Supreme Court Act amendments would drop the other shoe by virtually eliminating all appeals by right. However, Bill C–105, which would have accomplished exactly this, was abandoned in 1986, and the replacement Bill C–53, introduced the following term, was passed without the provisions further restricting appeals by right. Bushnell has suggested that this retreat must be seen as indicating something of a lack of confidence in the judges of the Court. Although the creation of a significant gatekeeper role is clearly revolutionary, it is equally clearly an unfinished revolution.

The impact of the reforms has been pronounced. In the 1980s, for example, the caseload of the Court averaged about 80 cases per year; the annual caseload for the 1970s was at least half again as high. The 1988–89 court year, which saw more than 120 cases decided, was an atypical trend–breaking period in two respects: first, a high number of appeals by right, the highest since 1974; and second, a high caseload, the highest in the 1980s. The two are clearly related, and many of the appeals by right seem to have been dealt with by short oral decisions that were usually unanimous, often consisting of a single paragraph elliptically endorsing the lower court's reasons for judgment. The general trend, however, has been toward a smaller caseload, and an extremely flexible — critics might say even an arbitrary — use of the discretion to grant leave. The Court does not give reasons for a refusal to grant leave, and commentators such as Eric Gertner have had difficulty determining the criteria which determine by which a specific application for leave is approved.

The final key date is 1982, the adoption of the Constitution Act 1982 including the Canadian Charter of Rights and Freedoms. Clearly, this is the most revolutionary change to affect the Canadian judiciary, with the Supreme Court of Canada carrying the ultimate responsibility. There are three reasons for suggesting that the Charter transforms the judicial role.

First, the broad scope of the entrenched rights involves the courts in a much wider set of public policies and controversies, from Sunday closing through compulsory union dues to abortion. Early indications are that the Court is anxious to leave far behind its weak and disappointing record on the 1960 Bill of Rights, and consequently the new jurisprudence asserting an expanded and aggressive role for the Court is starting from scratch.

Second, a finding that a piece of legislation is unconstitutional for Charter reasons differs in a very basic way from a similar finding in federalism disputes about the proper boundary between the exercise of federal and provincial powers. In federalism disputes, the Court demarcates areas of provincial and federal jurisdiction that are to be protected from each other by the courts. In matters involving the Charter, however, the Court demarcates an area prohibited to both levels to be protected by the courts; in other words, the Court both creates and polices its own turf.

Finally, the Meech Lake imbroglio has demonstrated that the new domestic amending formula is extremely difficult to use, especially with regard to matters, such as the amending formula itself, which can only be changed with unanimous consent. Given the distaste for constitutional amendment processes after Meech Lake, even amendments that can be brought about without unanimous consent seem unlikely to occur very often. Thus, even though the Charter and the division of powers can be amended with the agreement of Parliament plus seven provincial legislatures (necessarily including either Ontario or Quebec), the decisions of the courts appear unlikely to be disturbed often by amendment.

As well, eight years' experience has shown a strong political disincentive to use the "notwithstanding" section. (The "notwithstanding" clause in the Charter allows provincial legislatures or Parliament to override some judicial interpretations of Charter rights for five–year periods. This override provision was routinely used by the Quebec legislature when the Parti Quebecois was in power to draw attention to the fact that the Quebec legislature did not approve the 1982 constitutional changes. Since then, it has been used once by Saskatchewan to end a strike, and once by the Bourassa government in Quebec to maintain its outdoor–signs legislation intact.) Both these trends have encouraged the Court to use its dramatic new powers carefully, although the Court has not refrained from giving the Charter a somewhat expansive interpretation with regard to issues such as freedom of religion, equality rights, and the rights of persons accused of criminal offences.

Bora Laskin gave the Supreme Court a high profile; the Charter guarantees that the Court will never lose it. However, the Court that now confronts these challenges is in many ways fitter than it ever has been to cope with them. Its scholarly qualifications are impressive; a higher proportion of judges than ever before either took post–graduate studies in law, or taught in law schools, or both. Most of the judges bring with them to the Court a decade or more of experience on the provincial appellate benches, yet despite this the average age of the Court is relatively low — the current grouping is one of the youngest ever on the Supreme Court.

Paradoxically, after a record–breaking 12 Supreme Court appointments in 12 years, the Court now faces the potential of the reverse: the next decade or so will see very few new appointments. After facing, and admirably coping with, the problems of rapid turnover, the Court will now be faced with the reverse problem, virtually static membership over an extended period, with the concomitant difficulty of maintaining an openness to new ideas on both substance and process.

The Supreme Court is therefore an institution that has only recently come into its own after an exceptionally long apprenticeship, now enjoying a reputation and a stature that would have seemed unlikely a few decades ago. We will now consider the procedures that the Supremes (the slightly sardonic nickname appears to be ubiquitous among the judges lower in the judicial hierarchy) have evolved to deal with their new responsibilities.

Decision–making in the Supreme Court

As might be expected, much of the workload of the Supreme Court of Canada consists of appeals from the provincial courts of appeal, which accounted for 75 to 80 per cent of the Supreme Court's work in the 1980s. Appeals from the Federal Court (and, much more rarely, the Court Martial Appeal Board) account for about 20 per cent of total cases; the residue is comprised (in descending order of frequency) of per saltum appeals direct from provincial superior trial courts, reference cases direct from the federal government, and rehearings.

Our research suggests that a province's share of the national population is a poor predictor of its share of the Supreme Court's caseload. Based on population, the appeal rates from Ontario and Quebec are relatively low (although they still rank first and second for numbers of appeals by province), while the appeal rates from Manitoba and British Columbia are comparatively high. In the 1980s, appeals to the Supreme Court of Canada were successful about 45 per cent of the time; the Ontario Court of Appeal was the strongest (that is, the Court most seldom reversed) and the Quebec Court of Appeal one of the weakest (that is, the most frequently reversed).

Hearings of the Supreme Court of Canada, like those of other Canadian courts, are open to the public. (Only once, under unique circumstances in 1990, did the the Court close a case to the public for security reasons.) Security guards check all the people who enter the courthouse, once when they enter the building, and again when they enter the main courtroom. But no one ever asks *why* you are there. You have a right to be there; you have a right to see Canada's highest court in action.

Like other courtrooms used by appeal courts, this courtroom often has few watchers, except for the relatively frequent class-room tours that Ottawa teachers have arranged. But the courtroom does not have the sense of emptiness to it that other appeal court-rooms do. This is because there are usually seven judges sitting at the front of the courtroom (with the chief justice always in the centre), and sometimes the full complement of nine.

The court alternates between sitting weeks and judgment–writing weeks. During the sitting weeks, the Court spends most of its time hearing actual appeals, although a considerable amount of time (17 days in 1987, according to Dickson [2]) is spent hearing applications for leave to appeal. These applications are heard in three–judge panels, and the Court will hear as many as a dozen a day. In the late 1980s the Supreme Court Act was amended to allow the Court, at its discretion, to dispose of leave to appeal applications entirely on the basis of written submissions. For most leave applications, the Court continues to hear oral arguments, although lawyers for each side are limited to 15 minutes.

Since the mid–1980s the Court has permitted lawyers arguing leave applications to do so from a remote location through closed–circuit television. Dickson notes that in 1987, in 77 cases this video–conferencing technique was used. Video–conferencing was apparently well–received by most lawyers, although as Bushnell (2) notes, the rate of successful leave applications has been some-what lower for the video–conferenced applications than for those argued in person. Video–conferencing was made available begin-ning in the fall of 1987 for use in actual appeal cases, and some lawyers, especially those representing intervenors, have taken advantage of this opportunity.

With regard to the actual appeals, the Court will usually hear one case in the morning and one in the afternoon (although on Fridays both cases may be heard in the morning). The chief justice sets strict time limits on the amount of time that counsel may speak. For most cases, counsel for the appellant and counsel for the respondent each have an hour, but occasionally they are given only a half hour. Counsel for intervenors, if there are any, are usually given a half hour.

In front of the large dais that the judges sit on is a broad wooden lectern for counsel. On the lectern are three small lights controlled by the clerk. A green light indicates that the lawyer may continue speaking. An amber light indicates that he or she has five minutes to finish the argument. A red light signals that time is up, and the lawyer has to sit down. This system of lights is a recent innovation introduced by Chief Justice Dickson. Before this, lawyers could theoretically speak as long as they wished, although the judges had ways of letting the lawyers know when they had said enough. During one Supreme Court hearing in the early 1970s, which we witnessed, a lawyer was droning on about nothing that seemed important, and Justice Bora Laskin turned his swivel chair to face away from the lawyer, leaving nothing to look at but the broad back of the chair. Soon another judge did the same. The lawyer quickly concluded his comments.

While the lawyers are presenting their arguments, the judges will often interrupt with questions for clarification, sometimes in pointed and penetrating terms. This is a major difference between appeal courts and most trial courts; a trial judge is frequently a bystander who intervenes at the margins, but the members of the appeal panel are more often aggressive participants who grill counsel fiercely, embarrassing them if they are poorly prepared or if the Court is in an unfriendly mood.

The judges are already familiar with the arguments, having read the factums and pleadings, and for most of them there are one or two key issues in each case. What they hope for from the oral arguments is clarification about these issues; if they don't receive this clarity, they will usually pursue the point and take exception if the issue is not precisely addressed. The kinds of questions asked by the judges, and their reaction to the responses given by counsel, will sometimes give an indication of which way the judges are leaning. After the hearing is over, it is not uncommon for all the lawyers involved to chat informally about who they think won the case.

We asked the retired judges we spoke with to describe the Supreme Court's decision–making. The answers were fairly uniform about the general nature of the process. They read the factums and pleadings before the hearing and listen carefully to the arguments during the hearing. Immediately after each hearing the judges go into a "conference." The conference room contains a large table, about 15 feet across, where each judge has her or his own assigned "pew." Beginning with the most junior and working up to the most senior judge, they give their opinions on the case.

After that, the senior judge (the chief justice if he is present, which was almost always the case except late in the Laskin period when the chief justice was ill) would assign the writing of the court's decision to one of the judges. As one judge said, "It was usually pretty obvious who that person would be." This is because some judges expected to write all the decisions with regard to certain issues, or because other judges were too busy writing other decisions, or because one judge appeared to have taken an unusual interest in the case. Often, someone volunteers to write the decision. If no volunteers are forthcoming, the senior judge simply assigns someone to write the opinion.

One retired judge — who was noted for his industry on the Court — said that occasionally he felt he could simply not take on another judgment. However, if the chief justice made the request, it was considered impolite to refuse. He said that his favourite strategy for avoiding being asked was to bend down and tie his shoes. Because he was bent over, the chief justice could not see him over the table, and would invariably ask someone else to write the judgment.

It should be noted that the pattern of the formal conference became firmly established only during the chief justiceship of Bora Laskin. Before that time, there was a period when the judges did not even have a conference on the day of the hearing. This is because one judge had an invalid family member to care for, and wanted to leave each day immediately after the hearing ended. After that particular judge left the court, conferences began to be held after each hearing, and it became the tradition to begin with the junior judge — in contrast to the pattern established by the U.S. Supreme Court, which always begins the conference by hearing from the senior judge.

It usually takes several weeks for the opinion to be written, and it is then circulated to all the judges. Each judge has the right to make comments and suggestions on the draft opinion, and often they do. It is then up to the original writer to try to incorporate as many of these suggestions as he or she thinks appropriate into the draft. The revised draft is then circulated. At this point, some of the judges might decide to write dissenting opinions, or separate concurring opinions. It is not so much that the dissenters are not obvious from the time of the original conference, but that some of them, after reading the draft judgment, might change their minds and decide to go along with the majority after all. The reverse situation, of a written draft of a majority decision losing support as it moves through successive revisions, is extremely uncommon.

The content of the majority judgment is eventually agreed to at another conference, and then all the opinions (majority, concurring, or dissenting) are gathered together. The judgment is then announced in open court and transcripts of the opinions made available for the public. (Recently, the necessity for announcing the judgment in open court has been abolished.) The time from the hearing to the release of the judgment varies from several weeks to many months, with the average being six to nine months. The judgment appears in *Supreme Court Reports* about six months after the release of the announcement of the judgment.

Within this general pattern there are a number of variations. Some judges make up their minds about the case after reading the factums, and others do their best to keep an open mind until after hearing the oral argument. Although this might seem inconsistent with the principle of the presumption of innocence, that presumption actually applies only at the trial stage. Most cases heard by the Supreme Court have already been considered by at least two levels of court — the trial court, plus the provincial court of appeal — and it is up to the appellant to persuade the Court that a serious mistake has been made, or that there are serious consequences for matters of national importance. Some dissenters begin writing their dissenting opinions the day of the hearing, and others wait to read at least the first draft of the majority opinion.

Depending on the personalities of the judges and especially the chief justice, conferences last from a few minutes to several hours. Under Chief Justice Laskin, the conferences tended to be very brief. One judge said the conferences were "often only six to eight minutes." He added, "Laskin had a very sharp and concentrated mind. He was an intellectual leader; he knew where he was going. He had a decisive mind. It was usually obvious to him what the outcome should be, and he didn't want us to waste time debating unimportant issues. When it got to be his turn, he would usually say, "well, it's clear that this is the outcome, and for this reason." He didn't do this in a heavy–handed way, but in a kindly way. It was a joy to work with him." This is a somewhat surprising account of Laskin, given his famous dissents on some important cases. However, it should not be forgotten that Laskin agreed with the majority more often than he dissented.

Under Chief Justice Dickson the conferences tended to take longer, and to take the form less of a "vote with reasons" than a discussion of principles and issues. This is partly because of the complex and ground–breaking Charter cases the court has had to deal with, partly because Dickson believed that new and controversial issues required full discussion, and partly because of the nature of the judges on the Court, who were apparently less likely to make up their minds on certain issues until after a full discussion with their colleagues. Because of the tendency of the judges on the Dickson court to debate issues with each other directly, comments were sometimes not made according to the usual junior–senior order, but ricocheted around the room in a more random and variable manner.

There has been a certain amount of friction on the Supreme Court between judges who have spent many years in private practice, and judges whose major background is in the academic world. The judges who came from private practice sometimes saw the academic judges as wasting time over trivial philosophical issues, while the academic judges saw the judges from private practice as not giving serious enough consideration to important legal and philosophical issues. This sort of tension is endemic to any panel court and is probably (in moderation, short of a major polarization) a good thing.

The judges said that they generally felt that if possible, the court should write unanimous judgments. This is because when lawyers read several concurring opinions for the majority, they sometimes have difficulty deciding which opinion carries the most weight and accurately describes the state of the law. The clearest and most unambiguous way to indicate the present position and probable future direction of the Court on a specific set of legal issues is in the form of a single unanimous decision of the Court. In spite of this consensus, there was rarely any pressure put on the judges to come up with unanimous decisions. The one exception was the patriation reference (see chapter 9), concerning which Chief Justice Laskin pushed hard, but in the end unsuccessfully, for a unanimous decision.

There are times when the unanimous opinion of the judges will be anonymously attributed to "the Court" as a whole, rather than being acknowledged as the product of the judge who wrote the first draft of the opinion. (The Latin term, which is used increasingly less in federal and provincial law reports, is *per curiam* or — the term used in the United States — *per coram*.) We asked the judges how they decided in which cases to release an opinion of "the Court." The answer was that there was no rule; sometimes there was a feeling among the judges that a decision from "the Court" would have a "greater impact." One judge mentioned a decision in which all the judges were so upset with the decision of a provincial court of appeal judge that they decided to write a strongly worded decision to "rap his knuckles." They agreed to write a decision attributed to "the Court" so as to protect the identity of the individual judge who drafted the decision.

One retired judge told us, "Judges sometimes tend to be prima donnas, and sometimes the prima donnas clash with each other." In one case several decades ago, two senior judges both hoped to become the chief justice after the retirement of the incumbent. The competition was so intense that the two "nearly came to blows at conferences." Then there was the time when Justice Locke didn't like the way Justice Rand wrote his decisions; Locke thought Rand's decisions were too difficult to understand. This sometimes led to heated debates between the two judges during conferences.

It is up to the chief justice to decide whether the entire court should hear a case, or whether a smaller panel of five or seven judges should preside. Before the chief justiceship of Laskin, panels of five and seven judges were often used. Laskin disagreed with this practice because of the possibility that on contentious issues, one panel might come to a different conclusion than another, and the outcome would rest as much on the luck of the draw of the composition of the panel as on the substantive merits of the case.

One of the retired judges gave an example of this happening. He mentioned a case originally heard by a five–judge panel in which the judges split three to two and decided to re–hear the case with the full court. (He said that Justice Abbott referred to this procedure as "calling in the reserves.") The full court agreed with the views of the original two dissenters.

This retired judge also mentioned the case of a chief justice from the 1940 or 1950s who intensely disagreed with the view of the law held by one of the justices. When making up the panels, the chief justice would purposely leave this particular judge off the panels in which that judge's view of the law might be an issue. This is clearly an exceptional situation, and we report it only as an illustrative anecdote; nonetheless, it does indicate the real core of discretion and power that may lie within the rather modest perquisites of the office of chief justice.

After Laskin became ill, the Court had to hear a number of cases with seven–judge or even five–judge panels just to keep a serious backlog from developing. Under Dickson, the majority of cases were heard by seven–judge panels.

Although Canadian Supreme Court judges, like their American counterparts, employ outstanding recent law graduates as their law clerks, the clerks in Canada play a much less important role. This may be because the smaller caseload of the Canadian court — it decides only half to a third as many cases each year with the same number of judges — allows Canadian judges to be more active and more closely engaged with each case they decide. (One could, of course, run the causal arrow in the opposite direction: one of the reasons why the caseload of the Canadian court is so much smaller than that of its U.S. counterpart is because the Canadian judges make so little use of their law clerks.)

Decision–Making in The Supreme Court

The dynamics of decision–making in the Supreme Court are markedly different from those in the lower appeal courts and the trial courts. Not only do the large panels of judges make the Supreme Court unique, but so also do the nature of the cases it hears and the high profile it commands. And this process is changing. Only some ten years ago the court was more of a "group of individuals." The judges announced their *individual* decisions in the conference, and an individual from the largest group would be selected to write the opinion. Today, judges tend to debate issues more with each other, and to reserve their own final position until after they have heard from their colleagues. The court is becoming more consensual, and less individualistic.

There are at least four possible, though somewhat inconclusive, reasons for the change. The first is that Canadian courts of appeal generally are changing their view of the appropriate way to deliver decisions; the multiplicity of opinions ("Everyone on the panel having a go at it," as one judge described it) is being replaced by a single judgment of "Justice X for the Court." Remember that almost all of the members of the Supreme Court of Canada in 1990 served as provincial appeal judges; to the extent that such an evolution is taking place, they would already have been part of it before their appointment to the Supreme Court.

A second reason may well be that the Charter of Rights issues taken up by the Court are so new and so difficult that the judges truly have no preconceived notions of how many of these cases should be decided — even after the hearing — and therefore seek guidance from each other. Many Charter cases raise new questions for the first time; the extensive experience of our judges with judicial precedent and past doctrine is less help in these cases than in other components of their caseload, and the process of decision–making may well reflect this novelty.

A third possibility is that the inclusion of three women judges on the Court has changed the dynamic of the decision–making process. As Madame Justice Wilson noted in her address at Osgoode Hall Law School, women tend more than men to find consensual decisions. One of the retired judges we talked to thought that the appointment of women judges to the Court was the major reason why it was switching from a more individualistic style of decision–making to a consensual style. The number of women judges on the Supreme Court of Canada — three out of a total of nine — is much higher than the proportion of women judges on any Canadian court of appeal and, so far as we know, is the highest proportion of any comparable court in the Anglo–American democracies. If there is a difference between women judges and men judges in the style of their decision–making, the Supreme Court of Canada is certainly the laboratory within which these differences are most likely to present themselves.

Fourth and finally, the personality and character of the chief justice may be extremely important, and much of the recent shift in style may be the product of the replacement of Laskin with Dickson. Some U.S. scholars (such as Walker et al.) have highlighted the leadership style of the chief justice as a major factor in the ebb and flow of dissensual behaviour on the U.S. Supreme Court. The performance of the Court as its new chief justice, Antonio Lamer, leads it through the 1990s will soon show if this last factor is the critical one.

Conclusion

The nine judges of the Supreme Court of Canada represent the apex of the Canadian judicial pyramid. For much of its 115 years of existence, it has languished in a not entirely undeserved obscurity, very much in the shadow of the British Judicial Committee of the Privy Council to which Canadian legal cases could be appealed, often bypassing the Supreme Court in the process. Only in 1949 did the Court become supreme in fact as well as in name, and only in the 1970s did it begin to occupy the position of prestige and significance on the national scene that its supporters had long hoped for. With the high profile has come considerable public exposure on matters of serious controversy, and the burden of this mixed blessing is what the Court must continue to confront in the 1990s.

We know something of the decision–making processes of the Supreme Court of Canada, which has responded to its new prominence by a willingness to make public the way that it approaches its new responsibilities. We know that it prefers to deal with as many cases as possible with large panels, often the full court of nine members; and we know that it has exhibited a strong tendency toward consensual rather than individualist processes in its decision–making, as evidenced by an increase in the proportion of unanimous decisions. We have speculated on the possible causes of this tendency, but without being able to predict firmly whether it is likely to continue or to diminish.

In a real sense, the strength of the Supreme Court of Canada is also its weakness. Because it controls its own docket, and because its judges have not surrendered considerable discretion and initiative to their own clerks, the Supreme Court of Canada decides only a small number of cases (80 to 125) per year, almost all of which are appeals by leave, meaning that the Supreme Court has decided to consider them for the importance of the legal issues they raise. Members of the Court can concentrate their considerable legal talents on this relatively small package of cases, and generate thoughtful, well–researched decisions. Their performance with regard to the new Charter, for example, has been impressive. But the price the Court pays is the obvious one: namely the small number of cases that it is able to handle each year, even as the caseloads of the provincial appeal courts have undergone a major increase. For every provincial appeal court decision reviewed by the Supreme Court in the early 1990s, there are 99 others left unexamined.

The impact of the Supreme Court on the provincial appeal judges, and through them on the trial judges, therefore depends on the role of precedent — that is, the principle that judges should base their decisions on the legal rules enunciated by the judges of superior courts.

Part III

Judicial Law–Making and Court Reform

8

The Problem of Precedent: Departing and Distinguishing

At the core of the English common law, and therefore of the Canadian law that is so closely modelled upon it, is the notion of precedent — the idea that the law is discovered, not made, and the primary place where it has been discovered and can be retrieved by lawyers and by judges is in the written reasons for judgment of other common law judges.

This an inherently decentralized view of the law, because there are thousands of common law judges in Canada alone, and thousands more in the other common law jurisdictions of the world. If we add to this the fact that past as well as recent judicial decisions can be cited as precedents, we can reasonably describe the sources of the common law as all but infinite. Small wonder that most of us feel daunted and overwhelmed by the complexity and the scope of law, and readily surrender to the knowledge and authority of the expert.

But the other reality of the Canadian common law system is and always has been the familiar hierarchy of courts, which can be diagrammed as a pyramid with the pure provincial courts on the bottom and the Supreme Court of Canada (since 1949) on the top. By drawing arrows flowing up through this hierarchy we can trace the flow of appeals through the system, with the "higher" courts having the power to reverse, to vary, or to "quash" (that is, annul and send back for retrial) the decision of the lower court. Of course, a higher court can also dismiss an appeal and thereby uphold the lower court decision, which is what usually happens. If we reverse the arrows to flow from the top of the pyramid down toward the bottom, we have neatly diagrammed the concept of binding precedent, which is the way in which the centralized and hierarchical structure of our courts is reconciled to the essential decentralization of common law precedent.

To put the point briefly: in a common law jurisdiction, a judge follows the precedent decisions of other judges because (functionally) this contributes to continuity and stability within the judicial system, and to the principle that similar cases should be decided similarly. For judges personally, the principle recognizes that the insights of fellow judges are helpful in dealing with difficult or unusual situations. However, not all precedent decisions count the same, and the decision of a court to which the judge's decision could be appealed (either directly, or by several sequential appeals) carries significantly greater weight.

By precedent, we do not simply mean the *outcome* of the case (guilty or not guilty, liable or not liable), any more than we narrow things down to the final score when we talk about the championship game of our favourite sport. Rather, what judges look for are the principles of law and the constant fine–tuning of definitions and rules that goes on when the angular purities of the law confront the lumpy contours of daily human life. But some judicial decisions take the form of lengthy essays on the law, touching on a multitude of legal points and niceties; "following" a precedent decision is sometimes as simple and straightforward as reading a simple "how–to" manual but often it is far more complicated and difficult. In other words, the simple diagram of binding precedent we've suggested is too simple; it does not explain the process of the transmission of ideas from upper to lower courts, but only outlines the terms in which that explanation is to be sought.

Let us illustrate what we mean by "the problem of precedent". First, consider two different ideal types of Supreme Court of Canada decisions. These two types are really polar extremes, between which actual examples will be ranged on a continuum. Decision A is a unanimous decision by the Court; it is delivered by a single judge in a 15–page judgment, carefully and logically written; it builds upon a line of cases, tying together strands of judicial interpretation and doctrine that have been emerging for some time; and it has been followed up by two or three subsequent decisions that uphold its central principle but clarify related problems that have arisen.

Decision B is a decision of a badly fragmented Court, the seven judges coalescing behind no fewer than four different opinions that take strong exception to one another, a majority of them voting to uphold the provincial appeal court decision but for sharply different reasons. Let us further suppose that this decision does not address a number of collateral legal issues, or addresses them in a confused manner. The decision itself came out of the blue, the result surprising legal observers and meshing poorly with previous jurisprudence; and the Court has refused leave to appeal for several cases that seemed well–designed to permit a clarification of the questions raised.

No lawyer or judge would have trouble giving a dozen examples of each type, or of any point along the continuum between them. In principle, both A and B are decisions of the Supreme Court of Canada, binding precedent for all the judges of all lower courts. In practice, A will (and should) carry considerably more weight, and B will probably tend to be neglected — not as an exercise of judicial insubordination, but as the application of simple common sense.

There has been considerable research in the United States (see, for example, the collection edited by Becker and Feeley) on the extent to which Supreme Court decisions are in fact followed by the lower courts. In general, the researchers have found that the transmission belts of judicial doctrine that link higher and lower courts are not as tight as legal theory would have it, and that the factors contributing to the strength or weakness of higher court rulings can be discovered and described. We know of no comparable literature in Canada; our analysis of interviews with a random selection of judges is at best a limited beginning.

To highlight the problem of precedent from a different angle, imagine that you are a provincial superior trial judge, and that after years of distinguished legal practice you have accepted appointment to the bench as a service to the law and to your society. (The idealistic motives are convincing, because we know you didn't take the appointment for the money.) You are sworn to provide the fairest possible decision according to law to the individuals whose disputes march through your courts one after the other, and you take your duties seriously, as almost all judges do. Is it a fair or a credible representation to suggest that you are satisfied if you find a solid relevant sentence in a higher court decision, and simply echo it? Given that the appeal court decisions "from the top" can so often be divided or unclear, and that the trial court decisions "on the bottom" are made by dedicated and experienced legal professionals proudly aware of their own independence, this is not likely to be the case.

Rather, the key to understanding the operations of the hierarchical Canadian court system lies in a balanced understanding of the notion of precedent, and in the tension between obedient subordination and independent judgment that it engenders. However, in questioning judges about the extent to which they follow precedents, we found that we confronted them with a dilemma in the form of a question that had two wrong answers and no right one. To announce a powerful role for binding precedent and a strong reluctance ever to evade it has overtones unattractive to most judicial professionals, as if they were unwilling to think or decide for themselves. Conversely, too opportunistic an attitude toward the use of precedent and too great a readiness to substitute one's own judgment for that of a higher court smacks of judicial insubordination and a disrespect for law. From the sometimes reluctant and always carefully nuanced responses of judges to this set of questions, we will try to provide a realistic description of the role of precedent in the contemporary Canadian court system.

The Value of Precedent

When we bluntly asked the Alberta judges, "What is the value of precedent or *stare decisis*?" a solid majority spoke of precedent as an important and valuable part of judicial decision–making. We asked them how they felt about the suggestion (taken from Parker's introductory criminal law textbook) that "A good argument could be made for abolishing the use of precedents in all criminal cases because the words of the Code should be interpreted with the predicament of this accused only in mind." Most judges rejected the idea out of hand.

> Precedent is like having someone give you advice, or blaze a trail. (Provincial Court judge)

> Whenever a question of law is at issue precedent is very valuable because citations and quotations are the only way to resolve it. (Provincial Court judge)

> I came from a commercial law firm and therefore used precedent a lot as a lawyer, so that style has simply carried over to the way that I perform as a judge. I just can't imagine functioning without precedent. (Court of Queen's Bench judge)

Nine judges were somewhat more sympathetic with the idea contained in the quote from Parker, even if they could not accept it altogether. All were Provincial Court judges, mainly in the family and juvenile Division. (In 1984, as a result of the federal Young Offender's Act, Youth Court replaced Juvenile Court in Alberta as in other provinces, but all juvenile court judges stayed on only with a change in their title.)

> In technical questions, precedent is absolutely critical, it is invaluable. In more practical and judgmental matters such as custody and child welfare and maintenance, precedent doesn't help much. (Provincial Family and Juvenile judge)

> If another case is very similar, then you can use it [precedent], otherwise it doesn't help much, and the rule of precedent can create real problems if you try to apply it too flatly. (Provincial Court judge)

> Precedent is useful just in the small percentage of cases where there is a question of law, just in the grey areas, or in areas that don't come up very often. Once you get used to

it and develop your own routine, you don't have to consult precedents very often. (Provincial Court judge)

The different caseload and responsibilities of the Provincial Court and the superior courts are again highlighted by the responses of judges to a question about which courts they rely on as preferred sources of precedents. These responses are shown in Table 8.1. Of the Provincial Court judges, only two mentioned anything other than the three courts directly above them — that is, the Alberta Court of Queen's Bench, the Alberta Court of Appeal, and the Supreme Court of Canada. As well, some half dozen Provincial Court judges indicated that even Supreme Court of Canada decisions were rarely relevant to the sorts of cases that they decided, and so they seldom had to consult them. In contrast, only two of the Court of Queen's Bench judges did *not* cite some other court in addition to the courts directly above them: that is, the Alberta Court of Appeal and the Supreme Court.

This result is what would be expected given the nature of the jurisdiction and caseloads of judges on the various levels. Provincial Court judges deal with cases that are less likely to raise difficult questions of law and they must deal with them within a restricted time frame; they are less likely to have either the need or the time to consult a range of precedents, and when they do so, they are more likely to be able to find a satisfactory guide in the decisions of courts directly above them in the line of appeal. Superior trial judges deal with more difficult questions of law within a broader time frame; they are more likely to have the need and the time to consult precedents, and they are more likely to be confronted by questions difficult or unusual enough to call for a wider range of citations.

Other than courts higher in the appeals hierarchy, the most frequently mentioned category was other Canadian appeal courts, with Ontario's mentioned by the largest number of judges. Other Commonwealth courts, especially the higher English courts, were mentioned by a comparable number of judges, although court of appeal judges are more likely to make the suggestion than are trial court judges. Only one judge other than an appeal judge mentioned U.S. precedents. Three judges spoke of checking European court sources, especially on Charter cases, and a single judge spoke highly of some of the justices on the South African court. The conclusion that suggests itself is that (as might be expected) the higher the court, the more frequent and the wider the range of the judges' preferred sources.

Table 8.1 Courts Cited by Alberta Judges as Preferred Sources for Precedents				
	Provincial Court	Queen's Bench	Court of Appeal	All Judges
Supreme Court of Canada	17	19	7	43
Alberta Court of Appeal	18	20	na	38
Alberta Queen's Bench	17	na	na	17
Other Canadian appeal courts:				
Ontario	2	14	3	19
B.C.	0	4	2	6
Manitoba	0	4	1	5
Saskatchewan	0	4	1	5
Quebec	0	3	1	4
N.S.	0	3	0	3
United Kingdom	1	7	9	17
Australia	0	3	4	7
New Zealand	0	1	4	5
United States	0	1	7	8
Europe(charter)	0	2	1	3
South Africa	0	0	1	1
Never consult U.S.	0	2	1	3
Never consult British Columbia	1	3	0	4
n =	21	20	10	51

How strictly are precedents followed?
Departing and Distinguishing

A significant amount of research has been done in the United States on judicial impact theory — that is, on the extent to which the impact of an appeal court decision is or is not modified or resisted in the process of being transmitted through the trial courts to the relevant public. If the strict implications of the rule of precedent and *stare decisis* are that the lower courts operate as a transmission belt conveying appeal court decisions neutrally and automatically through the system, both common sense and actual practice suggest that this is an ideal from which there is considerable opportunity for departure; to extend the metaphor, the transmission belt may not be all that tight. Two items in our questionnaire (one on willingness to depart from appeal court decisions, and a second on the attitude toward how and when to distinguish decisions) tap the judges' impressions of how tight the transmission belt is for the Alberta judiciary.

Of the trial judges interviewed in Alberta, 29 — or three–quarters — indicated that they would *never* depart from a decision of a higher appeal court, even if they disagreed or had serious reservations about it. For these judges, the doctrine of *stare decisis* firmly applies in its most literal terms, and the principles of appeal court doctrines are to be carefully recognized and scrupulously followed at the trial court level.

For 16 of these judges, the duty to follow precedent strictly is stated very flatly and unambiguously, and we consider these judges to be *loyal followers* of precedent:

I am professionally bound to follow the decision of higher courts, although I am not bound on *obiter*. I can ascertain from reading what the basic principle is, and I will not depart from that philosophical direction regardless of my personal feelings. But I will distinguish on the nit–picking things that are really not the central thrust of the decision. (Court of Queen's Bench judge)

Binding means binding; the public is entitled to certainty and consistency in the law. (Provincial Court judge)

The Supreme Court of Canada must be followed; the litigant is entitled to that, and the judge is not entitled to do anything else. (Court of Queen's Bench judge)

Six other judges spoke of their unwillingness to depart in such nuanced terms that we consider them *reluctant followers* of precedent:

I am still in the early stages of being a judge and feeling my way through on this kind of thing, so I am reluctant to stretch the limits too much. I have had some real problems with incest cases, and with the guideline decisions from the Court of Appeal; I still tend to think of it as punishing the family more than the offender, and I have real doubts about the sentencing tactics. I try to get around whenever I can, but it is more a question of shading differences than simply not following. (Court of Queen's Bench judge)

If I disagreed with Supreme Court or Court of Appeal, I would reluctantly follow, and possibly if I felt very strongly about it, I would indicate and defend my reluctance. In a really strong situation, I might go out of my way to distinguish, because you can always distinguish if you want to although it won't always hold up on appeal. (Court of Queen's Bench judge)

The most that you can do is to build on dissents for future change; Laskin's dissents used to be a pretty good source for this. The trial judge must follow binding precedent, but can add qualifiers, such as "I am aware that the law is such–and–such, but I also take note that..." and then stick something in from a dissent. If the guy wants to appeal, give him something to hang his hat on. (Court of Queen's Bench judge)

Seven judges indicated that they would not depart from a higher court decision, but in terms far short of enthusiastic loyalty. We think of them as evading precedent within the formal rules of precedent, the rhetoric of firm adherence juxtaposed to a readiness to ignore or gloss over unattractive or inconvenient precedents. This group consists almost entirely of Provincial Court judges, perhaps because this is the level most ready to feel that a degree of flexibility is necessitated by their proximity to (and the appeal court's remoteness from) the often sordid realities of everyday life. In some cases, their reluctance to closely follow higher court decisions arose less from principled objection than from a feeling that the appeal courts were too unrealistic in their expectations and had no idea what it was really like to conduct a trial. (Given the high proportion of appeal court judges who have been elevated from the superior court trial benches, this is a somewhat surprising complaint.) We call this group *evading followers*, with the paradoxical overtones intentional.

> I would never depart, but would distinguish cheerfully. (Provincial Court judge)

> I believe in the practical approach — if you have a situation where the law as a result of precedent is not favourable to the interests of the accused, then you have to distinguish; this happens regularly, and it is never hard to find the grounds. (Provincial Court judge)

> All trial courts in Canada have some real trouble with some appeal court decisions, and there was one case in particular where we had to work pretty hard to distinguish it out of existence. (Provincial Court judge)

> This is not a hypothetical question. I have disagreed profoundly with decisions of Courts of Appeal. I have to respect them, but I can usually work around them. This is not very frequently a problem, because our court doesn't deal with as many legal technicalities as other courts tend to. (Provincial Court judge)

If a large majority of judges indicated that they would follow even higher court decisions with which they disagreed, albeit with some reluctance, other trial judges spoke explicitly of a more independent role. Two judges, one on each of the trial benches, said they would be willing simply to ignore a higher court decision if they felt strongly enough about it. For these judges, the transmission belt is very loose indeed; we will call them *departers*.

> I have done it, because I feel I have to do it if someone is being hurt by following the precedent; I'll do it if I think it

is the just thing to do, but I have to feel pretty strongly about it. (Provincial Court judge)

The Court of Appeal can always reverse, so in principle I would be willing to ignore a precedent if I fundamentally disagreed with it. But the question is hypothetical, the situation has never arisen. (Court of Queen's Bench judge)

But an alternative point of view was put in terms neither of directly following nor explicitly defying higher court decisions. Instead, this view presented the process of precedent and of judicial decision–making generally as a matter of discussion and persuasion in which both trial and appeal courts participated. A higher court decision was not a command but a reasoned argument, calling not for blind obedience but for a choice between agreement and reasoned dissent. Ten judges, seven of them from the Court of Queen's Bench, rejected the follow/depart dichotomy in favour of a perception of a give–and–take process; we will call them *debaters*.

You have to treat it as an ongoing dialogue. In my judgments, I am giving reasons for applying the law the way I have applied it. If the Court of Appeal reverses me, I just think of it as not having been convinced by my reasons and therefore applying its own rationale. If they don't persuade me, then in subsequent cases I try to get back some of the difference, try to do a better job of persuading the Court of Appeal why I think it should be done my way. The dialogue goes back and forth, not in terms of my explicitly rejecting Court of Appeal decisions, but not in terms of treating them as engraved on tablets of stone either, just nibbling away at the differences and trying to nudge them onto a different track closer to the one that I have in mind. (Court of Queen's Bench judge)

You have to be very cautious. There has been only one case in 14 years where I felt I could not follow the higher court decision. I departed from it and explained why, and lost on appeal. Once you are overturned, the point has been made and you don't do it any more. (Provincial Court judge)

Table 8.2 presents the responses of trial judges to the question about departing from appeal court precedents. The order of the categories can be read as a continuum of increasing departure from the official norm of strict adherence.

Table 8.2 Following/Departing Higher Court Precedent by type of court

Judge's View of Precedent	Court of Queen's Bench (procedural)*	All Provincial Court Judges	Provincial Court: Criminal & Small Claims (decisional)*	Provincial Court: Family & Youth (diagnostic)*	Total
loyal followers	9	7	(6)	(1)	16
reluctant followers	4	2	(2)		6
evading followers	0	7	(2)	(5)	7
debaters	7	3	(3)	(0)	10
departers	1	1		(1)	2
Total:	21	20	(13)	(7)	41

* These categories were developed by Kerwin, Henderson, and Baar, as noted in chapter 5.

The most distinctive group seems to be the diagnostic court judges, most of whom can be categorized as "evading followers." Other trial judges, both Queen's Bench (procedural) and Provincial Court (decisional), split between the loyal followers and the debaters (the first group being marginally larger for Court of Queen's Bench and significantly larger for Provincial Court). If we take the continuum literally to create an Adherence Index by assigning a value of 1 for loyal followers, 2 for reluctant followers, and so on through a value of 5 for departers, then the average value for all trial judges is 2.4, while the average value for diagnostic judges is 3.0.

Length of service on the bench does not seem to alter the response to the question of following or departing from higher court precedent. The clustering of evading followers in the more senior levels is entirely an artefact of the happenstance that the

Table 8.3 Following/Departing Appeal Court Decisions, by length of service on bench					
Orientation Toward Precedent					
Length of Service Categories	loyal followers	reluctant followers	evading followers	debaters	departers
transition (<5 yrs)	8	3	1	4	1
established (6–15 yrs)	6	3	3	4	1
committed (16+ yrs)	3	–	3	2	–
abstainers (never make law)	10	2	2	4	–
dabblers (sometimes make law)	5	4	4	5	2
enthusiasts (often make law)	1	–	1	1	–

diagnostic judges interviewed also cluster in the longer service categories. The average value for transition judges is 2.2, for established judges 2.5, and for committed judges 2.5, entirely consistent with the hypothesis that length of service makes no difference to the response. (If we exclude diagnostic judges, the average response for transition judges is 2.2, for established judges 2.3, and for committed judges 2.0.) This is counter–intuitive, in that we anticipated that longer–serving judges would show a greater degree of independence as a result of their growing experience and concomitantly increasing confidence in their own knowledge of the law, as well as a hands–on awareness that appeal judges are not infallible.

How Do Judges Depart from Precedent?
Ignoring precedent is the most straightforward and self–conscious form of treating higher court precedents with the automatic lock–step adherence that the formal doctrine of *stare decisis* seems to imply. Judges ought not to ignore precedents; according to the doctrine of *stare decisis*, all relevant precedents deserve mention in judicial decisions.

However, as all lawyers know, even at the level of the Supreme Court of Canada obvious precedents are sometimes simply not mentioned in the decision, and sometimes the omission is intentional. It is also possible to take note of a precedent authority, but to declare it "per incuriam," meaning that it has been discovered that the judges in the precedent case did not have as much relevant information before them as the current court does, and that the previous judges surely would have decided differently if they had been fully informed. (Freely translated, "per incuriam" means "the other court goofed"; the Supreme Court tends to use more oblique phrases such as "this is no longer good law" which at least does the courtesy of assuming that it once was). However, this sort of judicial finger pointing is unusual, the more so by a trial judge toward an appeal court.

A further way of evading precedent concerns the distinction between *ratio decidendi* — an integral and logically essential part of the reasons for the decisions — and *obiter dicta* — judicial asides in the written decision of no binding effect. However, in 1980 the Supreme Court of Canada suggested in *Sellars v. The Queen* [26] that anything it said in the case, whether *obiter* or *ratio*, was binding on lower courts. As a result, this distinction may no longer be so important, at least for Canadian jurisprudence.

Another device (its function unambiguously stated by the provincial judge who volunteered "I would never depart, but would distinguish cheerfully") is that of distinguishing a higher court decision. Gerald Gall defines distinguishing: "If [a judge] finds that the precedent case has a material fact or facts absent in the instant case, or alternatively, the instant case contains a material fact or facts absent in the precedent case, he [or she] will then be in the position to deny the necessity of following the precedent case." We found a very sharp division between two different sets of judges in the way that they spoke about distinguishing — whether it was a technical exercise conducted impersonally on perfectly objective criteria, or whether it was a discretionary exercise that left the judge a degree of latitude to be employed for a variety of purposes.

When asked, "When and how do you distinguish a binding precedent?" a majority of judges gave responses that were narrowly technical and careful; we call these judges *technicians*.

You have to be very cautious how you distinguish; it would almost put you in contempt of the higher court to ignore its decision or to refuse to follow it just because you disagreed. (Provincial Court judge)

You distinguish only where the facts are clearly different; distinguishing is not a device for getting around things you don't like. (Court of Queen's Bench judge)

You will look very hard for an interpretation that makes sense for a decision of a higher court that looks bloody wrong, but you can't go out of your way to distinguish in a contrived way. (Court of Queen's Bench judge)

However, even the wording employed by many of the 22 judges who gave this response — you cannot or should not distinguish simply in order to avoid or evade a precedent — implies an awareness of the opportunity to get around an unwelcome or unattractive precedent. Fourteen other judges indicated, often very candidly, that they sometimes used the devise of distinguishing in precisely this way; we call these judges *opportunists*.

It is almost always possible to distinguish fairly convincingly if you really feel that you have to. This has happened to me personally, and I know from reading other judgments that it happens in other courts; for example, a judge may just dismiss a Supreme Court decision as obiter to get around it when it is perfectly clear it wasn't obiter at all, but we don't do that sort of thing in Alberta. (Court of Queen's Bench judge)

There are many ways to distinguish, and you can usually get around a decision if you really want to. (Provincial Court judge)

If I don't like the precedent, then I distinguish; it is never hard. (Provincial Court judge)

**Table 8.4 Attitude Toward Use of Distinguishing, by
Degree to which Appeal Precedents are Followed.**

Orientation Toward Precedent	technicians	opportunists	no response
loyal followers	11	3	2
reluctant followers	5	1	–
evasive followers	–	7	–
debaters	5	3	2
departers	1	–	1

Table 8.4 gives the breakdown between technicians and opportunists for the various types of courts. (Five judges gave responses
to the question on distinguishing which were not really on the
topic, and which could not be categorized in this way.)

The style in the use of distinguishing seems to have some
connection with the degree of loyalty in following appeal court
decisions. The average Adherence Index for technicians is 2.1,
and that for opportunists is 2.7. Most loyal followers of upper
court precedent are also technicians in the use of distinguishing.
The overlapping of these two groups seems logically plausible,
although it is surprising that Court of Queen's Bench judges
outnumber provincial judges by almost two to one in this group
of loyal followers and technicians. It approaches tautology to
observe that evasive followers are always opportunists for the
simple reason that a generous use of the device of distinguishing
is the way that they avoid the impact of unattractive or unconvinc-
ing higher court precedent. These two groups — loyal fol-
lowers/technicians, and evasive followers/opportunists — account
for fully one–half of the judges responding to both questions.

When we link the questions about departing and distinguishing,
we can identify three major blocks of trial judges. The first bloc,
including 16 judges (twice as many from the Provincial Court as
from the Court of Queen's Bench) are either loyal followers or
reluctant followers of higher court decisions. The second group,
including ten judges (mostly Court of Queen's Bench) treats precedent as an ongoing conversation, and an unattractive precedent
as an invitation to join the conversation. This group divides on the
question of whether distinguishing is to be treated technically or
opportunistically. The third group, including seven long–serving

judges — all on Provincial Court and mostly in the family and juvenile division — are unwilling to depart openly from precedent but opportunistic in the use of distinguishing as a way of avoiding unattractive precedents.

Conclusion

Because the appeal courts cannot review every decision made by every trial court theoretically under their appellate jurisdiction, binding precedent (the rule that lower courts must follow the decisions of the courts above them in the judicial hierarchy) is the effective process whereby judicial doctrines of the provincial courts of appeal and the Supreme Court of Canada are transmitted throughout the court system.

Although it constituted something of a loaded question (what judges would dare consider themselves not bound by binding precedent?), our query about the value of precedent and the possibility of departing from precedent drew a variety of thoughtful and carefully nuanced replies. We found some judges who followed faithfully (if not always happily), others who would follow their conscience if it led them away from the higher court decision, and still others who would cheerfully match their alternative interpretation against that of the higher court in an ongoing dialogue.

Although most judges treated distinguishing in a technical fashion governed strictly by objective rules, others candidly admitted the degree of discretion involved in distinguishing and used it more opportunistically. Our interviews clearly demonstrate the need for the kinds of studies concerning judicial impact and adherence to precedent that have been conducted extensively in the United States, to gain an understanding of the substantive and contextual factors that enhance or diminish the following of appeal court precedents by trial judges.

9

Should Judges Be Legislators?

How often do we hear journalists rave, in their infinite wisdom, about a 'government of judges' that would have taken over the country; an insidious power held by nine unknowns, half–gods or demons, for whom no–one voted and that are really hard to get rid of?

Their argument goes something like this: The Charter makes it illegal for governments to infringe upon certain personal rights and freedoms. But the Supreme Court of Canada now has the final word in determining just what those rights and freedoms are. Therefore, the Supreme Court is in fact making the law rather than Parliament or the provincial legislatures.

— Madame Justice Claire L'Heureux–Dubé

When the law is unclear — as it often must be because of the enormous variety of situations that can arise — judges must clarify it before they can apply it. The essence of law is definition, not command, and an important part of the written reasons for judicial decisions is the honing and polishing of definitions. Judges have always had this job to do, and the more vague and general the law, the more that judges "legislate." To a certain extent, this "filling in the cracks" is simply part of the division of labour between legislature and judiciary, and it would be irresponsible for the judges to upset the balance by backing away from this duty.

This legislative or policy–making role of judges becomes more visible and more critical when the law being interpreted is part of the Constitution. Constitutional cases attract more media attention and thereby create a more intense, immediate, and widespread public reaction, both from those who support and those who oppose the substance of the court's decision. In addition, because constitutions can sometimes be difficult to amend (as Canadians have recently discovered thanks to Meech Lake), or are unlikely to be amended due to the other priorities that governments have, judges often have the "final word" about what the constitution means. To refer again to an example used in our preface: when a judge decides that preventing an animal from being "at large" may not require the use of a leash (honing the definition of "at large"), that is one thing; but when a panel of Supreme Court judges decides that fundamental justice requires a hearing in person, dismantling the country's procedure for refugee review [27], that is something else.

Given that all judges are legislators to some extent, they do have a certain amount of choice about how they will shape the law. Some judges believe that they should reduce this choice to a minimum and make law as little as possible. To paraphrase Edmund Burke, they believe that if it is not necessary to legislate, then it is necessary not to legislate. An example of a judge who believed strongly in judicial restraint is (now retired) Supreme Court Justice William McIntyre. In the Morgentaler case [23], McIntyre wrote that there was no clear "right to an abortion" contained in Section 7 of the Charter that guarantees to "everyone" the right to "security of the person." As a result, he said that judges should interpret Section 7 narrowly and let Parliament's abortion legislation stand until Parliament itself decided to change it: "The courts must confine themselves to such democratic values as are clearly found and expressed in the Charter." The majority of judges disagreed. They thought that Canadians wanted a broad interpretation of Section 7, and they saw in the old abortion law a clear violation of women's right to security of the person. They struck down the abortion law, a decision that had the same effect as if Parliament had repealed it.

In another contrasting case, the Supreme Court was faced with having to decide whether the right to "freedom of association" in Section 2 of the Charter included a union's right to strike.[18] Again, McIntyre advocated a restrained approach to the interpretation of the Charter. Since "freedom of association" did not clearly include a right to strike, the courts should interpret the Charter narrowly and defer to the labour legislation already put in place by Parliament and provincial legislatures. This time the majority of the Court agreed with him. Chief Justice Brian Dickson and Justice Bertha Wilson dissented, arguing that unless unions had a right to strike (except with regard to essential services), the right of union members to associate with each other was hollow.

Law–maker or law–interpreter?

Do judges simply interpret the law, or do they make law? In this form, of course, the question is oversimplified, even absurd. The source of the formal documents that we can identify as law is the legislature, in the form of statutes, or the executive, in the form of regulations. Clearly, judges do not "make" law in the same sense that legislatures or cabinets do.

However, properly translated, the question is more about the relative role and function of judges and other legal officials, and understood in these terms it is neither absurd nor simple. Do judges "simply" interpret the law — that is, extract the meaning of the framers from a document and apply it to the circumstances before them — or do they under some circumstances and to some extent reach beyond the document to some other source of value and meaning? Is law simply what someone else puts on a piece of paper, passively applied from the bench, or does the judge legitimately and necessarily play an active rule in creating the final meaning of the rule–as–actually–applied? This active role, too, is not always a case of judges substituting their own will and preferences for those of the legislature; if judges did not "make law" we might find that many law cases ended with a judge declaring that the law is not sufficiently clear to apply to the situation at hand, an outcome that would be even more frustrating.

The distinction between "making" law and "interpreting" law is a familiar one in the legal community. None of the judges interviewed objected to the question or thought it inappropriate, although two said it was too abstract to permit an answer, and many said it was difficult to answer in such dichotomous terms. By a considerable margin, Alberta judges preferred to see themselves primarily in the role of law–interpreter, although their responses can be divided into three distinct and different categories: "abstainers" (no law–making role); "dabblers" (occasional law–making role) and "enthusiasts" (frequent law–making role). Not surprisingly, the judges' responses were to some extent a function of the court on which they served.

Table 9.1 Approach to Law–Making by Bench

Orientation to law–making role	Court of Appeal	Queen's Bench	Provincial Court	Total
abstainers	–	8	10	18
dabblers	5	11	9	25
enthusiasts	5	2	1	8
Total:	10	21	20	51

"The Abstainers": No Law–Making Role

Eighteen judges, all from the trial benches, flatly rejected any significant law–making role whatever. As one of them said, "The Appeal Court may have some limited scope for law–making, but the trial courts have none at all." For these judges, it was their duty to find the facts and to apply the law, and not to go beyond this approach in any way.

> I am only and definitely an interpreter of the law. This is an important part of the principle of the independence of the judiciary; the legislature makes the law and the judges apply it. This is why the judiciary is independent and the legislature isn't, and any judge who goes beyond this is in error. I do not think that the role is changing over time, or that the Charter makes any difference to this principle.

I see myself as clearly and definitely an interpreter of the law. We often run into cases where we think the law is bad, but we must apply it as we find it; the judge can suggest how the law should be changed, but that is as far as he should go. The Charter will give the judges more work and problems, but the role remains the same.

Although our questionnaire made no explicit reference to the Charter of Rights, most judges interpreted the question as relating to the Charter's impact and reiterated the limited role of the trial judge even in this new context. This is not, of course, to imply that these judges were stolid or unimaginative, because all spoke of unusual cases mixed in with the more routine points of law that arose before them, and of the intellectual challenge of resolving the questions that they raised. Instead, it was more a question of the judge's frame of mind. One judge said, "It might be true from one point of view that interpreting in a novel situation is a kind of 'making' law, but the judge shouldn't think, 'I am making law.' You have to be less wilful and more passive about it."

"The Dabblers": Some Law–Making Role

Half of the appeal judges and almost all of the trial judges who did not reject a law–making role altogether described themselves in a way that we have chosen to label as "dabblers": that is, they saw themselves primarily as interpreters of the law, but conceded that they saw some significant scope — and for some a growing scope — for a more extensive role.

Half of the dabblers saw the dividing line between the two roles as being fairly firm, to be crossed only on infrequent and unusual occasions. Although judges possess some discretion, and the opportunity for the exercise of judicial power this involves, they should not be too anxious to use it. "Only in the most unusual of circumstances would I make law, and hard cases make bad law," one judge said. For these individuals, common law lawyers and judges have always had "a touch of the legislator" and this is how the common law evolves, but by the same logic the creativity should be restrained and moderate, patiently incremental rather than boldly original. The law–making role of judges is largely "by default" because legislatures move slowly and sometimes "deliberately dump a problem in the lap of the court by being vague."

In general, the dabblers concede that judges must and do make law, sometimes, but they add to this that judges should also be as passive as they can be, and no more (but no less) aggressive in drawing out or forcing meaning than they have to be.

> Too many judges want to strive for a particular result, but this is a bastardization of the judicial process. Only rarely is there a real choice; 99.7 per cent of the time, it is enough to apply straightforward self–evident law, and the case will determine its own outcome. This role is not changing, although the Charter gives greater opportunity to those who are already so inclined.

Other judges, mostly from the appeal bench, similarly stressed the law–interpreting role but spoke with candour of a law–making role that was a regular part — and for some an increasing part — of their conception of the duty of a judge. They acknowledged that there was a line between the two types of judicial role, but they thought it was one that a judge had to be prepared to cross as the situation required, and that this would not happen infrequently.

> All courts make law, but we on the Court of Appeal do so more than others. Judges are reluctant virgins, reluctant to admit that they make law and that they are perceived as making law. The law–making role of judges is increasing steadily. This would be so even without the Charter, but it is even more so the case because of it. (Court of Appeal judge)

> A judge has to be more than an interpreter of the law. You cannot just interpret what the legislators said because you know more about the circumstances in which the law is being applied than they could have known. The great judges of the past made law, and that was a good thing. In some

cases, judges have to make law, although they should not go out of their way to do so. I get the impression that many judges think of themselves as interpreters of the law, but I have no idea why this is the case. I think, and hope, that the Charter may reverse this tendency. (Court of Queen's Bench judge)

Others, mostly trial judges, described things differently, seeing themselves basically as interpreters of the law who are obliged by the entrenchment of the Charter to play a larger role regardless of their personal inclinations. To whatever extent there might have been a line drawn in the past between interpreting law and making law, the Charter had eroded this distinction. There is "no question but that the Charter gives all judges an expanded role" and that "judges will be forced to make law to a greater extent than has been the case in the past."

At the time the interviews were conducted, the Charter had been in place for only one or two years, and most of the judges were surprised about how little impact it had on the number and the type of cases that they heard; the situation may well have changed since then. A group of trial judges that we interviewed later about the impact of the Charter and the Young Offenders Act said that the broader provisions for legal representation and the greater opportunities for raising technical questions had both served to increase the amount of court time needed to dispose of the average case. (Gabor, Green, and McCormick.)

"The Enthusiasts": Extensive Law–Making

A minority of judges, mostly from the Court of Appeal, were "enthusiasts" who spoke much more confidently of a law–making function that was not something to be tackled only in unusual cases, or only because of the Charter, but rather a major component of a judicial role. "The judge has to be both, and both flow into each other," explained one judge. Or as a Queen's Bench judge put it: "The court is becoming (and for me it already is) a Court of Equity, and I feel this is the right direction to go; the finding in every case should be fair on balance."

For another judge, the legislative process was "just too slow" and this obliged judges to act — to such an extent that they would be letting down the system if they did not seek out adequate remedies through interpretations not contemplated, let alone carefully and explicitly provided for, by the legislature. Law–making is another way of describing a court that is flexible, that can adjust to change in a continuous fashion. According to this judge, the more innovative appeal court judges in England, past and present, served just as effectively as the Charter as a spur in this direction.

Law–Making and Judicial Activism

Although the interviews clearly suggest that many judges see some law–making as a legitimate component of their duties, this by no means implies that they see this as an activist role for the judiciary in promoting the causes of social reform or political challenge. In fact, quite the reverse is true. Most judges, even those who see themselves as law–makers, are extremely reluctant either to let cases before them range far afield to raise broader social issues, or to use the discretion within the law directly to promote such causes. Most feel that "the courts can get themselves into a lot of trouble" by becoming too flexible and permissive in allowing policy arguments, that they "should not let themselves be used" in this sort of effort. One told us, "My basic attitude is: if you want to give a speech, rent a hall. The court is there to apply the law, not to provide a soap box."

This is simply not the job of the courts. If you stop and think about it in those terms, a judge has a lot of power, because the law has a lot of power and the judge declares the law. But the judge merely exercises power, the power is not 'his', and you can keep that distinction only if you are very careful what you let into the courtroom, what you give yourself a chance to apply that power to. (Court of Queen's Bench judge)

Only a minority of judges take the opposite approach, suggesting that taking change in society into consideration is "just part of the law–making function, and you cannot avoid it." Even they

Table 9.2 Judicial Law–Making and Judicial Activism: Alberta Judges

Orientation toward law–making	Orientation to activism or restraint			
	restraint	activism	(no answer)	total
abstainers	12	4	(2)	18
dabblers	16	4	(5)	25
enthusiasts	3	3	(2)	8
Total	31	11	(9)	51

tended to draw an important if somewhat imprecise line. One of them stated, "The court has a real function in defining social issues, but you have to be careful not to be an activist court."

The notions of judicial activism and judicial law–making clearly have some logical connection, but the responses of the judges show that some caution is necessary in linking the two. Judicial restraint and a purely interpretive role seem to come in a logical package, while judicial activism is more congenial to a law–making role; but other combinations are possible as well.

For example, a judge might feel committed to a law–making role but limit this exercise to interpolation or incremental common–sense adjustment rather than the advocacy or encouragement of social change. Conversely, a judge might feel that the only appropriate role is that of interpreting rather than making law, but reveal an openness to social issues and a willingness to be creative in a variety of ways more procedural than substantive. Cross–tabulating the responses of Alberta judges to these two questions shows that the elaboration of this variety of possible responses is more than an exercise in abstract logic.

Most of the judges interviewed who indicated some support for the idea of an activist judicial role on social issues felt that it is seldom or never appropriate for judges to make, as opposed to interpret, the law. Conversely, half of the judges who see law–making as a significant part of the judicial role believe it is inappropriate for judges to promote social change. Clearly, when this set of judges talks of law–making it is more a logical or technical or incremental exercise than a statement of a political or social program.

Although trial judges are even less likely than appeal judges to see a judicial role in social change, this tendency is less pronounced among Provincial Court judges than among Court of Queen's Bench judges. The hierarchy of courts is not also a pure hierarchy of activism. This tendency of Provincial Court judges to be a little more activist than their cousins on the section 96 trial court is perhaps a reflection of a "people's court" mentality. Susan B. Silbey suggests that "the lower courts are more particularistic, empirical, individualized and responsive to local communities" and more willing to respond within the law to "a litigant's perception of his trouble, hurt and pain" than the more procedurally regular and rule–bound higher courts. The responses of the Provincial Court judges we interviewed support this idea.

Clearly, however, it would be misleading to overstate this point. In general, Canadian judges seem to see themselves as having little or no legitimate law–making role (and even more so outside the specific context of Charter challenges), and as equally disengaged from the promotion of social or political causes. Any image of judges thirsting to use the Charter to turn Canadian law and society on its ear is miles wide of the mark. Even a phrase like "reluctant revolutionaries" seems too strong by far to catch their mood.

Supreme Court of Canada Judges

The retired Supreme Court of Canada judges whom we interviewed were for the most part advocates of judicial restraint. One judge, when asked if he saw his role as that of law–maker or law–interpreter, said that it was clearly that of law–interpreter. "I *never* felt my job was to make the law; rather, it was to decide cases according to the law. We have to stick to precedent. It is no part of a judge's function to legislate."

However, when asked if the role of judges was changing he said, "Yes. The Charter of Rights has changed everything." Then he noted, "However, the Supreme Court of Canada is pulling in its horns now. I think they're beginning to realize the danger of writing dramatic general statements. They know now that if they do [write such statements], they'll suffer for it later."

What he was referring to is the fact that the Supreme Court tended to give the Charter a broad application until 1986, after which it began to interpret the Charter in a much more restrained fashion. Of the first 15 Supreme Court decisions under the Charter, to April 1986, the rate of "wins" by persons asserting Charter rights was an astounding 60 per cent. Since 1986, however, according to Peter Russell (1), the rate of individual "wins" has been only around 20 per cent. In the opinion of this retired judge, the Court realized the error of its ways during the first three years after the Charter and adopted a more restrained approach.

Another retired judge also favoured judicial restraint, but for a different set of reasons. "A lot of judges think they are 'Justinians'," he said, referring to the sixth century Byzantine emperor who codified Roman laws. "But there *aren't* any Justinians. The painstaking time which some judges take to set out 'the truth' in lengthy judgments doesn't help anyone. When I was practising as a lawyer before I was appointed to the bench, that became clear to me. I argued a number of cases before the Supreme Court of Canada, and the judges didn't impress me as being much brighter than the average lawyer." From his perspective, judges are in no better a position to "legislate" than legislators, so they ought to defer to the clear intent of the written law.

Bora Laskin was not as sanguine about the willingness and ability of legislatures to take appropriate action to update the law as those who advanced views like the judges mentioned above. His approach was illustrated in a 1976 Supreme Court of Canada decision that dealt with the law of trespass as it had developed through the common law. (*Harrison v. Carswell*, [10]) A group of strikers had been picketing their employer whose office was in a shopping mall, as F.L. Morton relates. Harrison, the manager of the shopping mall, complained and Carswell, a picketer, was charged with trespass and convicted. The case eventually reached the Supreme Court of Canada. No doubt all the members of the Supreme Court realized that the judges who developed the common law of trespass could not possibly have foreseen the era of collective bargaining and shopping malls, and it was obvious that the law needed updating.

Justice Brian Dickson, who wrote for the majority, claimed that it was the job of the legislature to update the law, and the convictions were upheld. "If there is to be any change in this statute law … it would seem to me that such a change must be made by the enacting institution, the Legislature, which is representative of the people and designed to manifest the political will, and not by the Court," Dickson wrote.

Justice Laskin, dissenting, implied in his decision that legislatures were unlikely to deal with such issues, and that the judges had a responsibility to reshape such clearly outdated common law.

> [My] observations … carry into two areas of concern respecting the role of this Court as the final Court in this country in both civil and criminal cases. Those areas are, first, whether this Court must pay mechanical deference to *stare decisis* and, second, whether this Court has a balancing role to play, without yielding place to the Legislature, where an ancient doctrine, in this case trespass, is invoked in a new setting to suppress a lawful activity supported both by legislation and by a well–understood legislative policy…. This Court, above all others in this country, cannot be simply mechanistic about previous decisions, whatever be the respect it would pay to such decisions…. [This Court is] free to depart from previous decisions in order to support the pressing need to examine the present case on its merits.

In our interviews with retired Supreme Court judges, two of the judges mentioned their participation in the court's constitutional decision of 1981 as the highlight of their judicial career. This was clearly a case in which the court was invited to settle a critical policy question — one that was tearing the country apart. What was at issue was Prime Minister Pierre Trudeau's contention that according to convention, the Canadian Parliament *acting alone* could request the British Parliament to amend the Canadian constitution to include an amending formula and the Charter of Rights, and then abdicate the power ever to amend the Canadian constitution again.

Eight of the provinces argued that the convention was that such an amendment could not be requested without the consent of the provinces, and they took the federal government to court over the issue. The majority on the Supreme Court eventually decided that the provinces were right about the convention, but that conventions can be enforced only through the political process and not through the courts. Many regard this decision, which gave a partial win to the provinces and a partial win to the federal government, as the turning point that forced the first ministers back to the conference table where they reached a compromise solution to patriate the constitution.

One judge said that the decision "was a real joy to be part of. It was like a great friendly discussion in which we tried to find what's useful for the country." We asked the other judge whether the judges tried consciously to write a decision that would force the politicians back to the bargaining table. He said, "No. We were given a job to do and we did the best we could with it. I was convinced of the importance of the convention of provincial consent because I thought that it existed. We didn't think of it for political purposes."

What is interesting about these comments from two judges who advocate judicial restraint is that when placed in a clear policy–making role, as in this case, they did not shrink from it or complain. In fact, they say they enjoyed it. It would not be their choice to undertake such a role, but they would not avoid it when it was thrust upon them.

Judicial Background and Judicial Decision–Making

Studies conducted in the United States, according to Sidney S. Ulmer, have found background variables such as social class origin, age, previous political experience, and religion to be useful in predicting discretionary judicial decisions. An analysis of judicial decisions arising out of the Charter of Rights and Freedoms offers a unique opportunity to test the relation between background variables and judicial decision–making. Because the Charter is such a new law, few guiding precedents have been established by higher level courts. And because the wording of much of the Charter is more general than most statutes (in Noel Lyon's delightful phrase "vague but meaningful generalities"), judicial decisions about the application of the Charter involve an unusual amount of discretion about precisely where to draw the line. This being the case, it seems reasonable to assume that Charter decisions, even more so than the more routine and standard judicial decisions, will be a reflection of a judge's character and personal values.

Of the judges in the Alberta judiciary study, 49 had made Charter of Rights decisions up to October 1986. (We are grateful to Professor F.L. Morton of the University of Calgary for providing us with data on the Charter decisions for the Alberta judges.) This is not a high enough number of cases to produce statistically solid generalizations about the relation between background variables and judicial decisions. However, it is enough to allow a tentative comparison of certain background variables with the Charter decisions to receive an indication of whether certain hypotheses are worth pursuing.

First we compared the number of judges who had ruled in favour of an individual's claim against the state, based on a Charter argument, with the number of judges who had never ruled in favour of an individual claim. Of the 49 judges who had decided Charter cases, 20 had ruled in favour of an individual claim at least once, and 29 had always ruled against individual claims. Of the 49 judges who had decided Charter cases, 22 were Provincial Court judges. Of the 20 who had ruled in favour of a Charter claim at least once, 6 were Provincial Court judges, and the other 14 were section 96 judges.

We analysed the relation between Charter decisions and the variables that Ulmer argued might be important in predicting judicial decisions: social class origin, age, previous political experience, and religion. The only variable that resulted in an association which was on the borderline of being statistically significant (that is, probably not due to chance factors) was social class background as measured by the occupation of the judges' fathers. (Of the 49 judges who had made Charter decisions, 46 had indicated to us the occupation of their father.) Table 9.3

Table 9.3 Fathers' Occupations and Charter Decisions

Charter
Record   Father's Occupation

		Farmer–Labour	Professional–Business	Total
At least one	n	4	15	19
claim upheld		21%	78%	100%
No claims	n	14	13	27
upheld		52%	48%	100%
Total	n	18	28	46
		100%	100%	100%

Note: The statistical significance was calculated to be .04, or .07 after a procedure known as the "Yates correction." The significance calculation in this case means that only in about 7 cases out of 100 are such distributions of attitudes likely to be found simply due to chance, and not because social class background is a factor. (The Yates correction is a procedure that helps to compensate for the over–estimation of statistical significance that sometimes occurs in tables like this one, where only two variables with two values each are compared.)

displays the association between the judges' fathers' occupation, and the judges' Charter decisions.

The relation between social class background and Charter decisions appears to be in the opposite direction to what we might intuitively expect. According to these limited data, judges of lower social class origins are the least apt to uphold a Charter claim.

One potential explanation for this possible association is the common view in the social sciences that persons of lower social class origins tend to possess a higher proportion of small "c" conservative attitudes and values than those of the higher social classes. However, a recent survey of the attitudes of Canadians toward civil liberties issues by Paul Sniderman, Joseph Fletcher, Peter Russell, and Phillip Tetlock has cast doubts on this traditional view. It indicates that according to at least some indicators of civil liberties orientation, such as the extent to which the police need extraordinary powers to control crime, the average Canadian is less conservative than the political elites.

Another possible explanation for the association between social class and Charter decisions among Alberta judges is that a judicial decision in favour of an individual Charter claim, to the extent that the judge has discretion, could be interpreted more as an indication of political conservatism than political liberalism. Such an approach is illustrated by decisions such as those in the Canada Elections Act case.[14] In this 1984 decision, Mr. Justice Medhurst of the Alberta Court of Queen's Bench struck down a provision of the Canada Elections Act that prohibited advertising for or against political parties by groups not under the party financial umbrella. This provision had been inserted into the elections act to make it possible to enforce the limits to campaign expenses provisions, and thus promote more equitable public participation in the electoral process by ensuring that the party with the richest supporters does not always win elections for that reason alone. (Greene [1]) Striking down this provision had a "conservative" rather than a "liberal" result.

Other such conservative Charter decisions are those in which criminal code provisions prohibiting certain offenses against women and girls have been struck down because they violate the sexual equality guarantees. As well, there are the many decisions that have benefited middle–class drinking drivers because police failed to inform them of their right to counsel before the breathalyzer test.[29]

Although it seems that it may be promising to develop and test hypotheses about the association between the social class background of judges and their Charter decisions, researchers should give further thought to the obviously complex relation between these variables. The benefits or disadvantages of particular Charter decisions for various groups in society need to be considered in the equation; obviously all Charter decisions do not have the same impact, although as a whole, they may tend to benefit some groups more than others.

Another question requiring analysis is whether judicial orientation toward economic issues accounts for the association between social class and Charter decisions, or whether other factors are more salient — for example the relation between ethnicity and social class. We tested for the association between the ethnicity of judges and their Charter decisions. The ethnicity variable was collapsed to two values: ethnicities associated with the political tradition of liberalism (such as English, Scottish, French), and those not as closely associated with liberalism (such as German,

Ukrainian, Polish). Of 19 cases in which a Charter claim was upheld, 13 were decided by judges whose ethnic origin was closely associated with the liberal tradition.

Because of the close association between ethnicity and religion, the development of hypotheses must consider the variable of religion as well. Our analysis indicated that 14 of 20 cases in which a Charter claim was upheld were decided by judges who adhered to one of the main–line protestant religions.

The two other variables found to have significant predictive value in U.S. studies are age and political activity. Our data indicate that there may be a tendency for older judges to decide in favour of Charter claims more frequently than younger ones. Of 20 judges who decided in favour of a Charter claim, 18 (or 90 per cent) were over 50. In comparison, only 20 of 29 judges (69 per cent) who made no decisions favouring a Charter claim were over 50. Although this tendency may seem counter–intuitive, John Hogarth found that older judges tend to have a "greater feeling of independence, self–reliance, confidence, and moderation." This set of attitudes may be a prerequisite for having the courage to rule unconstitutional a law or administrative action.

Those who have never belonged to a political party may be more likely to rule in favour of a Charter claim. Six of nine judges who reported never having had a political affiliation ruled in favour of an individual Charter claim. Those who had been affiliated with the Progressive Conservative or Social Credit parties were the least likely to uphold a Charter claim. Of seven judges in this category, only one had upheld a Charter claim. Of 38 former Liberals, 13 had upheld a Charter claim.

To explore the relation between judicial backgrounds and judicial decision–making is not to call into question the impartiality of the judiciary, or the ability of individual judges to make carefully reasoned decisions based on law and fact that have little or nothing to do with their backgrounds. Absolute impartiality is an impossibility because of the omnipresence of unconscious biases. What judges are expected to do, wherever possible, is to set aside the biases that they are aware of so that no litigant suffers as a result. Studies of the relation between judicial backgrounds and judicial decision–making, if carried out sensitively and carefully, could assist the judiciary in promoting impartiality by illuminating unconscious biases that may result from past experience. People who are aware of their biases at least have the opportunity to try to neutralize them in a decision–making situation.

The data gathered so far about the relation between judicial backgrounds and Charter of Rights decisions indicate that there may be a strong association between a lower social class background, and not upholding Charter claims. If this association is demonstrated in future research, it will lead to the paradoxical conclusion that the more representative the judges are of the general society (as opposed to just the business and professional classes), the less likely they are to uphold claims under the Charter of Rights — an instrument which some say is supposed to protect the average lower class Canadian from abuse of authority by the rich and powerful.

Conclusion:
The Human Element in the Judicial Process

If judges cannot help but be legislators at times, most take on the role only reluctantly and only where they have no other option.

When judges do make policy, they do so with few research resources at their disposal. They rely on their reasoning powers, what they can glean from relevant case law, and what they are given by the lawyers arguing the case. Sometimes, if their workload in a time of rising caseloads permits, they allow intervenors to take part in a case and present a greater variety of "social facts." But in general, judges are not encumbered with an abundance of social research to assist them in making their decisions. What are their decisions based on, then?

We believe that most judges do their best to weigh all the evidence before them and to make a decision based on what they consider to be the strongest point of view. But their *interpretation* of the evidence will depend, to some extent, on the totality of their background experiences. Judges from working and farming backgrounds may be more likely to rule against Charter claims than judges from business and professional backgrounds. We can only guess what the reasons for this association may be. Perhaps judges from lower–class backgrounds prefer security and stability as represented by deference to a strong government; perhaps judges from the middle classes and upper classes have had stability in their upbringing, and have always been able to afford to experiment. Or perhaps middle–class and upper–class judges have had a more extensive education, and as a result of the link that some researchers have found between education and valuing human rights, they tend to stress Charter values more.

Whatever the explanation, judges will always have a policy–making role, and it will be up to each one of them to decide how far to take it. It should be the responsibility of judges to become aware of the factors in their own upbringing that might influence their decisions, and to try to set aside those influences that might not be pertinent. Finally, those of us who use the courts have to realize that judges are human beings too. When they are called upon to make policy they are making human decisions just like the rest of us do every day.

10

The Court Renaissance

Court reform is not a new theme. The need for it was alluded to not infrequently in William Shakespeare's plays, and it was a favourite topic of Charles Dickens. Indeed, over the centuries there have been numerous court reforms in the Anglo–Canadian system. In spite of this, some serious problems persist. These relate to the overwhelming incomprehensibility of the system to outsiders, the insensitive way in which litigants, witnesses, and jurors are sometimes treated, the (increasingly archaic) preoccupation with the physical presence of witnesses for oral testimony, the casual and thoroughly unmodern attitude toward the efficient use of time, and unnecessary delays in case–processing.

Unfortunately, what is required to address these issues is more than structural reform. What is needed is a change in the perspective in which the court system is viewed by some lawyers and judges so that the reforms, when they come, will actually serve the public — a transformation we call a "court renaissance."

Toward the Demythologization of Courts

Our interviews all indicated that judges place a premium on attempting to decide cases impartially. However, judges are human beings, not computers, and all of us have biases we are not conscious of that help to determine our decision–making processes. As Kathleen Mahoney and Sheilah Martin indicate, various studies of judicial decision–making in relation to disadvantaged groups have shown that male judges sometimes undervalue the testimony of female witnesses, and that stereotypes of women and minorities sometimes influence the judicial decisions. For example, the Marshall inquiry concluded that the Nova Scotia

justice system had treated Donald Marshall, Jr. unfairly because
of the conscious or unconscious stereotypes held by key personnel
in the justice system — possibly including some judges — about
Native Canadians.

The backgrounds of judges do not suit them particularly well
to the task of empathizing with the day–to–day situations of
Canadians who are not of British or French origin or who are
women, members of minority groups, poor, or moderate or low
achievers. These potentially bias–producing factors may be overcome to some extent through a judicial selection process that
encourages the appointment of more judges from groups that are
now under–represented in the judiciary. But as long as we draw
our judges from among the ranks of successful lawyers, it is
inevitable that judges will continue to be disproportionately from
higher socio–economic status backgrounds, and that they will be
individuals whose intelligence, industry, and interactive skills
allow them to rise toward the top of their society and their profession. High–school dropouts, the homeless, and the unemployed
will never be represented in the legal profession and on the bench,
even though the ethnic and social groups that tend to be over–represented in these groups may well provide a majority of the individuals who appear before the courts.

It is important to remember, however, that judges *believe* in the
importance of impartiality. Studies that analyse systematic bias in
judicial decision–making and identify the blind–spots or the unconscious preferences of judges should not be regarded as an
attack on the judiciary, but rather as tools that judges may employ
to help them recognize and overcome, as much as humanly
possible, these biases.

We asked the judges we interviewed whether their independence had ever been violated. Not one complained of attempted political interference in their decision–making, although
a few referred to some well–publicized events involving other
judges. For example, in 1976 it came to light that three federal
cabinet ministers had telephoned judges with regard to particular
cases the judges were hearing; Marc Lalonde in 1969, Jean
Chrétien in 1971, and Bud Drury in 1976. More recently, in 1989,
Jean Charest, Minister of Fitness and Amateur Sport, telephoned

a judge who was about to hear a case involving the eligibility of a Canadian athlete for the Seoul Olympics. But the absence of personal examples of violations of judicial independence from our interviews, and the very few public examples in recent years, indicate that the principle of judicial independence is respected not perfectly, but to a high degree in this country.

In spite of this good record, most Canadians we have met, upon learning of the role that political patronage sometimes still plays in judicial appointments, immediately criticize such patronage as contrary to the principle of judicial independence. As a matter of fact, once judges are appointed in Canada, they generally cut their formal political ties completely so that they are, indeed, independent — patronage is a reward for past services, not an anticipation of future favours. However, the patronage system creates the *appearance* of a possible lack of independence, and when the legitimacy of the courts is at stake, appearance is as important as reality. This is particularly important when a majority of provincial appeal court judges are elevated from the provincial superior trial courts, and a majority of Supreme Court judges are elevated from the provincial courts of appeal; it is harder to feel confident that the tentacles of favour and patronage stop at the door of the judges' chambers when so many judges can contemplate the attractions of movement to the higher benches. The perception of judicial independence would certainly improve, as well as the quality of the judiciary, with the institution of more non–partisan appointment procedures in jurisdictions that do not already have them, and with the extension of these procedures beyond initial appointments to promotions from lower to higher courts.

In 1987 the federal Department of Justice released a survey on the attitudes of Canadians toward justice issues. The survey showed that Canadians have mixed attitudes about the system's effectiveness and fairness. Three–quarters of the respondents thought that the law favours the rich, although the same proportion thought the average Canadian usually gets a fair deal under the law. An astounding 86 per cent agreed there was a need to make the justice system "more sensitive and compassionate," although two–thirds thought that most people were treated with respect by the system. With regard to family law issues, most respondents thought that there were too many cases ending up in court that could have been settled more humanely through mediation. Four–fifths thought that marital disputes should go to mediation first, and then to court only if mediation failed. Half thought that judges do not treat the victims of sexual assault fairly, and two–thirds thought that lawyers who defend those accused with sexual assault treat the victims of sexual assault unfairly. Some 90 per cent said that the justice system is too complex for the average person to understand.

How can the reality of the Canadian court come closer to the theory described in chapter 1? Courts are intended to perform a public service. However, because they have evolved until they are anything but "user friendly," and because they cling to an ethos and a style of language and formal interaction that is increasingly archaic, they have become institutions that function primarily as places where lawyers and judges can practise their private skills, and secondarily institutions that can provide an effective, effi-cient, and fair dispute–resolution service for ordinary citizens whose cases may not always be ideally suited to adjudication. As Peter Russell (5) puts it, "For too many lawyers and judges, judging is still not regarded as the provision of a basic social service but the exercise of a private professional craft."

What can be done to address this situation?

Renaissance

Court reform, from our perspective, involves more than tinkering with the structure of courts to make it more understandable, fair, and efficient, improving judicial selection procedures, and provid-ing more and better judicial training so that judges can select the most appropriate decision–making process for the task at hand. While all of these thrusts are important, we believe that one additional factor is essential. We call this "court renaissance," a phrase we hope will conjure up images of the rebirth of creativity that eventually swept all of a culturally moribund Europe begin-ning in the fifteenth century. All the reforms in the world will not make the Canadian court system more legitimate in the eyes of ordinary Canadians without a change in the attitude toward courts by some in the two key groups in the justice system: judges and lawyers.

It is important to recognize, as many Canadians do not, that the Canadian court system has been in the throes of dramatic change for the past 20 years — acquiring judicial councils for appointment and discipline of provincial judges, focusing administrative responsibilities in newly created chief judgeships, sharply upgrading the procedures of the purely provincial courts and the qualifications of the individuals who preside over them, creating and expanding quicker and more informal options such as small claims court, and replacing the paternalistic and intrusive juvenile court with the rights–oriented procedures of youth court — to identify only some of the changes. We acknowledge that the renaissance is already under way, although the innate conservatism of the legal profession may be containing some of its impact and limiting some of its gains.

Structure

Nine out of ten Canadians think the court system is too complex to understand. Ontario's recent review of the court system, the 1987 Zuber Commission, recognized this problem and recommended the merger of all provincial courts into one Court of Ontario which would have trial and appeal divisions. The provincial government has acted on this recommendation, but will be unable to follow through without the assistance of the federal government either through promoting all provincially appointed judges to the superior court level, or through cooperating in promoting a constitutional amendment that would unify family court functions at the provincial level.

An important variable in determining the success of the unification project in Ontario will be whether the regional and provincial courts advisory committees — composed of judges, lawyers, ministry personnel and possibly lay persons — will be able to find ways to implement the ideas and priorities of judges at all levels, trial lawyers, crown attorneys, court staff, and members of the public who are court users. (Greene [5])

Court unification is a prerequisite to a court renaissance. We applaud the Ontario government's initiatives and recommend them to the other provincial governments. It must be kept in mind, however, that court unification is not a panacea. The concept contains within it the seeds of new problems; for example, as the former lower court judges in a new unified court gain status and responsibility, there will be a tendency to transfer the more routine cases to officials — lower–status officials such as Justices of the Peace — persons who often have little or no post–secondary education. But court unification also opens up new possibilities, such as adapting the continental European approach of channelling less complex cases to the newer judges, and then expanding the range of cases these judges can hear as they master judicial skills. The Europeans use a system of judicial ranks and promotions to accomplish this, but more informal, less cumbersome procedures could be developed to accomplish the same goal. The greatest obstacle to such a reform might be the expectations of high–profile lawyers with 10 to 20 years' experience in private practice who, when appointed to the bench, would expect to deal with important and complex cases after a few weeks, as in the current system.

But structural reform is only the first step. There are many other reforms that need to be effected to make courts user friendly. For example, if you walk into a Canadian court house the first person you usually see is a security guard. Although security guards can and do provide plenty of information about interesting cases being heard that day in the court house, their appearance does not invite novices to make inquiries, and they are not trained to provide comprehensive and clear information about how the system can help those who may wish to enquire.

Imagine instead a court house which, as its most prominent feature in the rotunda, had an information desk staffed by people cheerfully prepared to help visitors use the services provided by the court in the most expeditious manner. Imagine a simple organizational chart near the information desk explaining the hierarchy of courts right up to the Supreme Court of Canada. Next to this display is an exhibit showing the average waiting time to trial and appeal, with a comparison to the ideal waiting time (90 days to trial, and 90 days to each subsequent hearing) and an indication of the progress being made toward achieving the ideal. Next to this display is a "suggestion and complaints box," indicating that comments will be forwarded to the appropriate body — the local courts advisory committee, the provincial judicial council, or the Canadian Judicial Council. Finally, there is a poster explaining how the local mediation centre (located in the court house for the convenience of the public) operates, and inviting litigants to try mediation before going to court, if appropriate.

For this imaginary scene to become reality, what is needed is a renaissance in the way lawyers and judges think about the role of courts in society.

Selection

Judicial selection procedures in Canada are variations on the general theme of executive appointment. The variations all have to do with various degrees of non–partisan involvement in recruiting potential judges, screening judicial applicants, or both. The current procedures still allow for political patronage as a significant factor in provincial judicial appointments in the Maritime provinces, and with regard to federal judicial appointments in the provinces and in the Federal Court.

It is fair to say that merit is now a more important factor than party affiliation with regard to most judicial appointments in Canada. The most recent innovations in judicial selection have come about in Ontario where, in 1989, the provincial government established a ten–person committee to recruit and screen candidates for the provincial judiciary. The committee is composed of three lawyers (one nominated by the attorney general, one by the Law Society and one by the Bar Association), one judge nominated by the judiciary, and six non–lawyers who are appointed by the attorney general because of a demonstrated interest in fair and non–partisan judicial recruitment, and representing all regions of the province. The chair is Peter Russell, the University of Toronto professor who pioneered the political science study of courts in Canada. The committee advertises extensively to encourage qualified lawyers with at least ten years of experience to apply for judicial appointments when there are vacancies. From March 1989 to August 1990 the committee received nearly 500 applications for

29 positions on the Provincial Court — a figure that indicates there is no shortage of prospective judges.

After drawing up a short list of the most qualified lawyers, the committee interviews each person on the short list. The committee members consider not only factors such as education and experience, but also compassion, respect for others, community service, a sense of humour, and so on — in fact, most of the qualities that judges admire most in each other. Political experience is not considered in a negative light, and may be accepted as an indication of community–mindedness. Candidates who are deemed to be well qualified after the interview are ranked. The list is presented, via the Ontario Judicial Council, to the attorney general, who makes the final selection but so far has appointed only the candidates most highly recommended by the committee. The whole process is as public as possible, while protecting the reasonable privacy of the applicants.

We applaud this appointment procedure, and recommend it to the other Canadian jurisdictions, especially those maintaining a partisan selection procedure.

Decision–Making and Training

Although the educational seminars conducted by the Canadian Judicial Centre, the Canadian Judicial Council, and the Canadian Institute for the Administration of Justice are to be commended, we think that these should be considered merely as the beginning of a trend toward more appropriate judicial education. A week–long seminar is not enough training for a criminal court judge who has spent all of his or her life practising in the area of private law. If, for lack of training, trial judges are prone to make the kinds of procedural errors made by the trial and appeal judges in the Donald Marshall case, then comprehensive training seminars for new judges several months in length would constitute a worthwhile expenditure of our tax contributions.

The Marshall inquiry concluded that the trial judge should have realized that Marshall's defence had not been adequately prepared and that some of the evidence was being withheld. The inquiry also concluded that the appeal judges had not carefully read the transcripts of the trial, or if they had, did not notice the serious procedural errors made by the trial judge.

Many newly appointed provincial superior court judges attend "baby judges" courses, although because of rigid and infrequent scheduling this training is likely to take place after rather than before the critical first months on the bench. As well, at least some purely provincial judges spend a week or more on circuit with a specific sitting judge, observing first hand and discussing the actual situations frequently encountered, before first taking on the formal responsibilities of the bench. Such activities must become more regular and formal. As professors, we know the experience of thinking that simply being a student showed us everything we needed to know about teaching, only to discover the hard way that the transition to the front of the classroom involved more than we had ever dreamed. The same is true of lawyers who become judges, except that the stakes are higher and the consequences more serious. This is especially true for the many lawyers whose practice involves little or no trial court appearances, for whom the transition is even more difficult no matter how great the ability or sincere the effort.

At the same time, perhaps we need to reconsider the notion of the 'one size fits all' judge — the principle, strongly adhered to in the superior trial courts, that there is no specialization, and every judge is qualified and prepared to hear every kind of case. Such an idea is, on the face of it, simply improbable. It is disconcerting to think that a difficult murder jury trial might be scheduled in front of a new judge recently touted as one of Canada's finest taxation lawyers, while in the next room an experienced judge with a strong background in criminal law struggles with a complex taxation case — and we do not exaggerate; this is the policy to which our superior trial courts are committed. However able and conscientious the two judges in our hypothetical example, such "learn by doing" is a disservice to both the judges and the parties who appear before them.

If one concern should be to make sure that new judges' previous professional experience and recent training mesh with the responsibilities they will face on the bench, another must be to ensure that this training and experience focus on the type of law they will need to know on the bench: in a word, specialization. The continental European court system — with a series of specialized courts, each with its own internal appellate hierarchy — probably represents too much of a good thing. But the Canadian judiciary might consider a policy of scheduling cases so that judges adjudicate the types of cases they are by experience and temperament best suited to handle.

This would also render more comprehensible the duties of non–partisan selection committees. Instead of an unworkably abstract decision as to whether a person is 'qualified' to be 'a judge,' these committees could address the more functional question of whether this particular applicant is the most qualified to be a criminal judge, or a family law judge, or whatever.

In addition to training about the mechanics of judging, educational seminars could incorporate a participatory learning process about the nature of the decision–making process itself. We found it remarkable that trial judges were unaware that so many different decision–making styles exist among them, or that the range of opinions on basic questions was so great. By sharing their approaches and strategies to decision–making, trial judges could enrich the trial process for each other, with the goal of constantly upgrading decision–making standards.

Court of appeal judges could examine the effects of the panel decision–making process on their judgments. For example, together with Carl Baar and Martin Thomas, we calculated the degree to which appeal judges in Ontario were likely to decide in favour of the Crown or in favour of the accused. Although the scores of most of the judges on this variable were about the same, there were one or two judges who had a tendency to be more pro–Crown, and one or two others who had a tendency to be pro–accused. We also found that the scores of the pro–Crown judges tended to be less extreme when they sat in panels with two pro–accused judges, and vice versa. (This finding parallels what Neil Tate discovered with regard to the dynamics of decision-making in the Supreme Court of Canada.) Appeal court judges could learn much about potential unconscious biases by examining such statistics in educational seminars and discussing their implications.

Several years ago, a Supreme Court of Canada judge remarked to one of us that very little seemed to be known about the dynamics of Supreme Court decision–making in panels of five, seven, or nine judges. For example, does it make a difference that in the conference sessions after a Supreme Court hearing, the judges speak in order of seniority beginning with the most junior judge? The judges decide on the question of leave to appeal in three–judge panels. Are some three–judge panels more likely to allow leave to appeal than others? Has the decision–making process been improved or weakened by limiting oral presentations to an hour? These kinds of issues could be considered by Supreme Court judges in participatory seminars involving the judges, either singly or as a group, and court analysts. These seminars — which, given the Court's workload, could probably not occur for more than a day or two a year — would be aimed at continually improving the decision–making process in the Court. The same considerations are clearly applicable to the provincial courts of appeal, given the clear trend toward the virtually exclusive use of three–judge panels.

Madame Justice Wilson, in her address at Osgoode Hall Law School in February 1990, suggested the establishment of judicially appointed task forces to investigate the extent to which gender bias and other forms of bias exist in the judiciary. In the United States, such task forces have been established in more than 20 states since 1982. Research has shown that these task forces have improved judicial education programs and have also helped to generate the kind of public awareness necessary for meaningful reform of the court system. The point is of course not to collect horror stories or to pillory the judges for their imperfection, but to gain the knowledge that will permit the identification of problems and the development of appropriate responses.

Much could be done to enhance judicial education, but again it depends on a renaissance in thinking about courts by judges and lawyers, including an awareness of the differences in perspective and responsibility that exist between them. A judge is not simply a lawyer who has been elevated to the bench to apply there the values, standards, and procedures learned in practice. Judicial rank implies admission to a new profession, its values and imperatives overlapping but by no means identical, and the delicate balance between splendid individualism and responsible conformity is too important to leave to ad hoc individual resolution.

As the tone of this book implies, the result of our interviews was a great respect for the intelligence, integrity, and professionalism of the judges we talked to, and an appreciation of the problems they confront and the spirit in which they approach them. However, as our basic theme of demystification also implies, we think it is important to remember that they are fallible human beings like the rest of us, individuals whose professional training and extensive experience often mesh less than perfectly with the onerous responsibilities they have accepted. We do no favour to the judges if we think of them as super–human adjudicators of Solomon–like capacities, or if we turn on them savagely when they fall short of such unrealistic expectations.

Judges and Judging

We are fortunate to live in a country in which judicial independence is almost always respected, where judges do their level best to be impartial, and in which the calibre of judges is high.

It is unfortunate, however, that the court system is cumbersome for litigants to use, that litigants are sometimes not treated with respect by court officials, lawyers, and judges, that judicial appointments are sometimes used for partisan political purposes. To bring about the changes that would help to make the court system more sensitive, efficient, and fair, we advocate a partnership of concerned citizens willing to press for reform and of concerned lawyers and judges who have already achieved a renaissance in their thinking about Canadian courts.

References

Note: References recommended as general reading for those who want a deeper understanding of the Canadian justice system and constitution are marked with an asterisk (*).

Abel–Smith, Brian and Robert Stevens. *In Search of Justice*. 1968.

Adams, George and Paul J. Cavalluzzo. "The Supreme Court of Canada: A Biographical Study." *Osgoode Hall Law Journal* 7 (1969): 61.

Alpert, Lenore, Burton M. Atkins and Robert C. Ziller. "Becoming a Judge: The Transition from Advocate to Arbiter." *Judicature* 62 (1979): 325.

Abraham, Henry J. *The Judicial Process: An Introductory Analysis of the Courts of the United States, England and France*, 5th ed. 1986.

Aubert, Vilhelm. "Law as a Way of Resolving Conflicts: The Case of a Small Industrialized Society." *Case Studies of Law in Western Societies*, 282.

Austin, John. *Lectures on Jurisprudence, or, The Philosophy of Positive Law*. c. 1863.

Baar, Carl. "Delay Reduction as Public Policy: Explaining Canadian-American Differences in the Pace of Criminal Cases." Paper presented to the interim meeting of the Research Committee on Comparative Judicial Studies, International Political Science Association, London, England, August 21, 1990.

Baar, Carl and Ellen Baar. "Diagnostic Adjudication in Appellate Courts: The Supreme Court of Canada and the Charter of Rights." *Osgoode Hall Law Journal* 27 (1989): 1.

Baar, Carl, Ian Greene, Martin Thomas and Peter McCormick. "The Ontario Court of Appeal and Speedy Justice." Paper presented to the Annual Meeting of the Canadian Law and Society Association, 1989.

Batten, Jack. *Judges*. 1986.

Becker, Theodore L. *Comparative Judicial Politics*. 1970.

Becker, Theodore L. and Malcolm Feeley, eds. *The Impact of Supreme Court Decisions: Empirical Studies*, 2nd ed. 1973.

Bouthillier, Guy.

(1) "Matériaux pour une analyse politique des juges de la Cour d'appel," *La Revue Juridique Thémis* 6 (1971): 563.

(2) "Note sur la carriere politique des juges de la Cour superieure," *La Revue Juridique Thémis* 7 (1972): 573.

(3) "Profil du juge de la Cour superieure du Quebec." *The Canadian Bar Review* 55 (1977): 436.

(4) "Profil du juge de la Cour des sessions de la paix," *Revue du Barreau* 38 (1978): 13.

Bushnell, S.I.
(1) "Leave to Appeal Applications to the Supreme Court of Canada." *Supreme Court Review* 3 (1982): 495.
(2) "Leave to Appeal Applications: The 1986–87 Term." *Supreme Court Law Review* 10 (1988): 361.

Canada. Department of Justice. *Survey of Public Attitudes toward Justice Issues in Canada* (prepared by Environics Research Group Limited). 1987.

Canadian Bar Association. *Report on the Appointment of Judges in Canada.* 1985.

Canadian Judicial Council.
(1) *Annual Report, 1987–88.*
(2) *Annual Report, 1988–89.*
(3) *Annual Report, 1989–90*

Carp, Robert and Russell Wheeler. "Sink or Swim: The Socialization of a Federal District Judge." *Journal of Public Law* 21 (1972): 359.

Champagne, Anthony and Stuart Nagel. "The Psychology of Judging." In Norbert L. Kerr and Robert M. Bray, eds. *The Psychology of the Courtroom.* 1982.

Cheffins, Ronald and Patricia Johnson. *The Revised Canadian Constitution.* 1986.

Cook, Beverly Blair. "Role Lag in Urban Trial Courts." *Western Political Quarterly* 25 (1972): 234.

*Conklin, William E. *Images of a Constitution.* 1989.

Dawson, John P. *The Oracles of the Law*, 3rd ed. 1968.

*Deschênes, Jules. *The Sword and the Scales.* 1979.

Devlin, Patrick. *The Judge.* 1979.

de Montigny, Jean and Pierre Robert. *Analyse Comparative des Législations et des Perspectives de Réforme.* 1973.

Dicey, A.V. *Introduction to the Study of the Law of the Constitution.* 1885. (6th ed. 1902.)

Dickson, Brian.
(1) "The Role and Function of Judges." *The Law Society of Upper Canada Gazette* 14 (1980): 138.
(2) "Remarks by the Rt. Hon. Brian Dickson, P.C. on the Occasion of the Mid–Winter Meeting of the Canadian Bar Association," Saint John, New Brunswick, March 1, 1988.

Dworkin, Ronald.
(1) *A Matter of Principle.* 1985.
(2) *Law's Empire.* 1986.
(3) *Taking Rights Seriously.* 1978.

Eberts, Mary. "Risks of Equality Litigation." In Sheilah Martin and Kathleen Mahoney, eds. *Equality and Judicial Neutrality: 89.* 1987.

Feeley, Malcolm. *The Process is the Punishment*. 1979.

Ferguson, G. and D. Roberts. "Plea Bargaining: Directions for Canadian Reform." *Canadian Bar Review* 1974: 497.

Fouts, Donald R. "Policy–Making in the Supreme Court of Canada." In Glendon A. Schubert and David J. Danelski, eds. *Comparative Judicial Behavior: Cross–Cultural Studies in Political Decision–Making in the East and West*: 121. 1969.

Frank, Jerome. *Law and the Modern Mind*. 1936.

Friedland, Martin L. *A Century of Criminal Justice*. 1984.

Gabor, Peter, Ian Greene and Peter McCormick, "The Young Offenders Act: The Alberta Youth Court Experience in the First Year." *Canadian Journal of Family Law* 5 (1986): 301.

*Gall, Gerald. *The Canadian Legal System*, 3rd ed. 1990.

Gertner, Eric. "The Supreme Court's Expanding Jurisdiction and Other Procedural Tales." *Supreme Court Law Review* 10 (1988): 417.

Gibson, Dale and Lee Gibson. *Substantial Justice: Law and Lawyers in Manitoba, 1670–1970*. 1972.

Gibson, Dale. "Unobtrusive Justice." *Osgoode Hall Law Journal* 12 (1974): 339.

Greene, Ian.

*(1) *The Charter of Rights*. 1989.

(2) "The Doctrine of Judicial Independence Developed by the Supreme Court of Canada." *Osgoode Hall Law Journal* 26 (1988): 177.

(3) "The Myths of Legislative and Constitutional Supremacy." In David Shugarman and Reginald Whitaker, eds. *Federalism and Political Community: Essays in Honour of Donald Smiley*: 267. 1989.

(4) "The Politics of Court Administration in Ontario." *Windsor Yearbook of Access to Justice* 2 (1982): 124.

(5) "The Politics of Judicial Administration: The Ontario Case." Ph.D. thesis, Department of Political Science, University of Toronto. 1983.

(6) "The Zuber Report and Court Management." *Windsor Yearbook of Access to Justice* 8 (1988): 150.

Grossman, Joel B. "Social Backgrounds and Judicial Decisions: Notes for a Theory." *Journal of Politics* 29 (1967): 334.

Hart, H.L.A. *Definition and Theory in Jurisprudence*. 1954.

Henderson, Thomas and Cornelius M. Kerwin, "The Changing Character of Court Organization." *Justice System Journal* 7 (1982): 449.

Heron, P.T. "Judicial Independence Aside, Has Walter Valente been Forgotten?" *Canadian Lawyer* 7 (1987): 12.

Hiebert, Janet. "Fair Elections and Freedom of Expression under the Charter: Should Interest Groups' Election Expenditures be Limited?" *Journal of Canadian Studies* 23 (1989).

*Hogarth, John. *Sentencing as a Human Process*. 1971.

Hogg, Peter.

*(1) *Constitutional Law of Canada*, 2nd ed. 1985.

(2) "Is the Supreme Court of Canada Biased in Constitutional Cases?" *Canadian Bar Review* 57 (1979): 721.

(3) *The Meech Lake Accord Annotated.* 1988.

Holdsworth, W.S. *A History of English Law*, 3rd ed. 1922.

Howard, J. Woodford. *Courts of Appeals in the Federal Judicial System.* 1981.

Jennings, Ivor. *The Law and the Constitution.* 1959.

Johnson, Charles A. *Judicial Policies: Implementation and Impact.* 1984.

Kerwin, Cornelius M., Thomas Henderson and Carl Baar, "Adjudicatory Processes and the Organization of Trial Courts." *Judicature* 70 (1986): 99.

Klein, William J. "Judicial Recruitment in Manitoba, Ontario and Quebec." Ph.D. thesis, Department of Sociology, University of Toronto. 1975.

Klein, Mitchell S.G. *Law, Courts and Policy.* 1984.

Knopff, Rainer and F.L. Morton. "Nation–Building and the Canadian Charter of Rights and Freedoms." In A. Cairns and C. Williams, eds. *Constitutionalism, Citizenship and Society in Canada*: 133. 1985.

Laskin, Bora.

(1) *The Institutional Character of the Judge.* 1972.

(2) "Some Observations on Judicial Independence," Address, Meeting of Commonwealth Law Ministers, Winnipeg, August 23, 1977.

Lasswell, Harold D. *Power and Personality.* 1948.

Lederman, W.R. "The Independence of the Judiciary." *Canadian Bar Review* 34 (1956): 769.

L'Heureux–Dubé, Madame Justice Claire. "A View from the Top," Notes for an Address to the Annual Dinner of the County of York Law Association, February 8, 1990.

Linden, A.M., ed. *The Canadian Judiciary.* 1976.

Llewellyn, Karl. *The Bramble Bush.* 1930.

Locke, John. *The Second Treatise of Government.* c. 1690.

Lyon, Noel. "The Teleological Mandate of the Fundamental Freedoms Guarantee: What to do with Vague but Meaningful Generalities." *Supreme Court Law Review* 4 (1982).

Martin, Sheilah L. and Kathleen E. Mahoney. *Equality and Judicial Neutrality.* 1987.

Maddi, Dorothy Linder. *Judicial Performance Polls.* 1977.

*Mandel, Michael. *The Charter of Rights and the Legalization of Politics in Canada.* 1989.

Manning, Morris. *Rights, Freedoms and the Courts.* 1982.

McCormick, Peter.

(1) "Judicial Councils for Provincial Judges in Canada." *Windsor Yearbook of Access to Justice* 6 (1986): 160.

(2) "Case–load and output of the Manitoban Court of Appeal." *Manitoba Law Journal* 19 (1990).

(3) "Caseload and Output on the Saskatchewan Court of Appeal: An Analysis of Twelve Months of Reported Cases." *Saskatchewan Law Journal* 53 (1989): 341.

McEvoy, John. "Separation of Powers and the Reference Power: Is There a Right to Refuse?" *Supreme Court Law Review* 10 (1988): 429–468.

*Millar, Perry and Carl Baar. *Judicial Administration in Canada*. 1982.

*Milne, David. *The Canadian Constitution: From Patriation to Meech Lake*. 1989.

*Monahan, Patrick. *Politics and the Constitution: The Charter, Federalism and the Supreme Court of Canada*. 1987.

Montesquieu, *The Spirit of the Laws*. c. 1750.

Morton, F.L.

*(1) *Law, Politics and the Judicial Process in Canada*. 1984.

(2) "The Political Impact of the Canadian Charter of Rights and Freedoms." *Canadian Journal of Political Science* 18 (1987): 31.

Morton, F.L. and M.J. Withey. "Charting the Charter, 1982–1985: A Statistical Analysis." Research Unit for Socio–Legal Studies, University of Calgary, Occasional Papers Series, Research Study 2.1.

Morton, F.L., P.H. Russell and M. Withey."The Supreme Court's First One Hundred Charter Decisions: A Statistical Analysis." Research Unit for Socio-Legal Studies, University of Calgary, Occasional Papers Series, Research Study 6.1.

Olsen, Dennis. *The State Elite*. 1980.

Pal, L.A. and F.L. Morton. "Impact of the Charter of Rights on Public Administration." *Canadian Public Administration* 1985: 221.

Panitch, Leo and Donald Swartz. *The Assault on Trade Union Freedoms*. 1988.

Parker, Graham. *Introduction to Criminal Law*, 2nd ed. 1983.

Pateman, Carole. *Participation and Democratic Theory*. 1970.

Peck, Sidney R.

(1) "A Behavioural Approach to the Judicial Process: Scalogram Analysis." *Osgoode Hall Law Journal* 5 (1967): 1.

(2) "An Analytical Framework for an Application of the Canadian Charter of Rights and Freedoms." *Osgoode Hall Law Journal* 25 (1987): 1.

(3) "The Supreme Court of Canada, 1958–1966: A Search for Policy Through Scalogram Analysis." *Canadian Bar Review* 65 (1967): 666.

Plucknett, T.F.T. *A Concise History of the Common Law*. 1940.

Porter, John. *The Vertical Mosaic*. 1965.

Ratushny, Ed. "Judicial Appointments: The Lang Legacy." In Allen Linden, ed. *The Canadian Judiciary*. 1976.

Royal Commission on the Donald Marshall, Jr. Prosecution. *Digest of Findings and Recommendations*. 1989.

Russell, Peter H.

(1) "Canada's Charter of Rights and Freedoms: A Political Report." *Public Law* (U.K.) 1988: 385.

(2) "The Supreme Court Decision: Bold Statecraft Based on Questionable Jurisprudence." In Peter Russell et al., eds. *The Court and the Constitution.* 1982.

(3) "A Democratic Approach to Civil Liberties." *University of Toronto Law Journal* 19 (1969): 109.

(4) "The Effect of a Charter of Rights on the Policy–Making Role of the Courts." *Canadian Public Administration* 25 (1982): 1.

(5) "Judicial Power in Canada's Political Culture." In M.L. Friedland, ed. *Courts and Trials: A Multi–Disciplinary Approach*: 75. 1975.

*(6) *The Judiciary in Canada: The Third Branch of Government.* 1987.

(7) "The Political Purposes of the Canadian Charter of Rights and Freedoms." *Canadian Bar Review* (Charter ed.) 61 (1983): 30.

(8) "The Political Role of the Supreme Court of Canada in its First Century." *Canadian Bar Review* 53 (1975): 577.

(9) *The Supreme Court of Canada as a Bilingual and a Bicultural Institution.* 1969.

*Russell, Peter H., Rainer Knopff and F.L. Morton, eds. *Federalism and the Charter: Leading Constitutional Decisions*, 5th ed. 1989.

Russell, Peter H. and Jacob S. Zeigel, "Federal Judicial Appointments: An Appraisal of the First Mulroney Government's Appointments." Paper presented to the Canadian Political Science Association and Canadian Law and Society Association, May 29, 1989.

Schmidhauser, John R. "The Circulation of Judicial Elites: A Comparative and Longitudinal Perspective." In Moshe M. Czudnowski, ed. *Does Who Governs Matter?*: 33. 1982.

Schubert, Glendon A. *The Judicial Mind Revisited: Psychometric Analysis of Supreme Court Ideology.* 1974.

Shapiro, Martin, *Courts: A Comparative and Political Analysis.* 1981.

Shetreet, Shimon. *Judges on Trial.* 1976.

Silbey, Susan S. "Making Sense of the Lower Courts." *The Justice System Journal* 6 (1981).

Slattery, Brian J. "A Theory of the Charter." *Osgoode Hall Law Journal* 25 (1987): 701.

Smiley, Donald V.

(1) "The Case against the Canadian Charter of Human Rights." *Canadian Journal of Political Science* 2 (1969): 277.

(2) *The Federal Condition in Canada.* 1988.

Smith, Jennifer. "The Origins of Judicial Review in Canada." *Canadian Journal of Political Science* 16 (1983): 115.

Sniderman, Paul M., Joseph F. Fletcher, Peter H. Russell and Phillip E. Tetlock, "Liberty Authority and Community: Civil Liberties and the Canadian Political Culture." Paper delivered at the Annual Meetings of the Canadian Political Science Association and the Canadian Law and Society Association, University of Windsor, June 9, 1988.

Tarnopolsky, Walter S. "The Evolution of Judicial Attitudes." In Sheilah Martin and Kathleen Mahoney, eds. *Equality and Judicial Neutrality*: 378. 1987.

Tate, Neil. "Explaining the Decision–Making of the Canadian Supreme Court, 1949–1985: Extending the Personal Attributes Model Across Nations." *Journal of Politics* 51 (1989).

Tollefson, E.A. "The System of Judicial Appointments: A Collateral Issue." *University of Toronto Law Journal* 21 (1971): 162.

Ulmer, S. Sidney.

(1) "Are Social Background Models Time Bound?" *American Political Science Review* 80 (1986): 957.

(2) "Social Background as an Indicator to the Votes of Supreme Court Justices in Criminal Cases: 1947–1956 Terms." *Midwest Journal of Political Science* 17 (1973): 622.

Underwood, Nora. "Rating the Judiciary." *Maclean's*, May 19, 1989: 56.

Underwood, Nora, with David Philip, Kerry Diotte, Doug Smith, Leigh Ogston and Valerie Mansour. "Disorder in the Court." *Maclean's*, April 24, 1989: 55.

*Vaughan, Frederick and James Snell. *The Supreme Court of Canada: History of the Institution*. 1985.

Walker, Thomas G., Lee Epstein and William J. Dixon, "On the Mysterious Demise of Consensual Norms in the United States Supreme Court." *Journal of Politics* 50 (1988): 361.

*Weiler, Paul. *In the Last Resort*. 1974.

Williams, Cynthia. "The Changing Nature of Citizen Rights." In Alan Cairns and Cynthia Williams, eds. *Constitutionalism, Citizenship and Society in Canada*: 99. 1985.

Williams, David. R. *Duff: A Life in the Law*. 1984.

Wilson, Bertha.

(1) "Decision–Making in the Supreme Court." *University of Toronto Law Journal* 36 (1986): 227.

(2) "Will Women Judges Really Make a Difference?" Fourth Annual Barbara Betcherman Memorial Lecture, Osgoode Hall, York University, February 8, 1990.

Wold, John T. "Political Orientations, Social Backgrounds, and Role Perceptions of State Supreme Court Judges." *Western Political Quarterly* 27 (1974): 239.

Woodward, Bob and Scott Armstrong. *The Brethren: Inside the Supreme Court*. 1979.

Wright, Blenus. "The Charter: The Supreme Court of Canada: The First Seven Years: Brian Dickson's Influence". Master of Laws dissertation, York University, 1989.

Zuber, Honourable Thomas G. *Report of the Ontario Courts Inquiry*. 1987.

Cases Referred To

Note: The following abbreviations are frequently used in the list below:
LCD: Peter H. Russell, Rainer Knopff and F.L. Morton, *Federalism and the Charter: Leading Constitutional Decisions*, 5th ed. 1989.
LCDSCC: Peter H. Russell, Rainer Knopff and F.L. Morton, eds. *Leading Constitutional Decisions of the Supreme Court of Canada. Produced and distributed by The Research Unit for Socio–Legal Studies, Faculty of Social Sciences, University of Calgary, on an ongoing basis.*
SCR: *Supreme Court Reports.*

[1] A.–G. Man. et al. v. A.–G. Can. et al., [1981] 2 SCR 753; LCD no. 62 (constitutional reference).

[2] A.–G. Ont. v. A.–G. Can., [1947] A.C. 127.

[3] A.–G. Ont. v. Winner, [1954] A.C. 541.

[4] Birks & Sons v. Montreal, [1955] SCR 799.

[5] Boucher v. Regina, [1951] SCR 265.

[6] British Coal Corporation v. Regina, [1935] A.C. 500 (P.C.).

[7] Chaput v. Romain, [1955] SCR 834.

[8] Devine v. A.–G. Quebec, [1988] 2 SCR 790; LCDSCC, no. 53.

[9] Ford v. A.–G. Quebec, [1988] 2 SCR 712; LCD, no. 52; LCDSCC, no. 53.

[10] Harrison v. Carswell, [1976] 2 SCR 200.

[11] Johanesson v. West St. Paul, [1952] 1 SCR 292.

[12] Lamb v. Benoit, [1959] SCR 321.

[13] Nadan v. Regina, [1926] A.C. 482 (P.C.).

[14] National Citizens Coalition v. A.–G. Can., [1984] 5 Western Weekly Reports 436.

[15] Ponoka–Calmar Oils v. Wakefield, [1960] A.C. 18 (P.C.).

[16] Re Charles Currie v. The Niagara Escarpment Commission, (1984) 46 Ontario Reports (2d) 484.

[17] Reference re Justices of the Peace Act and R. v. Currie, (1984) 48 Ontario Reports (2d) 609.

[18] Reference Re Public Service Employee Relations Act (Alta.), [1987] 1 SCR 313; LCD no. 49; LCDSCC, no. 22.

[19] Regina v. Big M Drug Mart Ltd. et al., [1985] 1 SCR 295; LCD, no. 42; LCDSCC, no. 5.

[20] Regina v. Drybones, [1970] SCR 282; LCD no. 37.

[21] Regina v. Edwards Books and Art Ltd., [1986] 2 SCR 713; LCD, no. 48; LCDSCC, no. 19.

[22] Regina v. Jones, [1986] 2 SCR 284; LCDSCC, no. 17.

[23] Regina v. Morgentaler, [1988] 1 SCR 30; LCD no. 50; LCDSCC, no. 35.

[24] Roncarelli v. Duplessis, [1959] SCR 121.

[25] Saumur v. City of Quebec, [1953] 2 SCR 299.

[26] Sellars v. The Queen, [1980] 1 SCR 527.

[27] Singh et al. v. Minister of Employment and Immigration, [1985] 1 SCR 177; LCD, 5th ed., no. 41; LCDSCC, no. 4.

[28] Switzman v. Elbling and A.–G. Que., [1957] SCR 285.

[29] Regina v. Therens et al., [1985] 1 SCR 613; LCD, no. 44; LCDSCC, no. 7.

[30] Tremblay v. Daigle, [1989] 2 SCR 530 (Supreme Court of Canada), on appeal from [1989] 59 Dominion Law Reports (4th) 609 (Court of Appeal for Quebec).

[31] Valente v. The Queen et al., [1985] 2 SCR 673; LCDSCC, no. 11.

Index